T0350896

Hidden and Devalued Feminised Labour in the Digital Humanities

Hidden and Devalued Feminised Labour in the Digital Humanities examines the data-driven labour that underpinned the Index Thomisticus—a pre-eminent project of the incunabular digital humanities—and advanced the data-foundations of computing in the humanities.

Through oral history and archival research, Nyhan reveals a hidden history of the entanglements of gender in the intellectual and technical work of the early digital humanities. Setting feminised keypunching in its historical contexts—from the history of concordance making, to the feminisation of the office and humanities computing—this book delivers new insight into the categories of work deemed meritorious of acknowledgement and attribution and, thus, how knowledge and expertise was defined in and by this field. Focalising the overlooked yet significant data-driven labour of lesser-known individuals, this book challenges exclusionary readings of the history of computing in the humanities. Contributing to ongoing conversations about the need for alternative genealogies of computing, this book is also relevant to current debates about diversity and representation in the Academy and the wider computing sector.

Hidden and Devalued Feminised Labour in the Digital Humanities will be of interest to researchers and students studying digital humanities, library and information science, the history of computing, oral history, the history of the humanities and the sociology of knowledge and science.

Julianne Nyhan is Professor of Humanities Data Science and Methodology at the Institut für Geschichte, Technische Universität Darmstadt, Germany and Professor of Digital Humanities at UCL, UK. A Fellow of the Royal Historical Society, she was formerly the Deputy- and Director of the UCL Centre for Digital Humanities (2018–2021) and Director of UCL's MA/MSc in Digital Humanities (2017–2021). Her primary research interest is in the history of digital humanities and oral history, areas in which she has published widely.

Digital Research in the Arts and Humanities

Founding Series Editors: Marilyn Deegan, Lorna Hughes and Harold Short
Current Series Editors: Lorna Hughes, Nirmala Menon, Andrew Prescott, Isabel Galina Russell, Harold Short and Ray Siemens

Digital technologies are increasingly important to arts and humanities research, expanding the horizons of research methods in all aspects of data capture, investigation, analysis, modelling, presentation and dissemination. This important series covers a wide range of disciplines with each volume focusing on a particular area, identifying the ways in which technology impacts on specific subjects. The aim is to provide an authoritative reflection of the 'state of the art' in technology-enhanced research methods. The series is critical reading for those already engaged in the digital humanities, and of wider interest to all arts and humanities scholars.

Transformative Digital Humanities
Challenges and Opportunities
Edited by Mary McAleer Balkun and Marta Mestrovic Deyrup

Medieval Manuscripts in the Digital Age
Edited by Benjamin Albritton, Georgia Henley and Elaine Treharne

Access and Control in Digital Humanities
Edited by Shane Hawkins

Information and Knowledge Organisation in Digital Humanities
Global Perspectives
Edited by Koraljka Golub and Ying-Hsang Liu

Networks and the Spread of Ideas in the Past:
Strong Ties, Innovation and Knowledge Exchange
Edited by Anna Collar

The following list includes only the most-recent titles to publish within the series. A list of the full catalogue of titles is available at: https://www.routledge.com/Digital-Research-in-the-Arts-and-Humanities/book-series/DRAH

Hidden and Devalued Feminised Labour in the Digital Humanities

On the Index Thomisticus project 1954–67

Julianne Nyhan

Routledge
Taylor & Francis Group

LONDON AND NEW YORK

First published 2023
by Routledge
4 Park Square, Milton Park, Abingdon, Oxon OX14 4RN

and by Routledge
605 Third Avenue, New York, NY 10158

Routledge is an imprint of the Taylor & Francis Group, an informa business

Access the [companion website/Support Material]: [insert comp website/ Support
Material URL]

British Library Cataloguing-in-Publication Data
A catalogue record for this book is available from the British Library

Library of Congress Cataloging-in-Publication Data
Names: Nyhan, Julianne, author.
Title: Hidden and devalued feminized labour in the digital humanities : on the Index
Thomisticus project 1965-67 / Julianne Nyhan.
Description: New York : Routledge, 2023. |
Series: Digital research in the arts and humanities | Includes bibliographical
references and index. |
Summary: "Hidden and Devalued Feminized Labour in the Digital Humanities
examines the data-driven labour that underpinned the Index Thomisticus - a preeminent
project of the incunabular digital humanities - and advanced the data-foundations of
computing in the Humanities. Through oral history and archival research, Nyhan
reveals a hidden history of the entanglements of gender in the intellectual and technical
work of the early digital humanities. Setting feminized keypunching in its historical
contexts - from the history of concordance making, to the feminization of the office and
humanities computing - this book delivers new insight into the categories of work
deemed meritorious of acknowledgement and attribution and, thus, how knowledge and
expertise was defined in and by this field. Focalizing the overlooked yet significant
data-driven labour of lesser-known individuals, this book challenges exclusionary
readings of the history of computing in the Humanities. Contributing to ongoing
conversations about the need for alternative genealogies of computing, this book is also
relevant to current debates about diversity and representation in the Academy and the
wider computing sector. Hidden and Devalued Feminized Labour in the Digital
Humanities will be of interest to researchers and students studying digital humanities,
library and information science, the history of computing, oral history, the history of the
humanities, and the sociology of knowledge and science"-- Provided by publisher.
Identifiers: LCCN 2022033151
Subjects: LCSH: Digital humanities. | Humanities--Research--Data processing. |
Information storage and retrieval systems--Humanities. | Humanities--Electronic
information resources. | Index Thomisticus. | Computers and women--History. |
Women in computer science--History. | Sex discrimination against women. |
Sex discrimination in employment.
Classification: LCC AZ105 .N94 2023 | DDC 001.30285--dc23/eng/20220825
LC record available at https://lccn.loc.gov/2022033151

ISBN: 978-0-367-68596-6 (hbk)
ISBN: 978-0-367-68598-0 (pbk)
ISBN: 978-1-003-13823-5 (ebk)

DOI: 10.4324/9781003138235

Typeset in Times New Roman
by Taylor & Francis Books

Dedicated with love to the memory of
John Nyhan (2 November 1953–25 May 2020)

Contents

Figures

Acknowledgements

The manuscript of this book has been a constant companion through years and seasons; births and bereavements; accomplishments and disappointments; a global pandemic; upheaval, relocation and a new beginning. I am indebted to colleagues, friends and family for the help and support they have given me as I pursued this project, occasionally in leaps, but mostly in tiny, back-and-forth manoeuvres as the sands continued to shift.

First and foremost, I thank the many lesser-known and overlooked individuals for the valuable contributions they made to building the data-foundations of what would become the digital humanities, a field where I and many others would ultimately be able to thrive. As set out in detail in the pages that follow, interviews with some of these individuals, specifically some of the individuals who previously worked on the *Index Thomisticus* project, are drawn on in this book. I will not rehearse individuals' details here but instead refer the reader to the particulars given in the Introduction and Bibliography. I thank interviewees most sincerely for their willingness to share their recollections of the incunabular years of digital humanities, as they encountered it and co-created it.

Next, I thank Melissa Terras, for it was she who first noticed and wrote an important blog post about the otherwise unknown female keypunch operators who were pictured in a folder of digitised photographs that we received in 2011 from Marco Passarotti of the Università Cattolica del Sacro Cuore, Milan, Italy. I received incredible help and support from Marco Passarotti throughout this project. Many aspects of the oral history and archival research conducted for this book would not have been possible without his help. Marco is, moreover, the hub who bridges those individuals with an interest in the history of the *Index Thomisticus* to those individuals who actually worked on the *Index Thomisticus*, day to day. This bridging work can be easily overlooked but without it our networks and scope for collective enquiry and recollection would be much reduced. Likewise, I thank Danila Cairati (the final secretary to Busa), who performed equally important bridging work that facilitated my initial and subsequent contact with individuals who formerly worked on the *Index Thomisticus*.

Close colleagues and friends offered helpful input to this work as it was in progress. I especially thank: Melissa Terras and James Cronin, who read manuscript drafts with great care, making intellectual connections and prompting me to include additional historicisations that have very much improved this book. Thank you to Steve Jones and Geoffrey Rockwell, not only for their seminal contributions to scholarship on the history of digital humanities, which I cite extensively in this book, but also for the ongoing help they gave me as critical friends of drafts that I sent them. Thank you to Andrew Flinn for surviving the millions of rambling discussions about this book that I have inflicted on him over the past years and also for introducing me to a world of scholarship and ideas that has made a profound impression on me and on this book.

This project has benefited from the expertise, kindness and open-mindedness of Paolo Senna, Librarian at the Università Cattolica del Sacro Cuore, where Fr Roberto Busa S.J.'s archive is housed. When I first visited the Busa archive in 2014 the documents it contained had not been catalogued; during my second research stay in 2018, I worked with a new tranche of unaccessioned documents. During both research trips, Paolo Senna not only identified documents that were likely to be relevant to my research from among a vast and seemingly inscrutable paper archive, he trusted me to work appropriately with those documents. In other words, without the benefit of his archival and research expertise, this book and the archival sources it draws on would be very different. Thank you also to Paolo Sirito, Director of the library of the Università Cattolica del Sacro Cuore and to Savina Raynaud, former Director of the CIRCSE Research Centre, Università Cattolica del Sacro Cuore. The archival photographs included in this volume are kindly made available under a Creative Commons CC-BY-NC license by permission of CIRCSE Research Centre, Università Cattolica del Sacro Cuore, Milan, Italy. For further information, or to request permission for reuse, please contact Marco Passarotti, on marco.passarotti AT unicatt.it, or by post: Largo Gemelli 1, 20123 Milan, Italy. Thank you also to IBM Archives, Somers, New York, especially Archivist Max Campbell who assisted me with numerous queries, sent digitised copies of archival materials and helped with the identification of some accounting machines. Reprints of archival materials included in this book are all "Courtesy of IBM Corporation ©". Thank you also to IBM Hursley Park Museum, Computer Conservation Society, UK, especially Peter Short, who also assisted in the task of identifying some of the accounting machines included in pictures from the Busa archive.

A number of individuals translated newspaper, archival and oral history sources that I have drawn on and cited in this book. I thank most sincerely for their translation work: Philip Barras, Giulia D'Agostino and Ana Vela. The texts they translated are indicated in the bibliography. Giulia D'Agostino also assisted with aspects of the literature scan and Alexandra Ortjola-Baird with citation checking and bibliography verification. Supplementary financial support was secured from the European Association of Digital Humanities; the Centre for Critical Heritage at the University of Gothenburg, Sweden and UCL; the Department of Information Studies UCL; and the Faculty of Arts and Humanities, UCL. This was used to fund translation work and my research stays in Milan. I am grateful for the support of Elizabeth Shepherd, head of department, UCL Department of Information Studies, who supported the research on this book in myriad ways.

During the years that I was working on this book, I was invited to deliver numerous lectures and keynote talks on my work in progress, in the UK, Italy, Germany, Sweden, the USA, France, Ireland, Luxembourg and beyond. I'm grateful to the organisers and audiences of those events, where many important and difficult questions were asked, some of which I have continued to try to answer in this book. For all this, all mistakes contained in this book are, of course, my own.

Thank you to my darling husband Reimar and my daughters and step-son: Clara, Iris and Joey. They tell me that having an academic in the family is not easy; I can't think why. Thank you also to my mother Eileen Nyhan. Remember, Mum, that one of these days, the sun will shine again and the soft wind blow again and a new kind of comfort and hope will follow.

Finally, it is important to say that the argument set out in this book is my argument, based on extensive research, analysis and thought. My argument is not necessarily one that is shared, in part or whole, by any of those mentioned above or in this book, in any capacity. While no argument can ever convince everyone, I hope that I have succeeded in my aim of approaching my work with sincerity and responsibility, and of being as fair as it is possible for me to be to all of the actors who participated in the *Index Thomisticus* project, and thus in the founding and emergence of the field now known as digital humanities.

Introduction

Scaffolded by absence

In 1958, on an early-autumn day in Brussels, Fr Roberto Busa S.J. (1913–2011) was photographed at the World's Fair, Expo '58 presenting his research (see Figure I.1).[1] Busa is believed by many to be the founder of the field now called digital humanities, which studies all aspects: technical, representational, historical, sociocultural, technopolitical and ethical of the remediation, generation, analysis and activation of humanities sources as data (e.g. Terras, Nyhan, and Vanhoutte 2013). Busa's research was partially supported by IBM, who furnished his research centre with data-processing machines and the paper punched cards they ran on gratis, or close to. Busa also depended on the expertise of IBM's staff,[2] especially Paul Tasman. Tasman was "a senior engineer in charge of a good deal of the nascent World Trade Corporation … who became Busa's collaborator and friend until his death in 1988. … Indeed, one could argue that Tasman, as much as Busa, helped to found a language-based humanities computing" (Jones 2016, 14). Thus, Busa's stand at Expo '58 was located in the IBM Pavilion, which is estimated to have attracted c. 100,000 visitors in its first six weeks (Jones 2016, 19).

One of the earliest to use electromechanical accounting machines, and later electronic computers to process significant quantities of text rather than numbers, Busa's research is an early example of the use of automation in the humanities. Today, he is perhaps most famous for the way he applied electromechanical and later digital technologies to the venerable work of concordance-making. An index or *index verborum*, "it is generally agreed [is] a list of words in a text followed only by their location … while the addition of context creates a concordance." (Burton 1982, 196). Busa's concordance focused on the writings of Saint Thomas Aquinas, one of the Catholic Church's most influential medieval philosophers and theologians. Aquinas' *opera omnia* amounted to around 11 million words, recorded in multiple, dispersed and informationally-siloed hardcopy works that interested Catholic theologians greatly. Busa's *Index Thomisticus* was initially anticipated as an analogue bridge across the corpus of Aquinas, allowing patterns and divergences in the millions of words it contained to be identified, tracked and ultimately interpreted. In an

DOI: 10.4324/9781003138235-1

oral history interview, one of Busa's staff members[3] explained the significance of what the *Index Thomisticus* sought to achieve:

> DR [Diego Righetti] Saint Thomas used to be the greatest theologist of the Catholic Church. He wrote a lot of things, about a lot of arguments … He had found the answers to a lot of questions. And it was difficult to find where Saint Thomas had answered to a single question. Father Busa made this megawork to help the theologists to find where Saint Thomas wrote about a given topic.
>
> (Righetti, Nyhan and Passarotti 2014)

The *Index Thomisticus* went on to be "derived from 179 texts, of which 118 are the works of Saint Thomas Aquinas, and 61 belong to writers associated with him" (Burton 1984a, 109).

In 1974, c. 24 years after the project's inception, the first volumes of the *Index Thomisticus* appeared. Publication would continue in 56 hardcopy volumes until 1980. In 1991, the *Index Thomisticus* was published on CD-ROM (Busa 1991). In 2005 the web edition was released (Busa and Associates 2005). In the course of the work on the *Index Thomisticus* the text of Aquinas and related authors had been lemmatised and morphologically annotated. In 2006, a project to enhance the *Index Thomisticus* with syntactic annotation, the *Index Thomisticus Treebank*, was initiated. Directed by Marco Passarotti, this project continues to add further layers of pragmatic and semantic annotation to the *Index Thomisticus* material, extending in rich ways the computational operations and interrogations that can be performed on the Latin language. Given the profound and unresolved issues of data and platform sustainability and obsolescence that digital projects continue to face, it is astonishing that a project that was initiated in the mid-twentieth century continues to be freely accessible online, and in ongoing development in the twenty-first century. Little wonder that Busa's achievements received national recognition from the Italian state in 2005 when he was awarded the Grand Cross of the Order of Merit of the Italian Republic. Indeed, in time, Busa became an "eminent scholar with a worldwide reputation" (Jones 2016, 4).

During his lifetime, Busa published around 350 outputs and presented his research at scientific, governmental, military-industrial and commercial events across the world (Nyhan and Passarotti 2019, 197–220). He is a figure of great renown in fields that care about computing as much as words, especially digital humanities and computational linguistics.[4] His work, and the epistemic virtues that he and his scholarship embodied, mean many things to many people and so have a multifaceted relevance to individuals and communities. Accordingly, his achievements and significance have been narrativised in many ways. Researchers tend to emphasise the ongoing connection between Busa's research and the present-day field of digital humanities, including its text-analytical subfields, which use computational techniques to find patterns in large collections of text:

[Busa and his collaborator Paul Tasman] figured out how to represent unstructured text so that it could be processed by a computer for the first time and then they figured out how to tokenize or process the data into words such that the words could then be manipulated to generate various types of indexes. In these two coupled innovations they developed literary and linguistic data processing.

(Rockwell and Passarotti 2019)

Researchers also emphasise Busa's contributions to building what would become the distinctive para-institutional entity of digital humanities: the centre (Jones 2019); his reflections on the hermeneutic potential of computing's *via negativa* and the influence of this methodological orientation on later digital humanities (e.g. Passarotti and Nyhan 2019, 4–5); his personality traits have been lauded and connected with the realisation of his scholarship (e.g. Burton 1984a, 120) and, by implication, the development of digital humanities more generally (cf. Jones 2016). Perhaps most of all, Busa has been celebrated by many—albeit in a somewhat unreconstructed lone scholar and founding father mode—as the progenitor of humanities computing and digital humanities. For example, when announcing the award that was set up in his name, the "Roberto Busa Award", the preeminent associations of the digital humanities at that time, the Association for Literary and Linguistic Computing (ALLC) and the Association for Computers and the Humanities (ACH) stated that Roberto Busa "is regarded by many as the founder of the field of humanities computing" (EADH 2011; Jockers 2011; Dawson et al. 2002).

Albeit from an early stage of Busa's career, the photographs taken at Expo '58 show the valence of his work with actors, agenda, commercial and economic interests and technologies far beyond what might be expected of the "harmless drudge" of reference-tool and knowledge management work. The IBM logos and the state-of-the-art IBM 305 RAMAC commercial computer that appear in some photos (Busa Archive #0134) attest to how Busa's enfolding of automation in the humanities was backed and part-funded by IBM (Busa Archive #0129). That senior Roman Catholic clerics also supported his work is signalled by their presence at his Expo stand. Figure 1 shows Efrem Forni, Italian Cardinal and Papal Nuncio, standing on a raised platform and engaged in some kind of demonstration with Busa, as their attentive audience looks on. The backing Busa received from the Catholic Church was not just symbolic and promotional, his religious order, the Societas Iesu,[5] seems to have essentially seconded religious brothers to work on the parts of the project that were deemed scientific or had management functions (e.g. Aggiornamento 1960; Memorandum 1965).

Yet, for all this, the photographs from Expo '58 are most interesting for who and what they do not show. They signal little, if anything, of the fact that Busa's presence at the Expo was scaffolded by absence. As Busa's *Index Thomisticus* was foregrounded at Expo '58, the large team of workers who

Figure 1 03/09/1958 World Fair Expo, Brussels.
Note: Roberto Busa is pictured holding the microphone. To his left stands Efrem Forni, Italian Cardinal and Papal Nuncio.
Source: Busa Archive #0127, CC BY 4.0.

executed it on a day-to-day basis were invisibilised. During the period c.1954–1967, Busa was assisted by a team that numbered, at its peak, about 65 individuals (Busa 1976, 1). The absence from view of Busa's team, those who executed and progressed his research on a quotidian basis was not a mere glitch of the Expo '58 photos. As this book explores, absence would become a through-line of Busa's reporting of his work, of much popular media reporting on it and of many of the digital humanities communities' later portrayals of it too. In this way, the photos of Expo '58 may be said to distil processes of exclusion and inclusion and expressions of social and epistemological hierarchy that would shape the emerging field of humanities computing and, in due course, digital humanities. These processes and hierarchies would factor in the responses being worked out to the new questions that the inclusion of computing in the humanities was raising, like: who would be deemed eligible to make knowledge in this new departure for the humanities, where machines and humans were being enfolded in research projects in new ways, which required existing definitions of who was and was not a scholar, and what did and did not count as research to be revisited. In turn, these processes and hierarchies arguably also shaped decisions about who and what would ultimately be admitted to the historical record, and to some extent, the collective memory of Digital humanities.

This book will explore this ground through a detailed study of one cohort of the *Index Thomisticus*' wider team. As invisible in the photos of Expo '58 as in the majority of the *Index Thomisticus*' academic outputs, they are the female keypunch operators who worked on the *Index Thomisticus* project when it was based in Gallarate, near Milan, Lombardy from c.1954–67.

Though they worked with electromechanical accounting machines that are quite alien to us today, the work they did remains a crucial task of digital humanities today, where "still, the greatest amount of labour time in digital humanities projects is in preparing texts: typing them, scanning them, scraping them, cleaning them" (Pasanek 2019, 372).

The female keypunch operators' contributions to the *Index Thomisticus* were devalued but highly consequential. It was they who did the fundamental work required to make the entire basis of Busa's research on Aquinas and other authors machine-processable. Their work resulted either in the direct output, or subsequent generation of some "12 million [cards] ... which filled a row of cabinets 90 metres long and weighed 500 tonnes" (Passarotti 2013, 17). They input

> natural texts containing 12,000,000 words in 9 different languages in the Latin, Hebrew, Greek, and Cyrillic alphabets, which deal with different, subjects, periods, and cultures: such as the Qumran manuscripts [commonly known as the Dead Sea Scrolls, which deepen our understanding of the bible] the works of St Thomas Aquinas, and abstracts of nuclear physics.
>
> (Busa 2019j[1968], 120)

They worked with Busa until, as he later wrote, "*I* completed the punching of all my texts" (Busa 1980, 85 [emphasis mine]).

It is important to state emphatically that this book does not seek to personally attack Busa. For the issues explored here are far more complex, far more human, than totalising judgements made at this remove can convey. Neither does this book claim that the *Index Thomisticus*' devaluing of feminised labour was somehow "worse" than the devaluing of feminised labour that occurred right across the domestic, private, public and religious arms of the society of that time. Likewise, this book is in no way proposing that Busa's contributions should be denied or cast aside (though some reassessment and recontextualisation of how they are reported may follow this book). Rather, this book seeks to recover the mostly overlooked feminised labour that underpinned one of the most influential projects of the digital humanities; to understand what Busa thought he was doing and why he approached the labour organisation of the *Index Thomisticus* in the way that he did; and to understand the consequences of this approach especially through the lens of how the generations of scholars who followed Busa reflected on this approach. In doing so, this book aims to add another story to the substantial corpus of stories that exist about the take-up of computing in the humanities and the professional digital humanities community that formed around this. The story told here was little known in any depth until this book, yet it offers vital insights into the substantive role that gender played in the formation and development of the field of digital humanities.

The Jesuit order, to which Busa belonged, has already begun the difficult work of reflecting on its treatment of women. Decree 14 of the Society's Thirty-fourth General Congregation states that the Jesuit order "has been part of a civil and ecclesial tradition that has offended against women ... [and has] often contributed to a form of clericalism which has reinforced male domination with an ostensibly divine sanction" and goes on to propose ways that the order can do better in future (General Congregation 34 1995). Given that the story told in this book took place more than 60 years ago, and has ongoing resonance today, yet has not been told in any depth until now, is it unreasonable to ask whether the digital humanities commitment to reflecting on its treatment of women and other individuals and groups of difference is as radically honest, and self-searching as is expressed in the excerpt from the Jesuit's Decree 14 above?[6]

Main thesis and aims

This book argues that gender, and its collocations with technology, and the analogue labour history of concordance-making in the humanities have been implicated, in ways that have previously been overlooked, in the emergence and development of computing in the humanities. This is argued through a study of the *Index Thomisticus* project during its earliest years, from about 1954 to 1967, which finds that gender and technology were directly implicated in the hierarchies of labour, esteem and knowledge production that shaped this formative project of the digital humanities. Thus, not only was a masculinist epistemology and master-narrative valourised by the *Index Thomisticus* project, here understood as an idiosyncratic precursor to the institutionalised fields of humanities computing and digital humanities that would follow, that masculinist epistemology and master-narrative has been unquestioningly reproduced in significant portions of the scholarship that has since been published by the wider, institutionalised scholarly community. All the while, the field now known as digital humanities has tended to emphasise its progressive, inclusive and revolutionary nature (e.g. Nyhan and Flinn 2016, 257–75).

Like the history of computing in the humanities, the wider history of computing has often been told through machine-centred and androcentric lenses. Albeit to the chagrin of some (Stanford online 2014), scholarship on the history of computing is now also:

> increasingly situat[ing] seemingly internal developments in electronic computing within their larger social, technological and political context. The result has been more rigorous, convincing, relevant explanations of how the computer shapes, and is shaped by, modern society.
>
> (Ensmenger 2004, 96)

Studies of the imbrications of gender in computational workers' zones of operation and horizons of opportunity have given crucial impetus to this (e.g. Ceruzzi 1991; Gürer 2002; Abbate 2012; Esmenger 2012; Hicks 2017). For example, Abbate's work on women in programming and computer science has shown how gender played "an unacknowledged role in the history of computing, shaping beliefs and practices on issues ranging from the nature of expertise to the organization of work ..." (Abbate 2012, 2). In the broadest sense, this book hopes to contribute to this wider conversation through the micro-study of the labour organisation of the *Index Thomisticus* that it undertakes.

The study presented here is more circumscribed than those of others, like Hicks (2017) and Abbate (2012). Its focus is a highly specialised academic computing project, which is linked with the emergence and development of what would, in time, become a new, international (inter-)discipline (see e.g. Schreibman, Siemens and Unsworth 2008). By focusing on a highly specialised project it has been possible to identify continuities and discontinuities between the wider history of computing and the *Index Thomisticus'* situated mobilisation of gender, and the other techno-social and historical scripts that it drew on, and devised, in the process of seeking and gaining legitimisation. This will be brought out later with regard to, for example, the discontinuities that will be observed between the liberatory potential of aptitude testing in the wider history of computing versus the role of such instruments in the *Index Thomisticus* project. This will also be brought out through the analysis of the additional motivations that the incunabular digital humanities arguably had for devaluing feminised keypunching labour, including the questions about scholarly and non-scholarly identity that were being raised by the integration of computing into the humanities and changing attitudes to the scholarly value of reference-work making (see Chapter 1).

In this way, this book exemplifies Mahoney's observation that "people engaged in new enterprises bring their histories to the task, often different histories reflecting their different backgrounds and training" (Mahoney 2011, 56), showing also how those particular histories can go on to exert a hidden, yet decisive and broad influence subsequently. Busa's "somewhere else" (Mahoney 2011, 56) was the analogue humanities and concordance tradition. This book invokes the division of labour that has existed since medieval times between scholars and amanuenses in the textual projects they pursued as an important and influential, if overlooked, precursor to the emergence of computing in the humanities. This book, moreover, positions this tradition as relevant to understanding the deep time of the disciplinary and knowledge-based inequalities with which gender would intersect in the *Index Thomisticus.*

Like the other studies mentioned above, this book views gender as intersectional. Intersectionality examines "relationships and interactions between multiple axes of identity and multiple dimensions of social organization – at the same time" (Thornton Dill and Zambrana 2016, 184). Thus, it will be argued that the devaluing of the work of keypunch operators arose at the intersections of historical and coeval socially constituted frameworks and phenomena like gender, expertise, labour and technology while also being driven by specific and situated motivations.

Thus, this book has four main aims. The first is to contribute to ongoing scholarship on the overlooked and devalued work, workers and genealogies of early digital humanities and computing science projects (e.g. Scheinfeldt 2014; Earhart 2015; Whitson 2016; Earhart et al. 2017). Inflections of the so-called "techie" versus "scholar", or "research leader" versus "rank and file worker" divide can be detected in the morphology and labour organisation of the field of digital humanities, and sites of knowledge production more broadly, to this day. This raises questions about when, why and, to some extent, how the nonhegemonic individuals and communities who have shaped computing in myriad ways can or even should be acknowledged? Towards this, the research presented here follows from the recovery, recording and translation of the recollections of self-selecting individuals about their lived experiences of contributing to the *Index Thomisticus* project, which is often portrayed as the work of one man. Beyond this specific context, the oral history testimonies drawn on in this book are also important additions to the wider oral history archive of women and other minority groups who worked on early computing projects and in emerging professional and academic communities.[7]

The second aim is to challenge the exclusionary terms in which the research, and the history of digital humanities, has sometimes been framed. References to Busa's work usually emphasise that it was, above all else, ground-breaking and pioneering, like the field of digital humanities itself (see Chapter 5). This emphasis has arguably impeded the development of more nuanced understandings of the many aspects of his work that represent a continuation—even a superimposition onto supposedly new circumstances—of traditional scholarly ways of working and valuing. Likewise, in the way that the *Index Thomisticus* project mirrored the male chauvinism that is widely detectable in computing setups of the period. This will be explored through a reconstruction of the organisation and treatment of the *Index Thomisticus* workforce, with particular emphasis on the role of female keypunch operator.

It will be argued that the *Index Thomisticus* workforce organisation was anything but novel. Rather, it mirrored and reinforced the asymmetrical relationships that existed between scholars and their assistants since early modern times, and the sexism that was rampant across much of the computing industry, alerting us to the longer and even contested histories of text technologies, information processing and labour organisation of which the *Index Thomisticus*, and thus computing in the humanities, is also part. In this way, this book explores—as the project of writing the histories of digital humanities gains momentum in the wider field—how an analysis of the "old" in digital humanities is as critical as the identification of the "new". For without this complementarity, the place of the digital humanities in the longer history of the humanities and the history of computing will remain obscured.

The third aim is to look critically at how power operated in and through the *Index Thomisticus* project. Morus has cautioned: "It is not a historian's task to judge how demarcations between scientific and non-scientific work should be made. It is a historian's task to enquire into how and why such discriminations are historically constructed" (Morus 2016, 108). This book accordingly seeks to consider how scholarly authority over the *Index Thomisticus'* female technical workforce was manifested and legitimated, especially the criteria and rhetoric that were used in academic and other publications to draw distinctions between the project's scholars and key-punch operators.

This book foregrounds perspectives from feminist technology studies and the sociology and history of science and identifies the historical and coeval contingencies that could be drawn on by the *Index Thomisticus* to diminish keypunch operators work. It also synthesises recent scholarship on the labour organisation that underpinned the history of concordance making, the feminisation of "the office", women's position in automation and machine translation research along with the more local context of the "Italian economic miracle" and the employment conditions associated with it. This book thus argues that the devaluing of feminised keypunch labour served a purpose, and that it was not merely an inevitable reflection of how things were or had to be. It argues that this devaluing played an important role in validating the position of a scholar whose mechanically and computationally-assisted research nevertheless required the input of a large team of co-workers.

It bears repeating that the aim is not to criticise Busa, or others in the digital humanities, for holding attitudes that are supposedly different to now. Rather, the aim is to "pay attention to how attitudes take hold" (Jordanova 2000, 49–50) and, indeed, how they can continue to keep their hold even on communities like digital humanities whose self-narratives nevertheless emphasise its liberatory character. This is all the more urgent when one considers the role that devalued, gendered and racialised labour plays in our present computing systems, infrastructures and economy.

Invisible workers, often in the global south, people of colour and even incarcerated individuals (Bauer 2015) conduct the often hidden and yet crucial labour that generates, curates, and moderates swathes of our digital ecosystem (Roberts 2019). Within the digital humanities itself, this work may be undertaken in situ, directly by project staff, or outsourced. Though this work is crucial for digital humanities projects it can remain as hidden as the corresponding work that is done in commercial and service rather than primarily academic contexts:

> The ready-to-hand corpora available online (Google Books, Hathi Trust, Lion, EEBO-TCP) are commodified and therefore hold within them still other alienations, including the labor of the typists in Manila and Hyderabad who keyed the TCP texts, the scanners in the Google Book warehouses whose thumbs we occasionally glimpse at the margin of a PDF.
>
> (Pasanek 2019, 372)

As we shall observe, traces of the individuals who keypunched the *Index Tho-misticus* have likewise been preserved through apparent aberrations or errors, which are not only constituted linguistically in Busa's texts, in his discussions of mistakes that keypunch operators made (see Chapter 5). Traces of the fact of the existence of these individuals also take the form of disembodied hands and fin-gers, which can be sighted in photographs included in newspaper articles about the *Index Thomisticus*, sightings which seem to foreshadow the disembodied hands and fingers that have been inadvertently scanned in the course of various, present-day mass digitisation projects such as Google Books (see e.g. Irani 2016; Wen 2014). For all the techno-utopian rhetoric espoused of automation and digitisation, they can reinscribe and restructure marginalisation and deleterious power dynamics (e.g. Moravec 2017; Conway 2015; Sherratt 2019) and the story of the *Index Thomisticus'* keypunch operators allows aspects of the historical antecedents of this to be examined. Mindful of the necessity to "avoid amal-gams that could introduce an artificial continuity that has no evidentiary basis between human computers, keypunch operators or today's women labourers in computing (with all the diversity within the milieus of industry, public and private research, education, etc.)" (Schafer and Thierry 2015, 1), it is the case that "Todays hierarchy of data labor echoes older gendered, clas-sed, and raced technology hierarchies" (D'Ignazio and Klein 2020, 116), that of the *Index Thomisticus*, and its female keypunch operators among them, as this book argues.

The fourth aim is an anti-aim of sorts. In line with Hicks, this study "attempts to avoid further lionizing computer skill in a way that gives automatic approval to its worth" (Hicks 2017, 16). Thus, this book does not argue that keypunch operators' contributions should be acknowledged because they were technically superior or innovative. Rather, it seeks to reveal and acknowledge the impor-tance of keypunching labour for what it was—everyday but essential. As Hicks has argued:

> As important as hardware may be, computing functioned due to vast arrays of human workers, expressed through workflow organization, operator's actions and software. Networks of labor and expertise extend into the systems themselves, constructing the social and technological bedrock on which all computing projects rest. Ultimately, these factors determine which computer projects succeed or fail.
>
> (Hicks 2017, 5)

This book hopes to show that an understanding of the everyday significance of feminised keypunching labour opens new interpretations of the history of computing in the humanities as an unequal, and certainly inegalitarian, yet nevertheless collective, connected and distributed process.

Likewise, by reconstructing the detail of the keypunching of the *Index Thomisticus*, and analysing the how and why of its devaluing, the book advances understandings of how knowledge was defined at the beginning of digital humanities and points to the limited categories of people who were deemed appropriate to make that knowledge:

> Paying close attention [to hidden workers] offers historians ways, therefore, of looking more closely at how scientific authority is constructed and how. … Going behind the individual focus provides a way of re-emphasizing the role of the collective instead. It gives historians an opportunity to demonstrate that the notion of science as the product of individual genius is itself a construct.
>
> (Morus 2016, 108–9)

For all this, a note on this book's emphasis on Busa is in order. While Busa's work does indeed represent an influential and important digital humanities genealogy, as noted above, other alternative genealogies are also being charted by the digital humanities community, revealing the wealth of actors, agents, materials and instruments, places and spaces that may be connected with the emergence and development of computing in the humanities. This literature can be understood as participating in a wider effort to critique and challenge the use of difference as a justification for the ascendency of one group over another in the making and use of digital tools, resources and algorithms (e.g. Losh and Wernimont 2018; D'Ignazio and Klein 2020). In its inquiry into how difference was constructed and encoded into a foundational computing project, this book seeks to offer important historical context to these conversations. And yet, notwithstanding this attention to difference, this book's diving board is the canonical Busa "founding legend" rather than the other genealogies that are now being brought to light.

This is not unproblematic. Yet, it is contended that much can be gained by looking both out from, and in at, the *Index Thomisticus* from what can be reconstructed of the perspectives, and from the recollections, of the lesser-known, female workers on his team. Though this necessarily entails a revisiting and even a recentring of a canonical founding myth, this book seeks to move away from the singularity of perspective that has emphasised individual, male scholarly achievement and knowledge-making above all else. Instead, this book seeks to accommodate previously overlooked questions of process, agency, labour and affect to the story of the *Index Thomisticus*. As has been observed of feminist scholarship more broadly, "the experience of the marginalized can give them an epistemic advantage because their lives spark lines of investigation that are invisible to those in the top strata" (Bowden and Mummery 2014, 30).

Significance

Many reflections could be presented on why it is important to interrogate the role that gender played in a formative, and influential, project of the digital humanities. One contemporaneous reflection, which points to the ongoing presentness of the past even for a future-facing activity like computing, will be presented here.

Digital humanities has been experienced and described as a field that is welcoming to women (e.g. Hockey and Nyhan 2016; Rutimann and Nyhan 2016). Yet at the aggregate level, equality of opportunity, recognition and representation for all in global digital humanities remains some way off. Sex-disaggregated authorship studies attest this. One quantitative analysis of a major digital humanities conference found that the "large gender gap for authorship is not mirrored among those who simply attend the conference" (Eichmann-Kalwara, Jorgensen and Weingart 2018, 73). Despite their participation in the wider field (e.g. Weingart and Eichmann-Kalwara 2017), with regard to the female authorship of research papers in the longest-established journals of the digital humanities, women also remain in the minority. The basis of this claim is an empirical analysis of a gender-disaggregated[8] dataset of the authorship of papers published in some of the longest-established journals in the field of humanities computing and digital humanities: *Computers and the Humanities; Literary and Linguistic Computing*, renamed *Digital Scholarship in the Humanities* and *Digital Humanities Quarterly* (Gao et al. 2022). The dataset in question covers the journals' publication lifespans from inception until 31 December 2017, if still active (none of these journals had publications that spanned the whole 52-year period, 1966–2017).[9] Among the 3,382 authors in the resulting dataset, 2,253 are men (66.62%); 976 are women (28.86%) and the gender of 153 individuals remains unknown. Of that cohort, though women are a distinct minority, the top two most productive scholars are women, and the top two most central and connected scholars on the co-authorship network are women, too. The male-skewed gender distribution of the field as reflected in publications has been gradually changing during the past 52 years. Figure 2 shows the annual percentages of unique female and male authors, and we can see a rising

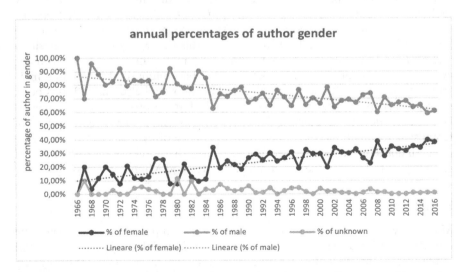

Figure 2 The annual percentages of unique number of authors disaggregated by gender. Retrieved from the journals Chum, DSH/LLC and DHQ (1966–2017).
Source: Gao et al. 2022

trend in the percentage of female scholars especially in recent years, although they are still the minority.

It is therefore important to look back to one of the foundational projects in the history of computational text processing, and to likewise acknowledge the continuing disparities of our present situation, to contribute to the ongoing and "radical task of self-critique in our present" (Quirke 2010, 12) and, perhaps, ultimately forge pathways towards more equitable futures for all who participate in computing.[10]

Analytical outlooks

Women and other minoritised groups have made seminal contributions to blue sky and applied research problems. Yet, like the *Index Thomisticus* keypunch operators, the details, and sometimes even the fact of their labour could be omitted from the scholarly publications, and other forms of reporting that were built upon their contributions, labour, skill and expertise. Scholarly and popular studies of the seminal, ground-breaking or otherwise remarkable contributions of women to the production of knowledge have been undertaken. Exemplary studies have been undertaken on, among others, the overlooked contributions of Rosalind Franklin to deciphering the double helix model of DNA (Maddox 2002); Henrietta Swan Leavitt, human computer at the Harvard Observatory who devised a way to accurately measure the cosmos (Johnson 2006); the work

Figure 3 29 June 1967, Busa's laboratory at via Galileo Ferraris 2, Gallarate.
Note: The female keypunch operators can be seen sitting at punched card machines and off to the side, presumably validating the accuracy of the cards. A male technician can be seen at the far end of the lab, operating what seems to be a sorting machine.
Source: Busa Archive #613.

of Alice Kober, which led to the decipherment of Linear B, with which Arthur Evans and Michael Ventris are usually associated (Fox 2014); the hidden stories of the black female mathematicians who worked at NASA and whose calculations put rockets and astronauts into space (Shetterly 2017); and the lived experience of female code-breakers at Bletchley Park during World War 1 (Dunlop 2015).

As with the history of computing, the history of digital humanities too has been refracted through teleological narratives of technical progress (e.g. Hockey 2004) and the achievements of famous individuals, Busa pre-eminent among them (e.g. McCarty 2013). Even in restorative (feminist) scholarship, extraordinary actors or actions can be emphasised. This can "favour figures who were already privileged relative to their contemporaries, and [who were] more visible in the historical record and other material traces of the past because of their education, wealth, or status" (Smyth, Nyhan, and Flinn 2020). In the context of the history of computing in the humanities, comparatively little attention has been paid to those individuals who used computing devices on a day-to-day basis to execute projects and research-tasks.[11]

The contention that keypunching work and workers merit recovery and acknowledgement is thus based partly on the proposition that the low esteem in which their work was held was neither a disinterested nor accurate assessment of it. The subjectivities of terms like "work" and "expertise"; the pre-eminence that has been attached to individualistic modes of knowledge production over the longer term; and the imbrications of gender and/or class, technology and/or the knowledge production regimes of disciplines all offer useful ways of thinking about why it was feminised keypunch operating work, in particular, that could be devalued, and why this devaluing may have appeared to have to been justified to those who participated in it or observed it.

Definitions of "work" and "labour"[12] are contextual and provisional: "What will count as work does not depend a priori on any set of indicators, but rather on the definition of the situation" (Star and Strauss 1999: 14). Factors that can cause work and workers to be denied or diminished include "power and status differences between employer and employee", where work and its outcomes are visible to the employer but the employee is invisible and becomes a "non-person"; where workers, like nurses, are visible but the work they do is overlooked; and through the "abstracting and manipulation of indicators", for example, when "[t]he products of work are commodities purchased at a distance from the setting of the work" (Star and Strauss 1999: 15). As we shall see, the invisibilising factors listed above all acted on keypunch operators, but the different viewers of their work, such as Busa, their *Index Thomisticus* colleagues, staff of IBM and successive generations of the international academic and computing community, watched the *Index Thomisticus* project from different lookouts and temporalities, so keypunching work was differently invisible to, or made invisible by, different actors. Neither did the invisibility of keypunching work have a bounded quality, rather, its invisibility was self-sustaining and -perpetuating: its omission from accounts of the

Index Thomisticus was sustained and amplified, however unintentionally or unwittingly, in masculinist histories of the field of digital humanities.

The inherent stability of the concept of "invisible work" has been questioned (Star and Strauss 1999), and renewed effort has been given to elaborating an analytical framework for it given the somewhat diverging definitions of the concept that are in circulation (Hatton 2017). Here the concept is used to convey how feminised keypunching labour was variously hidden or overlooked and framed as low-skilled despite evidence to the contrary. Accordingly, this book views work as social relation:

> To regard work as consisting of human interactions that are experienced within and shaped by social networks, social norms, and institutions and that are socially constructed power relations is to conceptualize work as social relation. The invisibility of work is therefore seen as constructed by these social forces, and the path to combatting problems of invisible labour is to change these social forces.
>
> (Budd 2016, 36)

This book furthermore understands the concept of invisible labour to be fascinating and slippery: its construction entails much irony and as a concept it necessarily participates in a dialectic of visibility and invisibility. The irony is that "… many overt tasks … go into making particular kinds of work invisible" (Poster, Crain and Cherry 2016, 9). The "overt tasks" that made the *Index Thomisticus* keypunch operating work invisible, including for example, the attempted erasure, or deformation of the female body in project reporting (see below), are also ironic in that they might be understood as a response to the visibility—the noticing—of the female body on the work floor and in the workflow of the *Index Thomisticus*.

Indeed, the presence of women in the *Index Thomisticus* project was questioned all the way, down even to the texts of Aquinas that keypunch operators were punching. Drawing on the views of classical authors like Aristotle, Aquinas' writings included such claims as:

> since the male seed produces a 'perfect likeness'—that is, a boy child—a girl child results from a defective seed. Women are 'deficient and misbegotten,' … inferior to men by nature except for purposes of procreation, and naturally subordinate to men because of their more limited capacity for reason.
>
> (cited in Noble 1992, 157)

Of the dominance that such claims were accorded by some in the learned and clerical circles who read them, and of the ensuing portability of these claims, Noble has written "it was not only … the unsupported prejudices of the medieval clergy which led to medieval and modern misogynism but also the medical and scientific assumptions of the ancient world that were incorporated into medieval thinking but with little challenge" (Noble 1992, 157). And without implying or claiming that Busa or those connected with the *Index Thomisticus* accepted such views, this foundational project of digital humanities can be viewed as a conduit for the successive incorporation of such views into yet newer contexts.[13] The young keypunch operators not only transcribed this misogyny but remediated it in the portable formats that made it computationally tractable in the emerging, global information processing network, which has, in turn, not only perpetuated but given rise to new forms and entanglements of misogyny and misinformation. Thus, the sighting of the invisibility of the female keypunch operators brings into focus their shared genealogy with the "uneven and exploitive set of social relationships that are rendered invisible through ... globalized technological infrastructures" (Noble 2019; see also Posner 2021).

The evaluative categories and the language used to articulate the nature of an individual's work can contribute to its invisibilising and devaluing too. The weight accorded to claims about, and the diagnosis of performances of "novelty", "innovation" and "originality" in academia is relevant to understanding why this is. Although the *Index Thomisticus'* female keypunch operators must have been among a select group of people worldwide to encode ancient and medieval languages and symbols onto punched cards, and to do so at scale, neither the novelty nor innovative nature of their work is acknowledged publications about the *Index Thomisticus*.

In contrast, albeit set in various rhetorical contexts, when discussing his own work, Busa often found it necessary to emphasise the novelty and originality of his contributions: "When in 1949 I proposed the use of computers for a wider, better, and more accurate exploration of speech and texts, I was the only person in the world who did this" (Busa 2019f[1964], 90; see also 2019e[1962], 80). Elsewhere, Busa connects originality not only with ownership and copyright, as we might expect, but with attribution and agency too:

> 'Doing' implies above all: ... having had the idea of something new or of some new service; ... describing its executive designs in detail; ... entrepreneurial deliberation; ... providing the raw materials; ... lastly, organizing the workforce to 'construct' it. Title and copyright are granted to the person who had the idea and developed the design.
>
> (Busa 2019q[1996], 187)

Yet, whatever about copyright, or the instrumental framing of a workforce in the above quotation, the fact remains that without a workforce, many projects cannot be executed or completed, as was certainly true for the *Index Thomisticus* project. This book accordingly critiques nebulous terms like "innovation", "novelty" and "originality" because:

> though essentially empty of substantive meaning, [those words are] used today to justify and rationalize a class system based upon claims of property in ideas. The system assigns most men and almost all women to

positions in the lower classes and preserves for a small group of self-recruiting males both hegemony over received knowledge and control of a variety of rewards and privileges. Among the various techniques of depreciation and dismissal of the work of women as intellectuals and scholars, one of the most prevalent has been the denial of its 'originality'.

(Carroll 1990, 136)

This book's proposition that feminised keypunching labour should be recovered and acknowledged thus seeks to move the wider frame of reference away from terms like "novelty", "originality", and the androcentric and property-based views with which scholarship can be implicated. Indeed, if it is flawed to continue to accept the devaluing of keypunching labour uncritically, then it is equally flawed to estimate that work with the very criteria used to side-line it. Though beyond the scope of this book to explore in depth, this raises questions about what might be restored to the historical record were knowledge production to be viewed from perspectives that acknowledge its interlinked and collaborative nature. Such perspectives might include that of a "feminist ethics of care", which emphasises "particularity, connection, and context" and "stresses the ways people are linked to each other and larger communities through webs of responsibilities" (Caswell and Cifor 2016, 28).

Literature on the history of science also offers useful ways of thinking about the invisible labour that haunts many academic disciplines, which have often valourised individualistic explanations and accounts of knowledge creation, such as that embodied in the canonical telling of the *Index Thomisticus* project. Large teams of individuals often supported the great men (and occasionally women) of scientific advancement, yet those teams were often eclipsed by their social and intellectual "betters" (see Russell, Tansey and Lear 2000). Nyhart has written how:

Since the late 1970s, historians of science have gradually come to accept a predominantly social constructionist account that views the development of scientific knowledge as depending heavily on particulars of local circumstances, people, epistemes, and politics, and that doesn't necessarily drive ever closer toward a single truth.

(Nyhart 2016, 8)

Contributing to the challenge of understanding "science in the past and explaining how it works now" (Russell, Tansey and Lear 2000, 237) studies have addressed, for example, the role of instruments (e.g. Baird 2004), infrastructure and laboratories (e.g. Latour and Woolgar 1986; Latour 1988) and controversies (e.g. De Freitas and Pietrobon 2010) in the social circumstances of knowledge production. There is also much attention on laboratory workers who held low-ranking posts and performed manual and largely invisible labour (e.g. Shapin and Schaffer 2011; Hartley and Tansey 2015; Barley and Bechky 1994; Iliffe 2008; Stewart 2008). As Morus has put it, "Following

Shapin's lead, historians of science have taken the task of making invisible technicians visible again to be central to the business of disassembling scientific knowledge-making and displaying its collective nature" (Morus 2016, 102).

Shapin's 1989 study of the invisible workers of Robert Boyle's experimental laboratory in early modern England showed that without them science could not have been made (Shapin 1989, 554–63). Yet few references to the fact of their existence, yet alone acknowledgements of their work are to be found in Boyle's publications or correspondence. This is partly due to the low regard in which their work was held: it was seen to require manual skill rather than knowledge (Shapin 1989, 554–5). Technicians were directed by Boyle and consequently viewed as lacking in agency and interchangeable in their roles without detriment to the workings of science (Shapin 1989, 557). The low ranking of their position was also influenced by the wider social milieu, and the gentlemanly conventions of seventeenth-century England, which meant that the remuneration they received for their work cast them as inherently untrustworthy. Scholars point out that numerous models now exist for "organizing scientific activity" (Iliffe 2008, 4). And though

> twentieth-century scientists are not gentlemen of independent means and do not employ ... junior laboratory staff themselves, to an extent their authority still derives from claims made on this historical basis. This may partly explain why modern laboratory support staff are sometimes as invisible as Boyle's assistants.
>
> (Russell et al. 2000, 240)

In Chapter 1 of this book, this idea will be explored with regard to the "laboratory" of concordance-making, and it will be suggested that cognisance of the amanuenses (or textual assistant)-scholar nexus that underpinned many textual reference works, like concordances, may help to explain further aspects of the historical basis on which the *Index Thomisticus'* feminised keypunching labour could be devalued.

The excesses of the radical social constructionist project have been critiqued by scholars like Haraway, who argue that the point should not be to deny objectivity in knowledge production entirely but rather to elucidate a feminist or embodied objectivity or "quite simply situated knowledges" (Haraway 1988, 585). That there should accordingly be a legitimate place in histories of computing in the humanities for situated knowledges and historicisation of, for example, experiential, affective, and embodied experiences of working with and in computing is not one that has been taken up substantively in the relevant digital humanities scholarship so far. This may be because computing, software and code has often been viewed as objective, neutral and hermetically sealed off from the influence of their creators and users (van Zundert and Haentjens Dekker 2017).

Yet, this perspective has been problematised by a wealth of scholarship, including feminist technology studies (FTS). This scholarship offers important ways of invalidating narratives of disinterested technological objectivity, and sheds light on how gender, and its intersectionality has been used in science and technology to legitimate the power of some while disenfranchising others.

In FTS scholarship, as in this book, gender can be understood and positioned as a critical and analytical category that is "constructed and negotiated within an historical, social and geographical context and accomplished through praxis" (Gunnerud Berg 1997, 266). While not seeking to essentialise gender (Wajcman 2010), FTS views technology and gender as fundamentally intertwined and often co-constitutive. Technology is an arena where gender is expressed, performed and even ratified (Wyer et al. 2013; Bray 2007, 38). Likewise, gender stereotypes can influence what counts as technology and who counts as a technologist or, more generally, an actor with technological agency (Linn 1987; Cockburn and Ormrod 1993). Thus:

> Men are viewed as having a natural affinity with technology, whereas women supposedly fear or dislike it. Men actively engage with machines, making, using, tinkering with, and loving them. Women may have to use machines, in the workplace or in the home, but they neither love nor seek to understand them: They are considered passive beneficiaries of the inventive flame.
>
> (Bray 2007, 38)

FTS theorises technology not as neutral, objective and detached but has shown how technological products and processes can be created "in the interests of particular social groups, and against the interests of others" (Wajcman 1996, 43) And it is from this perspective that this book seeks to understand the different ways that the work and workers of the *Index Thomisticus* project were portrayed, not only by Busa and the wider field of digital humanities but in broader societal contexts too. Indeed, neither scholars nor the societies they live and work in exist separately. It seems reasonable to suggest that there may have been some kind of reciprocal interchange between the *Index Thomisticus'* portrayal of the work of keypunch operators and that of their media depiction more generally.

That technology is not neutral, and that the same technology can be portrayed very differently when it is collocated with different social groups, and the individuals who constitute them, is attested in media images that depict Busa, his female technical staff, and the machines they used. Photographs of female keypunch operators at work are comparably abundant in public-facing publications, certainly in comparison with the number of mentions of them that occur in formal academic publications, written for a limited audience. This has also been observed of hidden or devalued manual workers in other fields, like archaeology:

> In publication, archaeological writers strategically excise [their digging workforce] individual identities, in their very names, and the collective

presence of workers. The main trace of their activity may be confined to colour photographs, in public-information web-sites, magazines and brochures, often oriented towards fundraising.

(Quirke 2010, 1–2)

Thus, the public-facing depictions of the *Index Thomisticus* that diminish its female keypunch operators were far from an exception or aberration and the diminishment of manual workers like those of the *Index Thomisticus* may have been naturalised through the ubiquity of this mode of depiction.

The visual diminishment of keypunch operators in the popular press took various forms, direct and indirect. In media images the conjunction of male scholar and automation machine seems to emphasise the complexity and sophistication of man and machine, and the work they are executing. So, in *Der Spiegel* when Busa is photographed sitting at a punched card machine, looking down at its keys, the scene is captioned: *"Text-Analysen durch Robotergehirne"* [Text Analysis using Robot Brains] (Der Spiegel 1957). Elsewhere, Busa and the keypunch machine are depicted intact, while a female operator is cut from the picture, save for her hands (La Croix 1957). This also occurs when Busa is not present, as when the keypunch machine is foregrounded and the keypunch operator using it is again cut to disembodied hands. The caption that accompanies one such image makes no mention of "Robot Brains", rather it relays, in the passive voice, how the scene depicts text being encoded onto punched cards (Colbans 1958, 34). Text and image work in tandem here, and elsewhere, to diminish the keypunch operator's knowledge, individuality and embodied use of technology: the passive voice that erases her in the photo's caption is echoed in the purported passivity of the disembodied hands to which she is diminished. The keypunch machine thus dominates the picture, while the identity of the person without whom it could not work is obliterated. At the same time, the machine is portrayed in a rather more prosaic way here as compared to when it is depicted alongside Busa, suggesting that it is not only readings of gender that such images frame, but readings of technology too.

If the esteemed scholar's association with the machine was, then, mutually enriching for man and machine, it seems that the keypunch operator may not have been pictured lest she diminish the machine, and the *Index Thomisticus* project that used it, by association. This alerts us to how the estimations of particular machines, and the gender associations they evoked were not necessarily fixed at this stage of computing in the humanities; rather they were performative. Thus, echoing Butler's scholarship on gender performativity (e.g. Butler 1990a, 1990b), very different portrayals and estimations of machines and their users could be invoked, via text and image, through human-machine collocations and enactments of labour. This may help to explain the apparent paradox regarding how and why Busa's texts could sometimes indicate that he himself, as cited above, had actually used punched card machines to do the work that was so devalued when it was linked with keypunch operators. This may also explain why the work of the *Index*

Thomisticus male technical staff, while they may be the least-mentioned of all *Index Thomisticus'* staff in Busa's academic writings, do not tend to be diminished on those rare occasions when they are brought into sight. Male technical staff connected with the *Index Thomisticus*, even when also using accounting machines (albeit for text processing rather than text input) tend to be referred to in broadly positive ways, for example, Busa emphasises the contribution that IBM technical staff made to the elaboration of his method: "it was nonetheless due to the open-mindedness and intelligence of the IBM people, who have honoured me with their patient confidence, that the method for such application has been found" (Busa 2019a[1951], 28). Meanwhile in media reporting, the male machine operators, as a group, are portrayed as consequential individuals, on course to use the knowledge they acquired in Busa's training school to automate the industries they were on the verge of entering, via management or senior administrator roles (see Chapter 3).

The point of images that diminish keypunch operators may also, of course, have been to make the *Index Thomisticus* seem "scientific", its work more analogous with that done in the laboratory. During and after the second world war, laboratory-based science, particularly in the United States, had delivered a smorgasbord of lucrative, if sometimes murderous outputs:

> The atom bomb, synthetic rubber, radar and other technologies were developed in a concerted effort by universities, the military and companies. The visible success of these programmes enshrined the linear model of innovation: knowledge production was crucial for innovation, and innovation was crucial for the development of industry and society. This ideology boosted the development of all laboratory types after 1945, even though innovation processes followed non-linear paths.
>
> (van Rooij 2011, 440)

Aligning the *Index Thomisticus* with "science" may thus have functioned to assert its similarly innovative and successful mode of operation. An attempt at such an articulation can perhaps be detected in the visual rhetoric of keypunch operators' corporeal diminishment. Regarding the early-modern laboratory it has been observed: "It is striking how often ... that work is seen to be performed by disembodied hands, rather than by a human labourer. ... Removing the technician from the picture was a way of showing where scientific authority really resided" (Morus 2016, 102). So too, perhaps, with the *Index Thomisticus* and the disembodied hands of its keypunch operators that can be sighted in media reporting on the project.

In any case, the stage-craft of these images suggests that Busa and the machine are doing the real work, the work that merits documentation and acknowledgement. As far as they may be noticed, keypunch operators are suggested to be as peripheral and interchangeable as pairs of disembodied hands, reduced to the stereotypical technician in scientific illustrations, and admitted grudgingly, in de-individualised and diminished form, to the long-sought after "world without women" of science and technology (Noble 1992). Thus, the *Index Thomisticus* project was not unique or even unusual in its androcentrism. Indeed,

> The modernist association of technology with masculinity translates ... into everyday experiences of gender, historical narratives, employment practices, education, the design of new technologies, and the distribution of power across a global society in which technology is seen as the driving force of progress.
>
> (Bray 2007, 38)

Accordingly, portrayals of women (and others, including men at lower levels of the class structure) as mere users of technology, and portrayals of important men as "... inventors, makers, and repairers" (Rothschild 1983, vii) can undergird accounts of the "great men", "grand narratives" and unrelated "firsts" that have sustained many histories of science, technology and computing (e.g. Basalla 1988, 21). And right across knowledge production settings, women are known to have provided low paid, overlooked and even "unpaid and invisible support for scientists and astronomers" (Iliffe 2008, 8; Nyhart 2016, 10), writers (Kirschenbaum 2016; Stillinger 1991; Price 2004), artists, choreographers and performing artists (Essin 2015; Becker 1998), and the library and information sector (Poole 2018), amongst others. Accordingly, this book seeks to contribute to ongoing conversations about the agency of previously marginalised individuals.

This book will argue that the work of the *Index Thomisticus* female keypunch operators was more varied and skilled than might be inferred from the mantle of "clerk" (Tasman 1957, 254) that was draped on them. But their work probably was not "seminal", "innovative" or "remarkable", the *raison d'être* of many restorative studies of women and minority or non-hegemonic groups. The nature of their training in Busa's centre, and the conditions that they worked under, which were characterised by a lack of autonomy and dearth of possibility for progression, would likely have precluded them from making such intellectual contributions. Why, then, should the *Index Thomisticus'* keypunching work be recovered and attributed to those who executed it, collectively or individually? Taking the conceptual perspectives outlined above as its jumping off point, this book will argue that by following the multiple threads that link the labour organisation of the *Index Thomisticus* to wider historical and contemporary conversations about invisible labour, technology, gender, and definitions of achievement, we can identify socio-cultural, historical and techno-scientific motivations for positioning their roles as transitory and subaltern, irrespective of their work's inherent complexity.

Research context

Until this book, the nature of the contributions that were made to the *Index Thomisticus* by female keypunch operators were almost entirely unknown.

Equally unknown was their lived experience of working in one of the earliest mechanically-assisted, "big data" projects in the humanities. Though omitted from the canonical historiographies of computing and the humanities, keypunch operators were numerically the most significant cohort among the *Index Thomisticus*' wider workforce, which reached about 65 individuals at its height.[14]

Busa often presented himself as a lone scholar in the sense that he was responsible for the ideation and execution of the substantive aspects of the *Index Thomisticus* (e.g. Busa 2019e[1962], 80). His writings do sometimes seem to minimise or deny the input of his scientific, clerical and IBM collaborators, for example, with claims like "I had to solve problems which no longer exist today. Without assistance and in addition to finding financial support, I had to develop and test a method which had no predecessor ..." (Busa 1980, 87). Still, it would be wrong to claim that Busa never acknowledged his collaborators.

Paul Tasman of IBM's role in devising and testing the technical processes that underpinned the *Index Thomisticus* was crucial. On the acknowledgements page of the *Index Thomisticus*, it is strange to note Tasman's absence from "*in re Scientifica et Editoriali* [scientific and editorial matters]". Instead, he is listed "*in re Oeconomica* [economic matters]", as are the "*Moderatores IBM*". But Busa did acknowledge elsewhere that Tasman's "role in this project has been an essential one: without his contribution it could have failed many times" (Busa 1980, 84; see also Busa 1957, 20; Busa 1958b, 187). Busa also acknowledged Cardinal Spellman's support of the project (Busa 1957, 20), "Mr. H.J. Krould, Chief of the European Affairs Division of the Library of Congress" for connecting him with Jerome Wiesner of MIT, who subsequently connected him with IBM in New York (Busa 1980, 84). We learn too of James W. Perry's matchmaker role for Busa in America (Busa 1980, 86). Busa names some IBM Milan managers and employees who assisted him: c.1949–51: "G. Vuccino, Cl. Folpini, A. Cacciavillani (I regret that I might have skipped over some names, but they know how grateful I am to them)" (Busa 1980, 84; see also Busa 1957, 20; Busa 1958b, 187). Busa wrote of the "team of ten priests who worked with me for two full years to design a Latin machine dictionary" (Busa 1980, 86) and of the Jesuit brother Federico Masiero who used an "American Davidson machine" to print on the back of punched cards (Busa 1980, 85). Busa frequently mentions the work of the male "scholars" on his team (those engaged in the "thought processing" mentioned above) and he communicates how much he valued their work (see Chapter 5). Also mentioned are those who helped with fundraising: members of the "Promoting Committee for the IT [who were] eminent Italian scholars" and the "group of friends, professionals and businessmen" who participated in the *Index Thomisticus* Finance and Administration Committee (Busa 1980, 85). On the acknowledgements page of the *Index Thomisticus*, a roll-call of 59 individuals honours their contributions to the project over the c. 30 years of its operation. A pattern is detectable, then, in Busa's acknowledgement and attribution practices. Efforts recognised are those of important men: clerics, scholars, businessmen, and politicians. Their association with Busa's research seems to lend it an additional air of authoritativeness and currency beyond what must often have been perceived as the arcane world of semi-automated concordancing.

It would be equally wrong to state that Busa never acknowledged the contributions of the *Index Thomisticus'* staff. They are collectively referenced in some published articles:

> At present the Center employs a group of close to sixty individuals: six for managing and secretarial work, fourteen for thought processing (Latin pre-editing group, Latin lemmatizing group, Hebrew group, and a soon to be arranged Greek group), four computer programmers, 32 to 37 for machine operations (key-punching the texts, verifying, listing, sight checking, punch-card processing, computer processing).
>
> (Busa 1964, 65)

And the keypunch operating work that is the focus of this book does sometimes get a fleeting mention in publications pertaining to the *Index Thomisticus*, for example, "A clerk copies the text ..." (Tasman 1957, 254). Mostly, however, words, images, technical plans and sketches are made confederate in the diminishment of keypunching work and those who executed it. The use of the passive voice, conventional in academic writing, may have sometimes unintentionally hidden the operators' presence: "The Centre at Gallarate is still today the one in the whole world that has put the greatest number of words on cards: there are to date about four million, and the number is increasing." (Busa 2019e[1962], 79). In all fairness, the first person plural personal or possessive pronoun, appropriate when reporting team-based work, may also have unintentionally obfuscated their presence: "we first punched, sequenced and numbered ..." (Busa 1980, 86). But other elisions are more difficult to attribute to the vicissitudes of grammatical voice or number. In these examples keypunching work goes totally unacknowledged and operators' identities are subsumed by Busa's so that we find various iterations in his writing of the claim that "I have now completed the punching of the 220,000 cards that represent all the lines of the *Summa Theologiae* of St Thomas" (Busa 2019c[1958], 66).

These verbal misrepresentations and obfuscations were sometimes given visual reinforcement in academic outputs as well as media reporting. For example, a diagram appended to the text of a 1960s conference presentation clearly depicts a male scholar in form and agency. The keypunch operator, meanwhile, is reduced to a disembodied, mention of a hand that intervenes between the circles and the frames that foreground the mechanical, material and scholarly, or rather, "authorized"[15] components of the *Index Thomisticus'* workflow (Busa 1960a).

Again, a pattern is detectable here: those who performed the mechanically-assisted capture and processing of the *Index Thomisticus* are rarely mentioned, and certainly not in a way that communicates the value of their work. As we shall see, it is computing machines, and performances of a certain kind of

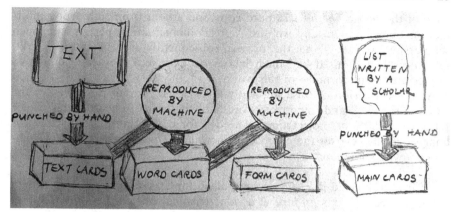

Figure 4 Author's impression of illustration included in "Zusammengefasste Darstellung der Erfahrungen des Centro per l'Automazione dell'Analisi Letteraria des Aloisianum" (redrawn for reasons of resolution)
Note: In Kolloquium: Maschinelle Methoden der literaryschen Analyse und der Lexicographie. 24–26 Nov. 1960. Pp. 6+26 (litografia).
Source: Busa 1960a.

scholarly identity, embodied in ideals of the scholar as a male who publicly and disinterestedly pursues higher knowledge, that is often valourised and echoed from publication to publication on the *Index Thomisticus*.

The feminist theory of co-liberation states that the detrimental impacts of inequality are not bounded to its immediate subjects: "men are often not even thought to have a gender, let alone prompted to think about how unequal gender relations seep into our institutions and artifacts and harm all of us" (D'Ignazio and Klein 2020, 35). In troubled letters from the late 1950s, Busa communicated the tremendous pressure under which he struggled, and his regrets at not having time for friends and family (Busa 1959d). He reports experiencing some kind of "nervous breakdown" around 1959 (Jones 2016, 164). Poignant references to the personal toll his work extracted occur in later periods too: "I have a lion by the tail. At first I was on the outside looking in, but now it is like being inside a remarkable prison" (O'Neill 1964, 3). However speculative the suggestion of the possible impact on Busa of striving to meet such an exacting reification of "the scholar", in addition to meeting the obligations of his Jesuit vocation, for keypunch operators the immediate impact was quite linear: they were largely written out of the abundant reporting, both project-internal and external, on the *Index Thomisticus* (see Chapter 5).

Underscoring how the *Index Thomisticus* is a work of scholarship on which the gendered, sociocultural conditions of its making are materially stamped, keypunch operators are neither individually nor collectively acknowledged in its paratexts. They are absent from the acknowledgements page of the *Index Thomisticus* hard copy and absent from supporting information on its present-day website.[16] A similar situation pertains in much scholarship written about the project subsequently (see Chapter 5). Yet, references to feminised keypunch labour do exist and they can help us to appreciate the importance of this work.

A later discussion of Busa implicitly invokes the "Pareto principle" or the "80/20 principle" and imperfectly foreshadows the often-heard data science refrain that 80% of project time is needed for data cleansing, and 20% for analysis. It also evokes the reliance of the *Index Thomisticus* project on feminised keypunch labour:

> I had completed the keypunching of all my texts before the opportunity of correcting texts on tape at a video-terminal existed. Less than 20% of the time was spent on the first punching and more than 80% on cleaning the input ... The ratio of human work to machine time was more than 100:1. Computer hours were less than 10000 while man hours were much more than 1 million.
>
> (Busa 1980, 87)

As we shall see, from behind, or under, such broad references to the work of an ostensible lone scholar, and sublimations of keypunch operators' time and effort into estimations of "man hours", some details of the rich arena of their operation can be uncovered. As will be set out in more detail in subsequent chapters, female keypunch operators were mostly attached to the "training school" that Busa set up in Gallarate in c.1956. In 1980, he wrote of the training school:

> For all those admitted, the requirement was that it was their first job. After a month of testing, only one out of five was accepted for a program of four semesters, eight hours per day. The success was excellent: industries wanted to hire them before they had finished the program. Their training was in punching and verifying our texts. To make the switch from the Latin to the Hebrew and Cyrillic texts, only two weeks were needed, and it was not even necessary to attach these new alphabets to the keys of the puncher. In punching these non-Roman alphabets, the process was less speedy but with fewer errors.
>
> (Busa 1980, 85)

This training school was, in turn, a division of CAAL (the Centro per L'Automazione dell'Analisi Letteraria, or Centre for the Automation of Literary (sometimes linguistic) Analysis) which Busa set up around that time too. CAAL's flagship project was the *Index Thomisticus*, though many other projects were also pursued under its aegis,[17] including a planned concordance to the non-biblical Dead Sea Scrolls (see Jones 2016, 139–68).

The keypunch operators' main task was to encode the pre-edited text of Aquinas and related authors onto punched cards using electro-mechanical IBM accounting machines, thus completing the essential preliminary work of the *Index Thomisticus*, of which Busa would claim sole authorship. They did this for the other multilingual text projects that CAAL undertook too, in an academic or service capacity. Thus, they keypunched alphanumeric texts that contained special characters and symbols that were neither routinely nor easily encoded at that time. From unconnected discussions of keypunching, it seems that the type of punching they did was highly demanding, perhaps the most demanding of all: "Alphabetic punching, that is, the punching of alphabetic characters, is slower than the punching of numeric data. Intermingled alphabetic characters, numeric data and special characters are the most difficult to punch and greatly decrease the speed of the operation." (Van Ness 1963, 37). In addition, they were tasked with the work of verifying, by sight or with the assistance of IBM verifying machines, the materials they had punched. Their work spanned right across Busa's 80/20 breakdown above, and further still (see Chapter 2).

As we shall see, keypunching labour work must have required intense concentration, attention to detail, manual dexterity and mechanical aptitude, including the ability to memorise multi-key combinations to encode text. It also required an ability to complete tedious, repetitive and ill-contextualised tasks, day-in, day out. Mental fortitude must have been requisite too: according to Busa's own portrayal, feminised keypunching was executed in an environment where mistakes, rather than achievements, were recorded and tracked (see Chapter 5). This book tends to use "women", so as not to sound disrespectful given the patronising register of "girls" in much of the trade and media literature on computing in the 1960s and later (see e.g. Light 1999). Yet the punched card operators literally were girls, many of whom were hired at 14 years of age, having completed the legal-minimum level of education in Italy at that time (see Chapter 4).

Oral history and archival evidence attest how some young women demonstrated their versatility, reliability and competence in roles beyond keypunching (see Chapter 4). Some took on significant tasks in the management, training and pastoral care of the male and female staff of CAAL. Yet despite demonstrable experience of workforce training, management ability and domain knowledge, women were not permitted to hold senior positions that were also acknowledged as such in the *Index Thomisticus*, or indeed in much of the wider world of computing and keypunching, as later chapters will evince. There is, moreover, some evidence that one keypunch operator helped to devise the bespoke key combinations that allowed the special characters and symbols of the *Index Thomisticus'* corpus to be represented on punched cards, as later chapters will also evince. In other humanities computing research projects, this was, indeed, valued as work that was significant enough to be reported on formally (see e.g. Dyer 1968; Wright 1972). At least one individual also liaised with external clients in connection with the keypunching contracts that CAAL completed for external universities, research centres and government agencies. Thus, feminised keypunching labour not only helped to constitute the *Index Thomisticus*, it seems to have generated a revenue stream for CAAL too. As we shall see, although one woman wanted to learn more, and to progress from the post of keypunch operator, she was obstructed from doing so (see Chapter 4). In an oral history interview, where the putting aside of a female manager was being discussed, the interviewee made an observation that seems applicable to the situation of the *Index Thomisticus*' punched card operators more widely: "TO [The Operator]: And so, in short, I would say this was the negative part, that Father Busa would have preferred a man in charge" (The Operator, Passarotti and Nyhan 2014).

In telling a previously overlooked story, this book shows that the labour organisation of one of the earliest humanities computing centres was founded on gender-segregated roles and gender discrimination. Tasks and responsibilities were not assigned according to an individual's knowledge and experience; rather, gender stereotypes played a decisive role in determining who could be admitted to which role and which technology they could use. Keypunch operators were seen as sources of low-cost and low-skilled labour, yet the tasks they undertook went beyond what might usually be associated with posts that create little value. As subsequent chapters will explore, their work was skilled, demanding and crucial to the everyday running and subsequent legacy of the *Index Thomisticus* and CAAL. Without their efforts there would have been no text on punched cards, then paper or magnetic tape and later, other storage forms to concord, analyse, transform and output, initially as hard copy, then, as we have seen, circulated on CD-ROMs, subsequently made globally accessible via a browser window and now enfolded in natural language processing and digital humanities projects that continue to work with this data, as indeed they should. Yet, keypunch operators were routinely side-lined and their agency and contributions to the *Index Thomisticus* have regularly been obscured. Subsequent scholarship has often presented the *Index Thomisticus* project as the work of a lone scholar (see Chapter 5).

Research methods

Through oral history, archival research, the analysis of newly accessible translations of primary and secondary sources and syntheses of secondary literature, this book examines the role that gender played in the elaboration of the data-foundations of the digital humanities, as seen through the lens of the *Index Thomisticus* project. In doing so, it also sets out a framework for the recovery and reconsideration of the devalued, feminised labour that was contributed to many mechanically—and computationally—augmented research projects pursued across the Academy, Library and Cultural Heritage sector.

A substantial part of the archival research that underpins this book was conducted on Busa's archive in the Università Cattolica del Sacro Cuore, Milan, Italy. What might be called the core of this archive, that is the first part of it to be deposited with the Università Cattolica in 2009, comprises Busa's own collection of the documents that he accumulated and preserved during his lifetime.[18] The core of the archive thus arguably represents the documentary view that Busa wanted to leave to posterity of his work and academic life.

Though the "'exclusions on which [archives] are premised [are] often dimly understood, all archives come into being ... as a result of specific political, cultural, and socioeconomic pressures and they frequently feature documents of the powerful and privileged" (Chaudhuri, Katz, and Perry 2010, xiv). During this research, one exclusion from Busa's archive was brought into view: little about the work or identities of the *Index Thomisticus*' keypunch operators is preserved in the core archive. The core archive contains a wealth of material pertaining to many aspects of the *Index Thomisticus*, but, aside from photographic evidence, documentary traces pertaining to the keypunching of the *Index Thomisticus* are few. And even self-consciously information-bearing archival documentation is framed by absence. Excepting two women who worked for him for many years, Busa did not record the identities of keypunch operators' in the explanatory handlist he prepared for the c. 900 photographs of his research-related activities that were accessioned to his archive. When keypunch operators are referenced in this handlist, it is with the catch-all *"Allieve-i del Centro"* [students of the centre].[19] By way of contrast, Busa often names individually the many important men (and a few women, usually present and acknowledged due to their connection with one of the important men who appear in the photographs).

A further tranche of documents was made available to the Busa archive in 2015, by brethren of the Aloisianum in Gallarate, Lombardy, where Busa worked and lived for much of his life. This tranche contained documents that shed light on some aspects of the labour organisation of the *Index Thomisticus* project, and the conditions under which its employees worked. Still, direct mentions of keypunch operators and their work are few.

That references to the *Index Thomisticus*' keypunch operators in documentary sources are far from abundant fits with wider patterns observed in archives "predominantly produced and preserved by men" (Bishop 2017, 767). The ensuing detriment of the "comparative lack of archival trace to secure [women] in the sightlines of history" (Burton 2008, 149) underscores the subjectivities of the archive. Individuals and communities tend to record and preserve what they value, and overlook what they do not, often with lasting consequences.

Butler's theorisation of gender has posited that it is constituted in enactment, in:

> a stylized repetition of acts ... which are internally discontinuous ... [so that] the appearance of substance is precisely that, a constructed identity, a performative accomplishment which the mundane social audience, including the actors themselves, come to believe and to perform in the mode of belief.
>
> (Butler 1990a, 179; see also Butler 1990b)

Schwartz and Cook have drawn on Butlers' gender performativity in theorising how "in performing their work, archivists follow a script that has been naturalized by the routine repetition of past practice" (Cook and Schwartz 2002, 171), thus helping to explain why such scripts can go unquestioned yet can also function as important loci for rethinking archival power. Methodological approaches that have been pioneered by feminist scholars can, moreover, bring some devalued or excluded actors into at least a partial view. By reading "against the grain", interweaving archival, secondary and oral history sources, and following the omissions, contradictions, imaginaries and multiple viewpoints this brings into view, this book aims to paint a fuller if still incomplete and sometimes tentative picture of the feminised keypunch labour that gave rise to the *Index Thomisticus*.

The oral history interviews that this book draws on were carried out on 1 April 2014 in the Aloisianum College of Philosophical Studies, Gallarate, Italy, with 9 of the female punched-card operators who had worked for Busa. Collectively, these interviews weave a thread from the period from shortly before the opening of CAAL (c.1954) to its close in 1967. All of those interviewed were contacted via Danila Cairati, Busa's final secretary, who knew many of the interviewees personally. Thus, the group were self-selecting in the sense that they responded to an open invitation to be interviewed. As for the numerical representativeness of this sample, it is difficult to say, for, such is the dearth of documentation, it has not been possible to establish how many keypunch operators worked on the *Index Thomisticus* during the years of its operation. It seems certain that those interviewed represent only a small fraction of the wider team of keypunch operators who contributed to the *Index Thomisticus* during the years it was based in Gallarate, Italy. Thus, through archival research, this book has also sought to reach beyond the cohort represented in the oral history interviews, and to get some sense of the experiences of the wider *Index Thomisticus* keypunch labour force.

Both the author and Marco Passarotti (a former student of Busa and Principal Investigator of the CIRCSE Research Centre, Università Cattolica del Sacro Cuore, Milan) were present at the interviews with the former operators, as was Cairati. As I have rudimentary Italian only, the interviews were conducted in Italian by Passarotti. They can be described as semi-structured in that a set of core questions were identified by Nyhan in advance of the interviews and raised in each interview. Passarotti also asked extemporaneous questions, to follow especially interesting or unexpected aspects of interviewees' recollections. The core questions were informed by Nyhan's wider oral history research on the history of digital humanities (e.g. Nyhan and Flinn 2016) and adapted with two aims in mind, namely, to prompt and record recollections of the nature and context of the feminised labour that underpinned the *Index Thomisticus* project along with recollections of the experience of having contributed to the *Index Thomisticus* project itself.

Passarotti is a native speaker of Italian with expertise in computational linguistics and digital humanities; he is also a former student and, indeed, friend of Busa. Therefore, he was well placed to translate the core questions, to identify and follow new leads in the interviews and to interact with interviewees according to the cultural and linguistic norms of Italian society. Yet, the choice of engaging as an interviewer someone whom the women were aware of as having had close connections to Busa is not unproblematic:

> An insider may have the credentials to get the interviews and to understand the situation enough to ask the right questions, but as insiders they may not acknowledge the shared tacit knowledge between them, they might avoid difficult and sensitive topics, or identify too closely with the community to present that community in anything other the most favourable light. If there are significant cultural, socio-economic and power differences, it does not mean that the interview will not be a success but it will almost certainly impact on the dialogue in some way and that difference ought to be located and understood.
>
> (Flinn and Nyhan 2016)

While a simultaneous style translation approach to the interviews would have been ideal it was beyond our resources. Instead, Passarotti tried, when feasible, to give me a succinct translation of the unfolding recollections but it was not possible to do so on a continuous basis.

When the interviews took place in 2014, every interviewee gave their informed consent for interviews to be recorded and released under a creative commons license. A small grant was secured from the European Association of Digital Humanities so that an Italian-language transcription, and translation could be made from the audio recording by a research associate, Ana Vela. I then set about the editing of the translated interviews (consulting with Vela, and a subsequent research assistant, Giulia D'Agostino for clarification where necessary and to identify para-textual aspects of the interviews (such as changes of emotion) hinted at in the transcripts (see e.g. Abrams 2016). In comparison with the audio files, the translated transcripts have been heavily edited to aid their readability. The type of editing that was done at this stage included literary-style interventions such as removing disfluencies of speech and deleting repetitious text.

In 2018, I returned copies of the interview transcripts, in English and Italian, to interviewees still living. Comments and corrections specified by interviewees and communicated to me were then integrated into the transcripts. At this stage, I communicated with interviewees in person and in writing, again with the help of Danila Cairati and Marco Passarotti, to further ensure that they were happy for excerpts of their interview transcripts to be included in this book. Everyone reconfirmed; one interviewee asked for their identity be anonymised. I have accordingly taken great care to anonymise their identity in this book, extending this beyond oral history interviews where necessary, by, for example, not writing about some trails and interconnections between the archival and oral history records that I know to exist to respect their request for anonymity in this book. More generally, where information of a personal nature has been recorded in archival documents about individuals connected with the *Index Thomisticus*, I have anonymised the identity of the individuals being discussed there, whether I have interviewed them or not.

Oral history literature emphasises the difficulties of cross-cultural interviewing (see Burton 2003) and the reliance on translators and other intermediaries it can require. Alone the use of verbatim transcripts is not uncontentious in oral history research:[20] the act of transcription can be seen as "a form of translation between the spoken and written word" (Andrews 1995, 49). A further layer of distancing is introduced when transcripts must be translated. Yet, as Ritchie notes, while "oral history becomes a lot more complicated if the interviewer and interviewee do not speak the same language, ... this is not an impenetrable impediment" (Ritchie 2014, 100). Though critical reflection on the oral history interviewing done for this book follows (see Chapter 4), the limitations of cross-cultural interviewing are here approached in a pragmatic way, that acknowledges that research projects require compromises of various kinds (e.g. Burton 2003). It is important to identify and discuss the compromises and limitations of cross-cultural oral history research; it is also the case that without such compromises, this book would not exist in its present form.

In its overarching aim, and in the methodological and ethical approach that has been taken to achieving this aim, this is a book of feminist oral history. A crucial concern of feminist oral history is how "the dynamics of power affect the process, content, and outcomes of interviews and the nature of the scholarship produced" (Srigley, Zembrzycki, and Iacovetta 2018, 2). As such, I was deeply uncomfortable with the prospect of adumbrating keypunch operators' voices once more, by positioning their interviews as data to be mined and reassembled as the foundations, and supporting beams of the authorial interpretations of aspects of this book, otherwise silencing what I have not included or obfuscating my interpretative interventions.

Part of this unease stems also from my positionality, given that I am a white, cisgender woman who by the age of 40 had twice been successful in her applications to full professor, in two highly regarded universities in the UK and Germany. Thus, my professional status and privilege is far closer to that of Busa than keypunch operators. While I wrote this book to learn more about the experiences that other women in my field have made, I became increasingly aware of the degree of reflexivity and cognisance of the ethical implications this required of me, given that my work is undertaken from a position of power and privilege within academia.

Accordingly, while excerpts from the interviews are interwoven into the chapters that follow, the interviews have also been published in full, online. This is to acknowledge that what follows is, while painstakingly researched and undertaken throughout with the greatest levels of care and integrity, my expert interpretation of the events analysed here. I do not propose or pretend that the interpretation set out here is somehow comprehensive or final. By making the oral history interviews freely available online, my hope is that they can also be read independently of this book, thus potentially accommodating a plurality of interpretative readings and historicisations of their interviews, and ultimately reminding us of the multiplicity of experience, interpretation (and recollection) that has contributed to the formation and development of digital humanities.

Since I began working in digital humanities in 2000 (as a 20-year-old text encoder in the Corpus of Electronic Texts (CELT) project, University College Cork (UCC), Ireland),[21] I have encountered, first hand, the essential and central role that text capture plays in many digital humanities projects. For if a hardcopy text is to be made machine readable—through the insertion of natural language codes assigned according to the rules of meta-mark-up languages commonly used in the digital humanities, like XML—the printed or written text it comprises must be ported to a binary format before anything else can be done. Such is the significance of text capture to CELT (and digital humanities projects like it), that its website includes a dedicated page entitled "How are texts made available?".[22]

Yet, as a young research assistant in CELT, it puzzled me greatly to observe that this work was sometimes acknowledged and attributed to named, in-house individuals, and recorded in the paratextual documentation of the digital editions that CELT made.[23] Other times it went unattributed.[24] Moreover, from the mid-2000s, the text capture necessary to execute some of the projects for which CELT was awarded funding, and, indeed, some of the projects that I would go on to co-lead, was outsource to expert companies, often in the global south (see e.g. Nyhan 2008; Ortolja-Baird et al. 2019). These companies not only transcribed the textual foundations of those projects, they sometimes also executed specified aspects of textual mark-up. So, some aspects of the XML mark-up of texts (a core activity of the digital humanities) was inserted "in house" by researchers in universities, museums, galleries and the other knowledge-production settings where digital humanities was and is pursued. Other aspects were inserted by anonymous workers in the global south, whose work could be costed on a tag per tag basis. This caused me to ponder, as I could find no guidelines and little discussion of this among the wider digital humanities community: when, why and how should this work of text capture, and even encoding, whether executed in house or outsourced, be acknowledged? How porous are the boundaries between the tasks that disciplines, in otherwise intensely hierarchical academic settings, designate as research-driven versus service-based? All the while, whether as a young or established researcher, I have observed and been party to, the ongoing ruminations and anxieties of my colleagues about how and whether digital humanities really is "scholarly" And I have observed the field's rarely acknowledged yet pervasive and certainly not unconnected ambivalence towards the computers it uses. The influential humanities computing scholar Willard McCarty, for example, has discussed having had a "stain of computing" on this carer (Crymble 2021, 6). In many ways, then, this book represents my first attempt to work through these questions, which I understand to be complex and interrelated. They are questions that have long bothered me and that bother me still.

Narrative outline

Chapter 1 considers the labour organisation of the *Index Thomisticus* against the longer trajectory of concordance-making, or the history of analogue, textual "big data" knowledge-management resources. It does this to better understand the contexts that the *Index Thomisticus* was both responding to and operating in when it encountered the questions about scholarly labour and knowledge production that the incorporation of newer technologies, like unit record equipment, into the humanities was raising. Chapter 1 thus begins the work of arguing that the divisions encoded in the *Index Thomisticus* project between scholars and technical staff were neither disinterested nor objective value judgements of the complexity of their respective work. Rather, these divisions were helpful in responding to the conundrum that the take-up of automation, and the large teams of workers it required, posed to the "great man", lone-scholar models of knowledge production valourised by the humanities. If the concordance tradition provided Busa with a labour-based template for the invisibilising of the technical workers on his team, it seems to be through the "feminisation of the office" (which, due to its associations with "big data", devalued labour and information processing technologies is understood here to be positioned downstream of analogue concordance-making) that the gendered technological dimension systematically entered the equation, a factor that this chapter identifies as being relevant to understanding why it was the work of the female keypunch operators, in particular, out of all the technical staff of the *Index Thomisticus*, that was particularly devalued in reporting on and about the *Index Thomisticus*.

The narrative structure of the book that follows seeks to juxtapose canonical portrayals of keypunch labour by Busa, Tasman and the wider humanities computing and digital humanities community (Chapters 3, 4, 5) with oral history and archival reconstructions and readings of the detail and nature of this work (Chapters 2, 3, 4, 5). Having historicised Busa's jumping off point and the labour organisation of the *Index Thomisticus* workforce, Chapter 2 reconstructs the methodology of the *Index Thomisticus*, and the detail of the "ghost work" contributed by keypunch operators, further weighting and contextualising it with regard to the human-machine distribution of the *Index Thomisticus* workflow. Thus, it is argued that while keypunch operators' work was largely quotidian, it was more skilled and more important for the *Index Thomisticus* than has been previously acknowledged and the devaluing of this work cannot have been based on an evaluation of its internal nature alone. Moreover, this chapter argues that the boundaries erected between scholarly and keypunching labour were more porous, and rhetorically useful, than previously recognised. The reconstruction of the technical elaboration of the *Index Thomisticus* presented in this chapter is probably the most complete to be synthesised so far. It has been assembled from a detailed study of Busa's publications and archival materials spanning the years c.1951–67, extended with more recent scholarship including that of Steve Jones, Geoffrey Rockwell and Stéfan Sinclair.

Chapters 3 and 4 continue to explore the new understandings of the work and workers of the *Index Thomisticus* project that can be developed by looking beyond the authorised picture set out in scholarly publications. Historical and epistemological questions are pursued in these chapters, which seek understand why and how the epistemic authority of keypunch operators as knowers and creators was denied, and the role of gender in this, while acknowledging that the *Index Thomisticus* was not unusual in the context of its historical moment in seeking to position feminised labour as it did. Chapter 3 thus seeks to sketch the organisational, spatial, relational, regulatory and knowledge-gatekeeping circumstances in which keypunch operators worked and through which the keypunch operator role was constructed. Chapter 4 draws on oral history recollections, focalising some keypunch operators' recollections of having worked in this important early project of computing in the humanities. Heretofore under-appreciated aspects, both national and international, of the *Index Thomisticus'* historical moment during the years under examination are also explored, like how it arguably benefited from the labour practices of the Italian economic miracle and how it conversed with Cold War questions and intersections of gendered labour, technology and language.

Chapters 3 and 4 contend that neither the *Index Thomisticus'* trajectory, nor the form of its day-to-day realisation was inevitable or predetermined. It is argued that the project was actively enabled and constrained by decisions that were made by Busa and others, which often reconstituted the knowledge- and gender-based inequalities of wider society while responding to worries about scholarly identity in the age of the (semi-)automated humanities. That the invisibilising of keypunch operators work, though not unusual, was far from an inevitable instance of how things had to be is argued with reference to archival reports of complaints raised by the male technical staff of the *Index Thomisticus*, which open ways of understanding the history of digital humanities as a space of contestation and discontent.

Having surveyed the complex, contingent and shifting circumstances in which the work of the *Index Thomisticus* was pursued, Chapter 5 returns to the literature on the *Index Thomisticus* project that was published by Busa and the subsequent humanities computing and digital humanities communities. The question why so many in the humanities computing and digital humanities communities appear to have accepted what is argued to be Busa's mythologising, thus replaying the "invisibility" that had already began in Busa's telling of the story of the *Index Thomisticus* is explored. The history of digital humanities is often told as the forward march of technological artefacts and techniques for wrangling words, yet this chapter emphasises the role that words and texts have played in the development of the field itself, not only, as we might expect, as vehicles for scholarly arguments but, in this case, as vehicles for scholarly performances of power and gatekeeping. Chapter 5 thus argues that the process of identity formation and meaning making in digital humanities has been linguistic as much as technical.

In this way, this book rereads the history of a formative project in the digital humanities as a history of gendered epistemology. It understands this gendering of epistemology as having directly impacted questions about whose voice would and would not be heard, and what would and would not count as work during the incunabular period of computing in the humanities and in the years that followed. The devaluing of keypunching labour is understood to have been intersectional, to have arisen in response to a range of factors that include: the specific and situated difficulties of pursuing digital humanities during this incunabular phase, when funding for staff costs was difficult to raise (Chapter 3 and 4); through more universal tropes, like the wide-spread devaluing of feminised labour in Italy and beyond during the years under study, meaning that young women probably seemed like obvious candidates to supply the cheap labour required (Chapter 3); and the politics of knowledge formation and economies of esteem within the academy which have often valorised great men, and their "innovative" work (Chapter 5), along with the inherently conservative aspects of developments like the feminisation of the office (Chapter 1), the Italian economic miracle (Chapter 3), and the cold war (Chapter 4), which were all entangled in the techno-social order that the *Index Thomisticus* itself sought to build (Chapters 3, 4, 5, 6).

As briefly set out in the conclusion in Chapter 6, it is through the exploration of such intersections that this book seeks to reveal a hidden history of gender politics in intellectual and technical work in the digital humanities, perhaps also speaking to the gender politics of intellectual work in the Academy more widely, in ways that remain relevant today.

In the course of this book, the reader is taken on a journey from the idealism of an enigmatic and yet initially reluctant scholar (Chapter 1), who pursued his digital humanities research in circumstances quite unfamiliar to present-day digital humanities (Chapters 3 and 4), to his later anointing as founding father of this field of professional enquiry, in what this book argues to have been an act of aetiological genealogy construction (Chapter 5). It is argued that keypunching labour was essential not only to Busa's work (Chapter 3) but to how his work came to be remembered, yet in ways that have remained hidden in plain sight (Chapter 5). Busa has often been positioned as essential to the digital humanities, and to the stories we tell about how the digital humanities came into being, in ways that have overlooked the rhetorical purchase of this positioning (Chapter 5). In this way, this book suggests that the work of keypunching and the highly malleable portrayals of Busa that have been put to work in the pursuit of disciplinary validation haunt the digital humanities, and broader understandings of the history and gendering of knowledge formation in the academy, in complex ways.

This book argues that the devaluing of feminised textual labour is not something that happened in a now finished and self-contained past; rather, the presentness of this past continues to be detectable in the scholarship, and hierarchies of esteem, of the field of digital humanities to this day. Humanities computing and digital humanities practitioners have often focused on elaborating digital workflows, new technological applications, and on valorising "great scholars", to the exclusion of those individuals who execute the rather more mundane aspects of digital humanities workflows on a day-to-day basis. As a result, as attested by this study of the *Index Thomisticus* project, our understanding of how digital humanities work has been and is actually *done*, on a day-to-day basis, remains incomplete. Ultimately, then, this book seeks to present an optimistic and empowering argument: better understandings of the field's history can prompt us to ask new questions about the voices that the field has and has not listened to and about definitions of work in the digital humanities and in knowledge production circumstances more widely. By asking such questions we may ultimately open new possibilities to do things differently, and more fairly, in future.

In an oral history interview, two former keypunch operators recalled how they occasionally wore blindfolds whilst working on the *Index Thomisticus* project:

> BV [Bruna Vanelli]: Of punching, the important thing was to do it blindfolded because you absolutely couldn't look at the keyboard.
> MP [Marco Passarotti]: You were blindfolded?
> BV Yes ... or else there was somebody there, perhaps [another member of staff], checking that you turned your head and didn't look. You had to punch a certain number of cards and then she would verify how many mistakes you'd made.
>
> (Brogioli et al. 2014)

In this excerpt, the blindfold is being discussed in connection with how it was used as an evaluative proxy of the accuracy levels that keypunch operators attained when encoding the text of Aquinas on punched cards. Yet, the blindfold can be read in a more figurative way too, conveying some of the core tensions that frame this book. They are tensions of absence and presence; of looking versus seeing and of being seen; of remembering, forgetting and being forgotten; of how these processes have informed what has and has not been deemed to be valuable work; and, ultimately, whose work has and has not been admitted to the historical record of knowledge production, as this book will now explore.

Notes

1 Against the backdrop of the cold war and the continuing technologising of warfare, the fair sought to promote "the positive uses of computing, its humanistic applications–for the expansion of knowledge, for example, and for better living and enhanced leisure time" (Jones 2016, 99).

2 In 1961, IBM was giving "free technical support to CAAL" through a "system of yearly points". IBM supplied Busa with data-processing machines "with a retail value of 1.500.000 Lire a month, [and made] financial contributions to keep the center running" (Jones 2016, 113). See also Thomas Watson's summary of IBM's contributions up to 1960 (Watson 1960).

3 This was recalled by Diego Righetti, a computer scientist who worked with Busa on the *Index Thomisticus* in the 1970s and made a major contribution to its typesetting in hardcopy. See Righetti, Nyhan and Passarotti 2014.

4 The field that has tended to be called digital humanities since c. 2006 has been known by many other names, including humanist informatics, literary and linguistic computing and (more commonly) humanities computing. Though differences between those fields do exist, their discussion is beyond the scope of this book. In this book, the terms digital humanities and humanities computing will be used more-or-less interchangeably, except if I am referring to the period before c. 2006 and humanities computing seems a more appropriate designation.

5 The Society of Jesus, also known as the Jesuits, is a religious order of the Catholic Church headquartered in Rome which has centred the study of science and technology as part of its missionary and educative activities. See https://www.jesuits.org/.

6 It was my friend and colleague, Melissa Terras (Professor of Digital Cultural Heritage, University of Edinburgh) who first noticed the unnamed female keypunch operators among historical images of the *Index Thomisticus* that Marco Passarotti shared with us in 2013, when Melissa and I both still worked in the Department of Information Studies, UCL. The highly cited blog post that Terras subsequently wrote about the female operators is, to the best of my knowledge, the first source to bring the forgotten keypunch operators to the attention of the contemporary scholarly community (Terras 2013). I had been working on the history of digital humanities, utilising an oral history methodology since 2011 (see e.g. Nyhan 2012), and so the enfolding of an oral history approach with archival research on Busa's archive in Università Cattolica del Sacro Cuore, Milan, Italy seemed like a potentially promising approach to finding out more about the keypunch operators, though it was not foreseen at this early stage that this would ultimately result in a book-length study.

7 See also, for example, interviews included in collections like the Computer History Museum Oral History Collection (https://computerhistory.org/oral-histories/); 52 oral history interviews conducted with women active in early computing in the United States and the United Kingdom, originally conducted for (Abbate 2012) and now included in the IEEE Oral History Collection, see (https://ethw.org/Main_Page); the Charles Babbage Institute Oral Histories (https://cse.umn.edu/cbi/cbi-oral-histories) and MIT's oral histories of "Women in Science and Engineering" and "Computers at MIT" (https://infinitehistory.mit.edu/collections), among others.

8 As stated in the article that underpins this discussion (Gao et al. 2022), we acknowledge the limitations of the binary model of gender that underpins our analysis and is prevalent in much of the bibliometric literature. Due to time and resource limitations, it was impossible for us to move beyond this limitation, except to extend the dataset with unknown / other in a small number of cases. We acknowledge the presence and parity individuals who are gender diverse.

9 Thus, the dataset includes *Computers and the Humanities* (1966–2004), *Literary and Linguistic Computing* (1986–2017) (renamed *Digital Scholarship in the Humanities* from 2015) and *Digital Humanities Quarterly* (2007–2017).

10 This task has been taken up by, *inter alia*, feminist digital humanities projects, such as Full Stack Feminism, which aims to devise "a feminist praxis throughout the 'full stack' (to include a feminist ethics of care, FAIR CARE principles, feminist epistemologies, decoding existing epistemologies) ... lead[ing] to an overall

intervention in the creation of more inclusive digital cultural heritage in digital humanities" (see http://ifte.network/full-stack-feminism/).

11 The overlooking of quotidian labour has also been observed by Hicks and others in connection with the history of computing more broadly. See e.g. Hicks 2017, 5.

12 Though the terms work and labour are sometimes differentiated, the terms are here used largely interchangeably.

13 Medieval writers' views on women did, of course, vary and misogyny was not the only order of the day. See Blamires, Pratt and Marx 1992.

14 Staff who operated keypunch machines seem to have consistently represented the majority of Busa's workforce. His publications report that in 1961 he had a staff of 30 people, of whom 22 were operating machines (Busa 2019d[1961], 72); and a few years later close to 60 individuals with "32 to 37 for machine operations (keypunching the texts, verifying, listing, sight-checking, punch-card processing, computer processing)" (Busa 1964, 65).

15 "Authorised" is here used with reference to aspects of the *Index Thomisticus'* workflow in a way that is analogous to Smith's definition of "Authorised Heritage Discourse", in the sense of how those aspects worked to "naturalize a range of assumptions about the nature and meaning of" scholarly identify and benefited from "a professional discourse that privileges expert values and knowledge" over discourses about what might be deemed non-expert values and knowledge, such as those of keypunch operators (Smith 2006, 4).

16 On the present-day website of the *Index Thomisticus*, the authorship of the work is given as "Roberto Busa and associates" (Busa and Associates 2005). Given the historical invisibilising of the keypunch operators work, readers of the website may well understand the term "and associates" to point to the names of the two web editors that follow this phrase and remain unaware of the large team who contributed to the *Index Thomisticus* during its lifetime.

17 For reasons of space, I don't usually address those projects here. For details of the publications that arose from those projects, authored by Busa, see Nyhan and Passarotti (2019, 197–220).

18 For overviews of the composition of the core archive see Nyhan 2014; Rockwell 2016; and for a discussion of the extended archive see Jones 2016, 6–7. Jones was present when this tranche of documents was delivered to the archive.

19 The masculine form of the Italian word for student "*allievo*" has the plural "*allievi*"; the feminine "*allieva*" has the plural "*allieve*". At this time, the masculine forms would generally have been used as the default form to refer to both sexes. The form that Busa gives in the handlist "*Allieve-i del Centro*", then, is a blending of the masculine and feminine plurals.

20 As Frisch has put it "Everyone knows that the core audio-visual dimension of oral history is notoriously underutilized" (Frisch 2006, 102) and this is arguably as true of digital oral history research as more traditional oral history research (Nyhan and Flinn 2014).

21 CELT was founded by Prof. Donnchadh Ó Corráin and led by him for many years. Dr Peter Flinn, Electronic Publishing Unit, UCC, provided technical expertise (see O'Sullivan 2020) and the project was funded in its earliest years by Professor Marianne McDonald via the CURIA Project.

22 See https://celt.ucc.ie/avail.html. I suspect CELT to have been relatively unusual for its time in addressing the capture of texts as prominently as it did.

23 See, for example, the header of the Annals of Ulster, where the names of the three individuals responsible for "Data capture, using OPTOPUS, and initial proofing and mark-up at the History Department, University College, Cork" are recorded (https://celt.ucc.ie/published/G100001A/index.html).

24 See, for example, https://celt.ucc.ie/published/L100005/index.html, where the chronological timeline set out under "Revision History" begins with the proofing of the electronic text.

1 On the histories of a history

The historical labour models of the *Index Thomisticus*

Introduction

A fascinating story about the *Index Thomisticus'* encounter with fire is often recalled at professional digital humanities gatherings. Passarotti, for example, has published the following version of it:

> The corpus [of the *Index Thomisticus*], recorded at that time on magnetic tape, was being moved from Pisa to Venice. Father Busa had organised the move. Everything was loaded onto two trucks, one of which accidentally caught fire on the motorway, shortly before arriving in Venice. Several years of work went up in smoke in just a few minutes. Father Busa told me that at first he was annoyed with his Boss, but then realised that the accident had been nothing more than a warning for him to be a bit more clever. The tapes of the two copies of the *Index Thomisticus* had not been divided equally between the two trucks, but rather mixed, partly in one and partly in the other. This episode is an example of the unassailable strength of Father Busa's faith, who saw every event in a divine light, able to provide a higher reason for the events of life.
>
> (Passarotti 2013, 20)

This same disaster was recalled, from a different perspective, in an oral history interview. In the oral history (re)telling of the story, which is captured below, an instance of the otherwise invisible and forgotten labour of keypunch operators is recalled. Excluded from the canonical version of this story, this labour was implicitly deemed ancillary and irrelevant to the real work of concordance-making and digital humanities. Yet, it was crucial for keeping the *Index Thomisticus* on track when Busa's plans met with unforeseen obstacles, as plans invariably do:

> GC [Gisa Crosta]: You know, when we were leaving for America, therefore, in Pisa, all the punch cards were placed on the magnetic tape, the old one. I don't know if you are familiar with those elaborators that were in Pisa.
> MP: Yes, yes, sure, the huge ones.

DOI: 10.4324/9781003138235-2

GC: ... we did not bring the cards, we brought the tapes.

MP: Yes, yes [to Julianne Nyhan] in the United States they took the tapes, not the punch cards.

GC: On the trip from Pisa to, I don't know, Rome, we boarded in Livorno, a bit earlier, the truck caught fire.

MP: Oh this is a famous story, this is a famous story ...

GC: Yes, but it's also famous because he stupidly ...

MP: ... This is famous, too. I wrote it in one of my publications.

GC: Right. So, then we had to go to Verona. And I went there.

MP: Oh, I hadn't heard this. This is interesting.

GC: One week working only by night, from here they sent all the punch cards to Verona ... and IBM in Verona gave us the elaborators at night. And I would insert all the punch cards in again until all of them were registered in the magnetic tape, from 9 pm to 5 am.

DC [Danila Cairati]: To make copies? Of the burnt ones?

GC: No, the magnetic tapes, the magnetic tapes burned but the punch cards survived. So all the punch cards were sent to Verona and I would reinsert the punch cards again every night from 9 pm to 5 am.

DC: You did ...

GC: ...The magnetic tape.

DC: The magnetic tape. For how long?

GC: A week. Then we went from the magnetic tape to the diskette ... and then also when we went to America [Boulder] I think ... I was happy but it didn't amount to anything. It was only expenses, that period.

DC: Maybe it was useful for him.

GC: Yes, useful for him. To become known.

...

MP: Unbelievable.

GC: Insert, insert, insert the punched cards.

MP: Unbelievable. Unbelievable.

GC: Insert, insert, insert [they laugh].

(Crosta, Passarotti and Nyhan 2014)

Crosta's account thus recalls another of the essential and yet previously unknown contributions that were made to the *Index Thomisticus* by its lower-profile staff, when they spent nights performing the onerous task of inserting punched cards into a machine that encoded the data they held on magnetic tape for subsequent transfer and processing. Their work thus saved swathes of the *Index Thomisticus* from oblivion and enabled its subsequent processing. Yet, this pedestrian and gruelling but essential and hands-on night-shift recovery work came to be left out of canonical versions of Busa's encounter with fire, such as narrated by Passarotti above, which emphasise Busa's heroic determination, fortitude and lone scholar status.

How could the work of keypunching be devalued and overlooked in this way despite its importance to the *Index Thomisticus*? What templates could be drawn on to position the work of keypunching as ancillary and subaltern? And who stood to benefit from this?

This chapter places the labour history of the *Index Thomisticus* in the longer trajectory of concordance-making, or the history of analogue, humanities "big data" resources, to better understand some of the contexts that the *Index Thomisticus* was both responding to and drawing on with particular regard to its workforce. Thus, this chapter explores the longer labour history of the concordance tradition, where the use of large, and almost invariably anonymous teams of workers, who supported the work of a person otherwise portrayed as a "lone scholar", was common. That Busa had an intimate knowledge of this tradition is argued in the course of a discussion that also sets out essential preliminary and contextual definitions of and reflections on concordances, while drawing attention to Busa's awareness of the devalued position of concordance-making in his day.

This chapter draws attention to the concordance tradition's dependence on large teams and its practice of invisibilising the contributions of the mostly anonymous individuals who executed the manual tasks of concordance-making. It argues that the concordance tradition provided a ready-made template for hiding the contributions of a large team in plain sight, and that this template was given new impetus as the concordance tradition was interfolded with the gendered labour practices connected with technologies like electromechanical accounting machines and, in due course, digital computing. As such, it is argued that the historical concordance tradition opened the way for Busa, and perhaps for some other humanities computing scholars too, to perform many aspects of the lone scholar persona while nevertheless depending on a large team of otherwise invisible co-workers, and it was through the so-called feminisation of the office and the devalued role of women in the burgeoning electronic computing industry that the gendered dimension was both brought into play and further reinforced. Though in some ways cutting-edge, the *Index Thomisticus* project was reconstituting both historical and contemporaneous class (in the sense of scholarly class), labour-esteem and gender asymmetries all the way down. It was drawing on local templates, like the concordance tradition, which had become naturalised in scholarly circles, and were not "imposed" upon these circles, as one might argue of processes like the feminisation of the office.

In this way, this chapter contends that the composition and framing of the *Index Thomisticus'* workforce became interconnected with Busa's scholarly legitimacy and identity, suggesting new ways of thinking about Busa's downplaying of the nature and extent of some human interventions in the workflow of the *Index Thomisticus* and the concomitant emphasis on his role and those of the scholars on his team. This issue was not played out on the pages of academic texts alone; it would become a core factor in Busa's articulation of the identities of those who contributed to the *Index Thomisticus* project. As subsequent chapters will argue, it would also shape the roles that humans played in CAAL and the *Index Thomisticus* project, and indeed, seems to echo through to sections of the digital humanities to this day.

Origins

In 1941, shortly after Italy had joined the second world war, the 27-year-old Busa was sent by his superior to conduct doctoral research at the Pontifical Gregorian University in Rome.[1] The pre-eminent pontifical university, its alumni and faculty were among the most powerful and revered ecclesiastics of the Catholic Church (Di Giovanni 2016).

By his own account, doctoral study was not Busa's choice, and he was sent unwillingly, so that "… up until the end of 1945, my principal interest was focused on philosophy and philosophical texts while I was surrounded by bombings, Germans, partisans, poor food and disasters of all sorts" (Busa 1980, 83). This text, and others, suggest that Busa may have had, at least in the earlier years, an ambiguous and compartmentalised stance on the scholarship that would become a major part of his life's work. Scholarship had not only been imposed on him by his religious order. During the formative years of his doctoral research, he seems to have perceived and experienced scholarship as a pursuit that was disconnected from the wider societal, political and techno-militaristic context of the second world war, against which he pursued his research, however remotely. Yet, as we shall see, the execution of the *Index Thomisticus* project would be anything but disconnected from the situated context in which it was pursued in post-war Italy.

It was to his doctoral research, and specifically 1946, the year of his doctoral defence, that Busa later traced the ideas that gave rise to the *Index Thomisticus* project and its automation.[2] His doctoral research was on the concept of "presence" in the works of Thomas Aquinas, an important concept not only in Aquinas' writings but also for the Catholic Church his writings influenced so profoundly. Aquinas' concept of presence, "strictly speaking … describes a feature of the *cognizer*, i.e., presence to an object. In other words, the statement 'The apple is present to my mind' is true on account of a feature of the mind, not because of some change in the apple" (Cory 2014, 117). The cogniser's "conceptual system", Busa believed, could be accessed through a study of their vocabulary and patterns of lexical usage (see Busa 1980, 83). As he put it: "[t]he structure and history of the spoken word are merely the manifestation of the structure and history of thought" (Busa 2019a[1951], 21). He accordingly searched for the words *praesens* and *praesentia* in the writings of Aquinas using "tables and subject indexes",[3] and determined that "such words in Thomas Aquinas are peripheral: his doctrine of presence is linked with the preposition *in*" (Busa 1980, 83). Under established circumstances, after a scholar had formulated a conjecture like this, they might next consult an index or concordance, so as to locate all instances of a given word in a text and develop their conjecture into a hypothesis or other form of problematic for further research.

Before digital text and personal computers unlocked affordances like interactive search, paper-based concordances and indexes allowed occurrences of some types of words and concepts recorded in manuscript and print to be located. The "keyword in context" arrangement of concordances further allowed the senses of a given word to be disambiguated without requiring recourse to the full text, which may not have been to hand even for those like Busa who had the rich collections of the Pontifical Gregorian University libraries at their disposal. The information so gleaned with indexes and concordances could then be sampled, annotated, compared, quantitatively analysed and so on, as the undergirding of literary, linguistic and other kinds of text analysis, for example, or for use in teaching (Dubé 1975, 27; cf. Raben 1969 on limitations of concordances).

Concordances to sections of Aquinas' output had been published by 1946[4] but, at that time, few concordances at all would have listed the function words like *in* that especially interested Busa. The bounties of function words that would have required harvesting far exceeded the material and labour resources of many paper-bound concordances and indexes, and Busa's mention above of "subject indexes" is indicative of the resolution of detail that was generally achievable. Implicitly recalling stories of how the limitations of printed mathematical tables had inspired earlier technical inventors like Babbage (e.g. Hollings, Martin and Rice 2018), and in what would become a characteristic pattern, Busa would not be put off. He dug in and made his own card-based concordance of Aquinas' use of the word *in*.

Irrespective of whether it was made in an analogue context or not, the making of a concordance involved the identification and excerption of the words to be listed in it, their possible lemmatisation and duplication, along with the particulars of their context. It was accordingly necessary to transcribe "...the complete work once for every word in the average context. Thus, if each reference is to be followed by a quotation averaging ten words in length, the complete work will have to be transcribed ten times" (Wisbey 1962, 162). The basic steps of concordance making can thus be summarised as follows: pre-editing, or the parsing of the text, (see Tasman 1957, 251); followed by the

1   transcription of the text, broken down into phrases, on to separate cards;
2   multiplication of the cards (as many as there are words on each);
3   indicating on each card the respective entry (lemma);
4   the selection and placing in alphabetical order of all the cards according to the lemma and its purely material quality;
5   finally, once that formal elaboration of the alphabetical order of the words which only an expert's intelligence can perform, has been done, the typographical composition of the pages to be published.

(Busa 2019a[1951], 27)

With dry wit Busa described his attempts to search and manipulate the "10 000 3" X 5" cards" that resulted as akin to playing "grand games of solitaire" (Busa 1980, 83).

Through this experience, Busa had encountered, first hand, the limits of paper-based research tools for harnessing abundance and facilitating manipulability and interactivity. This limitation was not a mere inconvenience for him, it was a barrier to his research, with its intertwined premises that, firstly, a "philological and lexicographical inquiry" (Busa 1980, 83) of the way Aquinas used and understood words (what we might today call his idiolect) should underpin an analysis of the concept of presence in his theology (Busa 1980, 83). And secondly that so-called "function words", like *in*,[5] should not be omitted from study because they "manifest the deepest logic of being which generates the basic structures of human discourse" (Busa 1980, 83). Busa must have realised that he would need to expand and deepen his forays into concordance-making before he could pursue his research on Aquinas.

The formal announcement, in 1950, of Busa's intention to elaborate a "Complete Index Verborum of Works of St Thomas" foresees a highly instrumental incorporation of technology into the work. The announcement requests from readers (in a way that sits uncomfortably with the more hermeneutically and critically-oriented digital humanities pursued today):[6]

> any information they can supply about such mechanical devices as would serve to achieve the greatest possible accuracy, with a maximum economy of human labor. (Father Busa has been in contact with IBM in New York, the RCA laboratories in Princeton, the Library of Congress and the Library of the Department of Agriculture, in Washington.)
>
> (Busa 1950, 425)

Busa's early emphasis on economy of labour and the vouchsafing of accuracy suggests that he was not only internalising tropes commonly circulated about the potential of technology to save labour and compensate for human frailty and inconsistency. He was also seeking to understand the potential of mechanisation through the lens of the analogue concordance tradition, and his experiences of its potential, limits and constraining factors. The tendency to seek to understand a new technology in terms of antecedent technologies or techniques is noted in scholarship on the history of technology, including computing: "Comparison of the computer with earlier technologies was ... also the means by which historical actors themselves had understood the potential of the new technology and shaped their own plans for its development" (Haigh 2011, 8). As prosaic as it may seem at first glance, it was the enfolding of mechanisation in the making of indexes and concordances that would allow Busa and others to study function words at scale, in ways that were previously impossible and would open new lines of quantitative research into areas like authorship attribution and stylometry over the longer term. The extent to which the enfolding of automation technology unlocked a maximum economy of labour for concordance-making or ameliorated the time-intensive task of verifying accuracy is debatable, however.

Concordances: a complex inheritance

As discussed above, Busa believed that an individual's "conceptual system" could be accessed by studying their vocabulary and use of language (see Busa 1980, 83). He cleaved to this philological tenet throughout his life,[7] and he was not moved to respond directly to the challenges raised to such conceptualisations by New Criticism,[8] leading Ramsay to opine:

> we do no injustice to Busa's achievement in noting that the contemporary critical ethos regards Busa's central methodological tenets as grossly naive. Modern criticism, increasingly sceptical of authorial intention as a normative principle and linguistic meaning as a stable entity, has largely abandoned the idea that we could ever keep from reading ourselves into the reading of an author and is no longer concerned with attempting to avoid this conundrum.
>
> (Ramsay 2011a, 3)

Still, Busa apparently was aware of the pitfalls of trying to infer what an author thought from their written record: "Each writer expresses his conceptual system in and through his verbal system, with the consequence that the reader who masters this verbal system, using his own conceptual system, has to get an insight into the writer's conceptual system" (Busa 1980, 83). For Busa, concordances were an important tool for gaining this insight.

And in some ways, Busa's emphasis on concordances was fortuitous. Concordances were authoritative information management tools with a pedigree that stretched back to the thirteenth century.[9] The Rouses have written of how reference tools like indexes and concordances appeared suddenly in the West, so that "before the 1190s such tools did not exist" and after 1290 they were commonplace (Rouse and Rouse 1991, 221). Concordances were first devised c.1230–1238 by the Dominicans at Saint Jacques in Paris, led by "Cardinal Hugo of Saint-Caro or Hugh of Saint-Cher" to facilitate access to the Bible for the preparation of sermons (Burton 1981a, 6). By the third iteration of their work, the Dominicans had mastered the selection of the details that would distinguish the concordance form: "... [the] third concordance of St Jacques, already in circulation by 1286, ... responded to the need for a verbal concordance of words-in-context, providing a brief context of (usually) four to seven words for each lemma" (Rouse and Rouse 1991, 225).[10] Their association with biblical scholarship remained strong in Busa's day and by the time he began his concordance to Thomas Aquinas, concordances to secular writers would have been available in substantial numbers too (Wisbey 1962, 161). Yet, for the most part, Busa's research required mechanically-assisted methods that were unorthodox to the humanities. Indeed, "the relationship of humanities and new technologies was confronted from the beginning by the higher status of interpretation, analysis, and abstraction over fabrication, application, and production" (Klein 2017).

Thus, the prospect of situating his research within the authorised concordance tradition may have been associatively beneficial for him.

Busa's emphasis on the concordance form may also have given his incorporation of automation somewhat of a head start. Of the various textual tools used by humanities scholars, mechanical and computational processes were first applied to concordances because their compilation had always been "a very mechanical process" (Hockey 1980, 41). Neither Busa, nor other pioneers who sought to automate concordances deviated substantially from the steps of concordance making outlined above: "Designers of pro-grams to do concordancing simply analysed the operations inherent in the process of hand-concordancing since the days of Cruden's work with the Bible and substituted equivalent computer routines ..." (Oakman 1980, 69).

For all this, the concordance form also brought with it distinct burdens. Although part of a long-authorised tradition, it became increasingly neces-sary for Busa to argue that this work could even be classed as scholarship. Important and widely used as reference tools were, the task of making them, and the work of editing, bibliography and lexicography they entailed was increasingly devalued. This is an issue still encountered by those who make digital editions, digital archives and other curated, digitally mediated collec-tions (see e.g. Schreibman, Mandell, and Olsen 2011, 125). The labour and gender-oriented associations of data compilation, such as the *Index Thomis-ticus* relied on, may have been relevant too: "The star of large-scale literary data-gathering rises and falls in different eras, [sometimes] the making of datasets was regarded as feminized and mechanical" (Buurma and Heffernan 2018).

Busa found it necessary to convince the reader that work "done in this particular space should not be "despise[ed] .... or [seen as a] 'waste' [of] energy which might have been utilised better elsewhere" (Busa 2019a[1951], 26) He continued in argumentative riposte:

> the great services which works of this kind render ... to knowledge; and the more so when, as we mentioned, due account is taken of the exhausting amount of work entailed and the sheer materiality of a great portion of it.
>
> (Busa 2019a[1951], 26)

And in an elegantly defensive flourish, Busa further elaborated the specialist academic knowledge that the work required and implied that those who did not appreciate its complexity were blinkered by their inadequate understanding of the "scientific enterprise":

> only those who have had a hand, or at least an eye, in this sort of work will realise that it is not a matter of purely material labour. To organise an unbounded mass of material, in function to definite services to be rendered to exigent disciplines, requires intelligence, training to foresee

and predispose, caution and vigour so as not to let oneself be induced to take those unwise steps … Nor can such work be successfully concluded unless one is competent or at least possess a well-grounded introduction to the reflective study of thought and expression, knowledge of the grammatical and metaphysical structure of the language, in short, philology with a smattering of philosophy. So much is to be said in defence of the "scientific" nature of such works …

(Busa 2019a[1951], 26)

Busa's strategy was not to deny that concordance making required a great deal of manual (or "material") labour. Instead, like a magician, he used attentional misdirection to shift the reader's focus onto the more "scientific" work that it also demanded. This entailed explicitly differentiating the "purely material labour" of concordance making from that which entailed "intelligence … training … caution … vigour" (Busa 2019a[1951], 26) and competency in philology and philosophy. This elaboration of the epistemic virtues of the scholar and scholarship itself, and its juxtaposition with the manual work of concordance-making evokes Gieryn's concept of "boundary-work" or the "ideological efforts by scientists to distinguish their work and its products from non-intellectual scientific activities" (Gieryn 1983, 782).

From at least 1951, Busa was implicitly and explicitly communicating the work of the scholar in oppositional terms to the work of those responsible for the "material" aspects of making concordances, or those individuals who operated the technical equipment required by the *Index Thomisticus*. This rhetorically-laden move helped him to defend the worth of concordance-making, and as this book argues, was sometimes used by him as an important aspect of his construction of the habitus of the humanities computing "lone scholar". As has been stated in connection with, for example, the emerging field of humanities data science: "Incorporating new computational, quantitative, and data-driven approaches into the way humanities research is conducted requires us to articulate and rethink the whole research process in new ways" (McGilivray et al. 2020, 15). Here it is contended that the rethinking of scholarly identity has historically been part of this process too, and that in Busa's writings we are seeing a certain idea of the scholar, often expressed in oppositional terms to technical workers, typically female, being worked out.

Of course, the ideal of the lone scholar presented another conundrum for Busa. From the early-modern period forward, the "lone scholar", or man who worked alone in a heroic and self-sacrificing quest had been held up as the ideal (Thornton 1998; Jardine 2015). So much so, that Blair argues that the lone scholar ideal has contributed to the obscuring of how the scholarship of those such as Erasmus, Robert Boyle and Thomas Aquinas, among others, was scaffolded by the contributions or labour of often anonymous assistants (Blair 2014). In the case of Thomas Aquinas, it was his companion, amanuensis and fellow Dominican, Reginald of Piperno who is thought to have transcribed Aquinas' lectures and is also thought, after

Aquinas' death, to have been responsible for the Supplement to the Third Part of the *Summa Theologiae* (Cross and Livingstone 2005). Blair argues that: "while few early modern scholars collaborated directly with peers, almost all relied on the help of others who were considered intellectual and social inferiors and were typically omitted from explicit mention" (Blair 2010, 104).

Despite the foreclosing of context and interconnection it requires, the lone scholar template continues to be the one that successive generations of scholars have worked with, and are sometimes assessed against (Whitley 2000; Kaltenbrunner 2015). It is a significant aspect of the basis upon which decisions about entry to, and subsequent progression in the Academy, and the humanities in particular, are regularly made. This continues to be a point of contention today for those who pursue digitally-augmented scholarship, because this scholarship often requires the input of teams that are large enough to represent the wide spectrum of expertise and praxis-based knowledge necessary to pursue this research (e.g. Rockwell 2011).

For Busa, the necessity of working with a large team came about not only through the range of expertise his project needed to function but also through its use of accounting machines, and, in due course, computers. And it might also be said that Busa was bequeathed this by the concordance tradition, where large teams where a necessity and, in ecclesiastical contexts, often a given (see Blair 2010, 103). Yet, what is not readily detectable from Oakman's otherwise perceptive statement (above) is that early concordance-program makers like Busa not only replicated the long-established routines and processes of concordance making, their routines continued to require, and to rely on, a significant quantity and input of human labour too.

In his earliest writings, labour, time, efficiency and accuracy savings were the modalities through which Busa sought to articulate the novelty of his work. Fashioning himself as an innovator, whose work would break the mould of established ways of concordance-making, he claims that his work would dispense with large teams of co-workers and overturn the labour-intensive methods that had been in use from medieval times to his day:

> It is at all events certain that from now on the history of concordances will no longer have to record figures like those of the past: five hundred Domenicans [sic] – can it really be true? – employed by Hugh de Saint Cher in 1200 in Paris for the first biblical Latin concordance; fifty monks occupied in preparing the biblical concordances organised by the Benedictines in 1700; five German universities cooperated to set in order by hand the ten million cards of the [*Thesaurus Liguae Latinae*] the end of the last century.
>
> (Busa 2019a[1951], 32)

Thus, he wrote that the concordance to the 13,000 pages of Aquinas that he was planning should be completed in four years rather than the fifty that might otherwise be expected (Busa 2019a[1951], 31–32). In short order, however, it would transpire that mechanical methods would not dispense with the need for large teams, and the *Index Thomisticus* project would become a multi-year one. But all was not lost.

On the need for a workforce

That the making of an index or concordance was an arduous, lengthy and tedious process that depended on a large team is indisputable. Whether in early-modern scholars' studies,[11] or Busa's post-war "data centre", manually-led transcription, implemented with pen, keypunch, keyboard and so on, is a through line of concordance-making from the thirteenth century to the founding of humanities computing and beyond. This "material" work was usually done by individuals who tended to be seen as inferior to the scholar whose name would be inscribed on the project.

Though more recent scholarship has cast doubt on whether handwritten slips were the medium on which the earliest reference works were compiled, that concordances and indexes were often transcribed by hand is not in doubt.[12] An innovation that must have lightened this burden is known to have been used from the sixteenth century, though it is difficult to gauge how commonly it was used from scholarship on premodern information management. A variation of the more common practice of cutting and pasting paper slips, it involved copying words onto sheets of paper.[13] Those sheets could then be cut up and recombined into the various word combinations and permutations that concordances required (Considine 2015, 488). Though the ability to combine and recombine slips was a boon, it must still have been quite burdensome to copy text longhand. In a 1548 publication, Conrad Gessner suggested instead that words could be cut from printed books onto slips because "much labour can be saved in this way" (Blair 2010, 214). It is known that Gessner cut texts from printed books as well as handwritten materials like correspondence. The printer Froschauer supplied him with books (often unsellable) for dismemberment (Blair 2010, 214); those without such connections may have found this technique a difficult one to finance and the "cutting and pasting of textual passages from printed books to save the labour of copying them was a technique used primarily by bulk compilers" (Blair 2010, 225). In addition to Gesner, Lawrence Beyerlinck and Theodor Zwinger probably also used this hack (Blair 2010, 225). Considine mentions other publications that were compiled in this way too, including a

> reversal of Kircher's concordance: ....published in the Netherlands in 1718, with an initial statement saying that 'it could not have put on this form, unless it had been cut apart page by page into the smallest possible parts, with amazing ingenuity and patience, and then put back together, page by page, piece by piece' evidently by pasting.
>
> (Considine 2015, 495)

Meanwhile, Miles L. Hanley at the University of Wisconsin, in the late 1930s:

> gummed sheets of paper with page and line number[ing?] [pdf difficult to read here] printed repeatedly in rows; when the text of James Joyce's Ulysses was typed on these pages, the numbers could be read underneath, and when each word was cut and pasted on a slip, its citation automatically came along. But the final produce of this operation was only a word-index, not a concordance … Hanley's technique has not been transferred to the compilation of concordances.
>
> (Raben 1969, 64)

Looking at Busa's 1951 outline of efforts known to him to automate the process of transcription, one is struck by the continuity of those earlier techniques of transcription and duplication. The technology of the typewriter was by then in use in place of the technology of the pencil or scissors, yet the work remained overwhelmingly manual. Methods that evoke the early-modern and modern duplication of slips overviewed above were still in use:

> A kind of mechanisation has been working for years so far as regards caption 2: the *T.L.L.* and the *Mittellateinisches Wörterbuch* use the services of Copying Bureaux, where one of the many well-known systems of duplicating are used; Prof. J. Deferrari of Washington used electrical typewriters which can make many copies; Prof. P. O'Reilly of Notre Dame (Indiana – USA) had each side of the page repeated as many times as there were words contained thereon.
>
> (Busa 2019a[1951], 27)

The technique that Lane Cooper developed at Cornell to work on the concordance to Wordsworth, which was published in 1911 echoes that of Gessner (described above):

> Cooper avoided much copying and reduced the possibility of error by eviscerating and cutting up printed editions of the text concerned, so that each slip had a printed line pasted on it. Rubber stamps with movable types were used for recording the numerical references. A concordance to Horace was produced in less than a year by this method, yet eighteen collaborators assisted in preparing the slips, and an unspecified number helped in alphabetical ordering, so that, although greatly reduced, the time and labour involved still cannot be termed insignificant.
>
> (Wisbey 1962, 162)

The keypunch operators of the *Index Thomisticus* used electromechanical accounting machines and rectangles of cardboard (that is, punch cards) to capture text, rather than the slips of paper, scissors and glue of earlier concordance workers, but the fundamental processes that were implemented with these tools may be viewed as a continuum. Indeed, the paper slip and the punched card can also be understood as iterations of the "paper machines" that made information "available on separate, uniform, and mobile carriers [that] can be further arranged and processed according to strict systems of order" (Krajewski 2011, 3) and prefigured the database. As we have seen, paper slips and cut-outs could be assembled into an infinite number of combinations and configurations; once the texts that Busa sought to interrogate were encoded onto punched cards, the same was possible. In fact, the eventual printing of a concordance-imposed fixity and linearity on the material, and crucially, negated the mobile and combinatorial nature of the paper-slip as information carrier (Krajewski 2011, 3). Paper technologies also continued to be used and generated by the *Index Thomisticus* project across the many stages of its work:[14] books (editions, facsimiles, lexicographical and other texts) guided the preparatory philological work while the millions of paper punched cards that were output by keypunch operators and machines required file cabinets and other containers to store and organise them. And this is to say nothing of the reels of paper and magnetic tape or the print outs of the *Index Thomisticus*, still in binary code, generated by the project.

Whether in the *Index Thomisticus* or other concordance projects, more examples could be enumerated and added to those set out above. Yet the key point is not the broad lines of continuity of the techniques and materiality per say; rather it is that these techniques were usually implemented by people whose identity, and even agency, is absent from accounts of implementation. As we have seen, scholars did not usually do this work themselves and "[i]n the composition of reference works the use of slips and of cutting and pasting favoured the delegation of some tasks (like sorting and gluing) to helpers who were considered unskilled (like women and children)" (Blair 2010, 229). And those individuals tended to remain as invisible as the keypunch operators of the *Index Thomisticus*. Before looking at some of those teams in greater detail, the following section will discuss the punched cards that were used by the technical team of the *Index Thomisticus*, to understand why this technology could require input from teams of individuals.

Punched cards and the humanities

Though not commonly used for humanities scholarship in the late 1940s,[15] punched cards were neither a new nor a rare technology when Busa sought to involve them in concordance-making. In use since the 1890 US Census of Population data, they were "one of the foremost computational techniques available before computers" (Agar 2006, 873). When the *Index Thomisticus* was initiated, punched cards were already so established that they had developed "from an ad hoc technology ... into a pivotal technology for managing advanced industrial nations in the 1930s and in the Second World War" (Heide 2009, 5).

Winter has asked, with an implied sense of wonder (Winter 1999, 9–10) how Busa came up with idea of using "tools developed primarily for science and commerce" (Tasman 1957, 249) for his work. Yet, in Italy and during his many trips to the USA,[16] Busa must have encountered punched cards in some of the many contexts where they were used to process information in the government, military, public utility administration and commercial sectors (Heide 2009; Campbell-Kelly 1990; Norberg 1990). In Italy, for example, the National Institute of Social Security had been paying pensions using IBM punched cards as receipts since 1934 (IBM Corporation 2003a). Initially used in special libraries and documentation centres, they were used in scientific research centres before the 1940s (Eckert 1940), widely taken up by academic and public libraries in the US, and university administration from the early 1950s (e.g. Williams 2002; Black 2007; Lubar 1992). In addition to these examples, Heide has shown that some large alphanumeric punched-card registers were proposed in 1935 by the Social Security Board in the USA (Heide 2009, 214) and implemented as an army payroll system in Germany as early as 1943 (Heide 2009, 238). Busa's use of such machines to capture and process text, in the first instance, rather than numbers, is often held up as a ground-breaking aspect of his research (see e.g. Jones 2016, 44). The novelty of this move deserves further research. For now, we can say that what distinguished Busa's use of accounting machines from governmental or other forms of centralised processing of alphanumerical text is presumably the volume of text that he processed and its unstructured nature.

For all punched cards prevalence, at present, our understanding of Busa's consumption junction[17] remains incomplete. Some brief and mostly later comments of Busa's claim his choice was "merely intuition" (Busa 2019a [1951], 28). He also mentions the cards' "multiple adaptability" (Busa 2019a [1951], 28) and implicitly evokes some of the technological affordances that his project required in his discussion of why he rejected the Rapid Selector, another technology he considered.[18] Later, in 1958, when well acquainted with punched cards, he wrote of their affordances for his project:

> Punched cards permit multiple coding of the same information, and they can be sorted and re-sorted rapidly. In addition, the great – even enormous – quantity of cards to be handled, and the possibility of making automatic printouts directly from the cards, dictated the choice of machine-sorted punched cards.
>
> (Busa 2019b[1958], 41)

Crucial enhancements, that arguably bolstered the potential of accounting machines in humanities contexts, had also been made to the machines in the years before Busa began his work. Printing capability was incorporated during the 1920s (Heide 2009, 4). Alphanumeric representation was introduced in the 1930s as "a direct response to the need for names and addresses and alphabetic descriptions on tabulator listings and the provision of several levels of automatic control enabled very sophisticated consumer statements and management reports to be produced" (Campbell-Kelly 1990, 146). Problematic for a project like the *Index Thomisticus*, representation of upper- and lower-case text and punctuation, and special characters, remained limited when Busa first took up the machines (Busa 2019a[1951], 31). Still, in contrast with the Rapid Selector, alphanumeric text could be encoded onto punched cards directly from the get-go.

The origins of Busa's interest in lexicostatistics and text analysis, and how this interest was shaped by the well-established quantitative affordances of accounting machines also requires further analysis than it has been given thus far.[19] Yet here too the statistical and accounting affordances of the machines could be adapted to the "quick comparative analyses of the composition and frequency of the vocabulary of various authors, useful for example in psychological research" (Busa 2019a[1951], 32) that he sought. Punched cards had also been used as a storage medium since the 1930s (Heide 2009), again important for a multiyear project such as Busa's that sought a scalable textbase (though the limits of punched cards as storage media would become apparent before long).[20]

Given Busa's above-noted early emphasis on labour saving, perhaps this was another aspect of what attracted him to punched cards? Heide has written how "Punched-card technology distinguished itself from the competing information technologies by facilitating more complex tasks, like producing statistics and printing invoices, with little human interference after the initial setup of the machines" (Heide 2009, 5). Irrespective of the sophistication of what could be achieved once text had been captured, for much of the time that the *Index Thomisticus* text capture was in process, c.1954–67, Optical Character Recognition (OCR) was not readily available to the project.[21] Thus, the *Index Thomisticus* could not automate the most fundamental stage of its workflow, namely text capture and substantial "human interference" would, after all, be required. This book examines the precedents that could be called on by the *Index Thomisticus* to solve this, from the longer history of scholarly reference tool development and from the then present-day context where women were routinely hired to work in keypunch pools to input data. Let us first consider the invisible workers of the concordance tradition. But the point is not to propose that there is a one-to-one interrelationship between the *Index Thomisticus* and one particular team of invisible workers. Rather, the point is to show how common these teams were in concordance making, an area characterised by intensely hierarchical working practices that often entailed asymmetrical relationships between scholar and amanuenses. It is also to suggest that Busa's knowledge of this tradition may have given him a template for similarly involving manual workers in the *Index Thomisticus* project. Busa, as has been shown, knew of the concordance tradition and of the place of amanuenses in it. In the labour organisation of the *Index Thomisticus* we arguably see the labour-bearing aspects of the concordance tradition realised in a new context, that of the centre he set up in Gallarate, Milan.

Invisible textual workers

The role of amanuensis (or textual assistant), the individual who assisted scholars in the making of reference tools and other textual tasks, was performed by a range of people, including paid or unpaid servants, secretaries, friends, peers, people in printing houses, students and family members (Blair 2014). The work that amanuenses did could include reading aloud, taking dictation, copying, summarising, excerpting, ordering and indexing, translating, running errands and so on (Blair 2010, 108–112; Blair 2014). For the early modern period, Blair emphasises how "variety and great informality characterised the nature of relationships and working arrangements ... with little advance negotiation about the nature of the work". Howsoever varied the specifics of amanuenses' work, by the seventeenth century their task was increasingly perceived as "mechanical" (Blair 2010, 108–111). Though Blair emphasises that in the early modern period "the boundaries between the tasks requiring judgement and those considered mechanical were fluid" (Blair 2010, 112), work designated mechanical was judged to be tedious, repetitive, of low-value and perhaps even detrimental to talent. It could therefore be delegated to amanuenses so that the master or scholar could proceed with the real and creative work undisturbed.

References to the work of amanuenses are not abundant. From the early modern to the modern periods mentions of them and their work sometimes occur in scholar's private papers, including correspondence, and in the paratexts of works like indexes, concordances and their close relations, dictionaries, which they helped to create too (Blair 2014). Those mentions can reinforce perceptions of their work as mechanical or unskilled, and seem to foreshadow how key-punching labour would be framed as unskilled by the *Index Thomisticus* project too (see Chapter 4). In 1664, Juan Caramuel, for example, discussed the making of indexes and advised that after the text had been marked to indicate words to be indexed, one should

> have an amanuensis copy out the passages using only one side of the sheet of paper, and 'have someone cut up [the sheets] with scissors into slips. Have someone do this, I say, do not do it yourself; indeed, this work is mechanical ... Then call four or six servants or friends and have them distribute the slips by letter and classes' on large tables.
>
> (Blair 2010, 110–1)

Similarly, J.J. Scaliger described the work he did in indexing Gruter as akin to that of a "servant" (Blair 2010, 111). Green's description of the later work of Samuel Johnson's amanuenses strikes the same note: "While the amanuenses were largely deputed to what must indeed have been lexicographical drudgery, Johnson himself took on the more creative task of preparing the definitions and the etymologies" (Green 1997, 221). The work done for the Oxford English Dictionary by young women assistants, Miss Skipper and Miss Scott, sorting the word slips into alphabetical order was initially considered so menial as not to merit mention:

> The efforts of [Miss Skipper and Miss Scott] pass unacknowledged in any of the earlier volumes of the completed Dictionary – a mordant commentary on the realities of Victorian life. However, the complete OED was published in the more liberal and enlightened year of 1928, their names did appear on the list of Assistants.
>
> (Winchester 2003, 112 fn7)

The bonds that existed between amanuenses and scholars could vary dramatically. Not all appear to have been as distant as those that shaped the *Index Thomisticus* (see Chapter 4). Some, such as Scaliger, developed close connections with their amanuenses (Blair 2014). Johnson is said to have stood bail on 12 March 1750 for Mary Peyton, wife of his amanuensis V.J. Peyton. He also paid for the Peyton's funerals (Green 1997, 221). Yet, "these relationships could also be fraught with tensions" (Blair 2010, 107). The servants of Scaliger and Montaigne stole their work (Blair 2010, 107). S.J. Herrtage, the earliest of Murray's assistants in his work on the Oxford English Dictionary was dismissed when "he was discovered to be a kleptomaniac" (Winchester 2003, 100 fn. 2). Erasmus found that his work had been published without his permission (Blair 2010, 107).

Scholars complained in print about errors and infelicities in their work that were apparently caused by their amanuenses (Blair 2010), a highly rhetorical move (Blair 2014; Shapin 1989). The possibility of ostensibly disowning one's mistakes by attributing them to amanuenses opened a world of possibilities for the scholar, who could disavow personal, managerial or scientific responsibility for errors made. It is particularly intriguing that one of the few sustained discussions extant of the work of keypunching does exactly this (see Chapter 5).

It is important to state that arrangements between scholars and amanuenses were not necessarily to the scholar's exclusive advantage. Amanuenses were sometimes recompensed financially, giving some individuals time and funds to pursue their own intellectual or literary pursuits. Payment could be a double-edged sword, however, as in some periods it was seen as a marker of individuals' non-scholarly and essentially untrustworthy status (Shapin 1989, 561). Some also benefited from the opportunity to learn from an experienced scholar. Amanuenses "could be treated as close to an equal; indeed, some of Erasmus' famuli may have been social equals, since working for another was often only a stage in the training of a student and future scholar" (Blair 2010, 106). Erasmus reserved the title of amanuensis for his three favourite assistants and it is known that Nicolas Cannius "worked with Erasmus on improving the index of the Adages for the edition of 1526" (Blair 2010, 106). The example of Hugo Grotius, whose family or "household academy" enabled his work, shows that the boundaries between amanuensis and scholar could be porous:

The household academy bore many other fruits: his wife Maria van Reigersberch (1589–1653), his younger brother Willem de Groot (1597–1662), his sister-in-law Suzanna van Reigersberch (1586–1640), his daughter Cornelia (1611–1687) and his second son Pieter de Groot (1615–1678) all became authors in their own right, often with his aid and encouragement.

(van Ittersum 2011, 525)

As we shall see, some of the *Index Thomisticus'* keypunch operators did recall that their training benefitted them subsequently, though none of the individuals interviewed were able to use their training as a stepping stone to the world of scholarship, as amanuenses had sometimes previously done.

Crucially, Blair holds that the role of amanuensis morphed yet continued from the early modern period to the modern in various guises:

In the nineteenth century, social and professional distinctions became more clearly defined. By 1900 many of the menial tasks, such as copying, taking dictation, filing, and even routine calculating had become feminized. ... Women were employed as secretaries in offices and by literary authors and also as "computers" to perform complex and tedious calculations, notably in astronomy.

(Blair 2010, 111–12; see also Price and Thurschwell 2004)

In the next section we will look in greater detail at the merging of the amanuensis tradition with the so-called "feminisation of the office", or "industrialisation of the office" which was underway from c. 1880. The *Index Thomisticus* converged with these processes through their shared labour practices, data-orientations and technologies, including their common use of sex-segregated workforces, office-technologies like electromechanical accounting machines and, in due course, electronic computers for data processing. So, while the concordance tradition sheds some light on the historical roots of the invisibilising and task-based segregation of the *Index Thomisticus* workforce, the feminisation of the office writ large further provides an important template for understanding the gender-segregation of the *Index Thomisticus*. And of course, the feminisation of the office overlapped to some extent with, and would subsequently influence, the gendering of the labour force who operated electronic computers in their early years, before many women would be pushed out of the field. As Hicks has written,

a common misperception is that women got into computing during World War II simply because men were at the front, but the gendering of computing work existed before the war, and before computers were electronic. The feminization of this work continued through and after the war, with women ... perform[ing] computing work with electromechanical and later electronic systems ...

(Hicks 2021, 140)

Thus, it is argued that the *Index Thomisticus*' take-up of the historical concordance labour tradition in the context of humanities computing was not a
carbon-copy of what had gone before. Developments that were then more recent,
like the gendering of mechanically-assisted office work, are also relevant to
understanding the divisions that were drawn by the *Index Thomisticus*, not only
between technical workers and scholars, but furthermore, between female technical workers and their male scholarly and technical counterparts. As we have
seen, at least in the earlier phases of his work, Busa arguably viewed scholarship
as something that stood apart from the social and cultural circumstances of its
pursuit. It seems ironic, then, that it may have been the *Index Thomisticus*' active
reconstitution of wider social and cultural narratives about gender, information-
processing work and technology that made the divisions that it drew between
scholars and technical staff appear to be natural and inevitable rather than a
situated response to the context in which one of the inaugural projects of computing and the humanities came into being.

The next section will overview the subsequent feminisation of the role of
"amanuensis" over the longer term. Data-input using office technologies like
the accounting machines that were also used by the *Index Thomisticus*,
would become, by the early 1900s, "almost entirely feminized ..."
(Ensmenger 2021, 41). But the gendering process did not stop there: "The
origins of the computer industry can only be understood in terms of the
larger history of industrialization; otherwise, the large number of women
workers and the particular organization of labour are inexplicable"
(Ensmenger 2021, 41–2).

Feminisation of the office and electronic computing (co-written with Melissa Terras[22])

With roots in women's participation in the industrialisation of light manufacturing and the second industrial revolution, late nineteenth and early twentieth century developments—like the take-up of unit record equipment in
workplaces and the abundance of documentation that resulted from the scientific management of workplaces—resulted in the creation of new kinds of jobs,
to which women were increasingly hired (Hartman Strom 1989). This "feminisation of the office" was not confined to industry or government departments
but occurred in research contexts too as women took on roles like that of
"human computer" in scientific laboratories and statistical bureaus (Grier 2005;
Iliffe 2008, 8). Just before construction of the ENIAC at the University of
Pennsylvania in the mid-1940s, for example, the University of Pennsylvania was
recruiting "women college graduates" only for its scientific calculating (Grier
2005; Light 1999, 463). As ostensibly new as the machines being used in these
contexts were, this approach to employment and labour mimicked the "industrial textile factory ... [where] a woman ... operated a highly specialized
machine to perform *one* specific task within a rigidly organised division of
labour" (Ensmenger 2021, 39, emphasis original). Ensmenger's emphasis on

women's confinement to *one* task and, indeed, *one* machine and the blocking of their progression to other roles is, of course, mirrored in the *Index Thomisticus*. This will be examined closely in Chapter 2, when the methodology and labour that underpinned the technical elaboration of the *Index Thomisticus* will be unpicked.

Women were desired for what were positioned as lower-rung information processing posts right across the academic, scientific, governmental and commercial sectors partly due to the wider economic and social circumstances that meant they could be paid less than males at the time of their hiring and over the longer term. The marriage bar that many firms operated meant that women were unable to continue working after marriage and so opportunities for promotion or advanced training were not extended to them (Hicks 2017, 49). Turnover of women staff tended to be low because employment opportunities outside of clerical contexts were limited, thus creating a "like it or lump it" situation with little prospect of amelioration (Hartman Strom 1989, 60). Firmly entrenched stereotypes of femininity[23] were also in play. In implementing the Hollerith punched-card system with the 1890 census, women were reportedly:

> more exact in touch, more expeditious in handling the schedules, more at home in adjusting the delicate mechanisms of the "electrical machines", and eventually 80% of those employed as census "computers" were women (though a more important reason for this may be that women, having fewer options, were more willing to take such work at the wages offered).
>
> (Nebeker 2009, 200)

This stereotyping could further inform the perception of women as suitable for such posts and, in turn, of the work requiring little ability and low pay (Hartman Strom 1989, 187–8). Moreover, this gave rise to "an important incidental benefit—as more women took jobs at depressed rates, the overall levels of wages for men might be reduced as well" (Hartman Strom 1989, 68).

Though viewed as routine, the work of human computers, for example, involved the capture and processing of data, and the manual undertaking of sophisticated calculations (Ceruzzi 1991). In some sectors, like astronomy, the work of women in roles like human computing was acknowledged for a time: "until the 1950s, published copies of photographs that each woman scanned bore her name" (Light 1999, 459). Yet, as women "became synonymous with office machine operators and their work became tied to typewriters, desktop accounting machines, and room-sized punched card equipment installations" (Hicks 2017, 9), they were conceptually disassociated from work that required thought. This may have further compounded the devaluing of women's contributions to areas including Science and Astronomy (e.g. Rossiter 1993) and the Arts and humanities more broadly (Carroll 1990), where mind tends to be privileged over body.

From the categorisation of feminised labour as physical, menial and lacking in specialisation there followed a routine denial of the value of this work and a divestment of an individuals' moral right to receive attribution for one's contributions. Various processes and actions gave rise to this. Female technical worker's identities were eroded by practices like a (male) lab leader's name appearing on publications which bore no mention of theirs:

> Technicians generally did not author papers or technical manuals. Nor did they acquire the coveted status symbols of scientists and engineers: publications, lecturers, and membership of professional societies. Ultimately these women never got a public opportunity to display their technical knowledge, crucial for person recognition and career advancement.
>
> (Light 1999, 459)

There also developed a deindividualising tendency to refer to women workers collectively, with reference to their lab leader or main instrument, for example, "Cecil's Beauty Chorus", "ENIAC girls" and "scanner girls" (Light 1999). By the 1940s, calculating projects were estimated in "girl-years" of effort (Grier 2005, 365 fn. 2), and many teams of scientific computers were referred to as "girl computers" (Grier 2005, 276). Thus, the possibility of offering low levels of financial recompense, and common stereotypes about women having lower technical ability than men, a docile nature, and an inherent propensity for precision may well have made young women seem attractive for the mechanical posts that Busa sought to fill, blending the concordance tradition and the feminisation of the office in a stream that would, in due course, merge with that of the electronic computing industry and emergent humanities computing.

The modern-day conception of the "young, male and technologically inclined" (Ensmenger 2012, 23) specialists who program computer software is one that dominates today's computing industry, both in perception and practice.[24] However, "the computing professions, at least in the early decades of commercial computing, were surprisingly accepting of women. It was only later that the computing occupations became highly masculinized" (Ensmenger 2012). It was no coincidence that many of those to first work with digital computers were women: as calculating assistants were replaced by electronic devices, the stereotypes of the gender and type of worker best placed to undertake computational work remained the same,[25] and many digital software engineers were recruited from the scientific computing field (Light 1999; Sydell 2014). In 1957, IBM "produced an elaborate recruitment brochure for college-educated women, entitled 'My Fair Ladies' after the recent Broadway hit" (Abbate 2012, 65), that included images of women who worked as programmers or researchers. The work assigned to women typically covered computer operation and programming (Hicks 2017), which was seen as lower in status and less difficult than the hardware-oriented work that men did (Light 1999). The employment of many women in the early days of computing was thus tied to an assumption that computational coding was a straightforward and simple task that could be assigned to clerical workers (Light 1999, 458; Ensmenger 2010, 29; Abbate 2012, 7 and 25–6).

Abbate has written about how the "dominant view of technology [as] a masculine field structured the entire process of job recruitment" in computing (Abbate 2012, 64). This is exemplified in, for example, the workplace structure of the ENIAC project, where male computer engineers performed the ostensibly intellectual and skilled job of looking after the hardware. Women performed the devalued job of dealing with the software:

> The ENIAC women, the computer programmers, as they would later be known, were expected to simply adapt the plans of computation already widely used in human computing projects to the new technology of the electronic computer ... The ENIAC women would simply set up the machine to perform these predetermined plans; that this work would turn out to be difficult and require radically innovative thinking was completely unanticipated.
>
> (Ensmenger 2012, 14–15)

Of course, the actual nature of the work that women did could be entirely different to how it was portrayed. They became skilled at both operating and maintaining the ENIAC: "Since we knew both the application and the machine, we learned to diagnose troubles as well as, if not better than, the engineer" (Betty Jean Jennings, quoted in Light 1999, 471). Their expertise was, all the same, viewed as sub-professional (Turner 2014). Jean Jennings Bartik, a programmer of the ENIAC,[26] recalled of its launch "People never recognized, they never acted as though we knew what we were doing. I mean, we were in a lot of pictures" (Sydell 2014). Yet media outlets did not name the women[27] who appeared in the press photographs of the systems[28] (Sydell 2014). It was not until the 50th anniversary of the ENIAC that the contributions of its female programmers began to be recognised:[29] historians had previously focused on the achievements of the male engineers rather than the "support" of the female programmers (Light 1999). Although the field has "developed a rich literature from academic, journalistic, and participant perspectives" (Abbate 2012, 5) it has biased the activities of men, equating computing with hardware, rather than software, when women rarely had the chance to build computers (Abbate 2012, 6).

Widespread personnel issues in recruiting enough skilled programmers for the computing sector made it a common destination for the female workforce until well into the 1960s (in 1967, *Cosmopolitan Magazine* urged their readership to become "computer girls" with the potential for high salaries, job satisfaction, and the chance to meet plenty of eligible males, quoting Admiral Grace Hopper saying "Women are 'naturals' at computer programming" (Mandel 1967)). After that period, the sector became increasingly professionalised and masculinised, with increasing use of aptitude testing and personality profiles as barriers to entry which embodied and privileged "masculine characteristics" (Ensmenger 2012, 77), the "explosion of unscrupulous vocational schools" (Ensmenger 2012, 79) which encouraged women into secretarial and clerical roles and a convenient bias towards "traditional male privilege" (Ensmenger 2012, 79), all leading to "the increasing assumption that the average programmer was also male" (Ensmenger 2012, 79).

These developments in the computing profession created new barriers to female participation, and "an activity originally intended to be low-status, clerical–and more often than not, female–computer programming was gradually and deliberately transformed into a high-status, scientific, and masculine discipline" (Ensmenger 2012, 239), leading to the stereotypes and workforce we now associate with the computing industry today. Even if the keypunch operators of the *Index Thomisticus* do not seem to have had the opportunity to work with electronic computers, the wide-spread devaluing of women's work with unit record equipment, and the apparent further validation of this devaluing in electronic computing contexts, remind us that the *Index Thomisticus* is far from the only project that has been recorded with photographs filled with unknown young, female workers. Thus, in the context of the *Index Thomisticus*, as in other areas of computing and knowledge production, the devaluing and "long term invisibility" of women's contributions was fostered (Light 1999, 459; see also Rossiter 1993) and even compounded by events and traditions that preceded, ran parallel with and even continued after their time as keypunch operators.

Feminisation of concordance automation

It should hardly come as a surprise that as the concordance tradition merged with that of the feminisation of the office and, in due course, electronic computing, on those occasions when the "concordance amanuenses", was brought into view, they were indicated not only to be someone of "lower status" than the scholar. They were often indicated to be female too. Perhaps influenced by Busa, but surely also drawing on common sources, disparaging references to those who assisted concordance projects can be found in the wider humanities computing literature. In 1965, for example, with what might be termed genre-characteristic derision, Parrish referred to the team of 67 people assembled by Lane Cooper some years earlier:

> By lashing on squadrons of graduate students and discontented Ithaca housewives and junior colleagues (incidentally, three of these people died during the operation), Professor Cooper accomplished the immense labor of cutting and pasting, stamping and alphabetizing, hundreds of thousands of slips of paper in less than a year. It was a labor that might have taken one man twenty years.

(Parrish 1967, 57)

Aspects of Parrish's description, such as the subsuming of the efforts of these individuals by the identity of the scholar is reminiscent of the portrayals of amanuenses discussed above. An important figure who worked at an early stage of humanities computing,[30] it seems reasonable to assume that Parrish probably also employed assistants to punch the texts he concordanced. Definitively establishing this would require further fundamental research, as Parrish too tends to switch to the passive voice when discussing the work of keypunching, for example, "As we ultimately worked out our technique for a pilot run on the poems of Matthew Arnold, the process went roughly like this. The lines of Arnold's verse were punched on IBM cards, one line per card." (Parrish 1962, 5). In any case, from a report written by J.A. Painter, an IBM programmer who worked with Parrish, it might be concluded that the work of keypunching concordance projects did not qualify even as work, as punching is portrayed merely as a precursor to, and excluded from discussion of the tripartite stage that is indicated to have constituted the "real work":

> The poetry is transcribed to punched cards, one line per card, together with some identifying information. ... In this work there has been a fairly rigid division of labour. First there is the problem solver, or user, who realized a computer could be used to prepare a poetry concordance and initiated the entire operation. Next there was a programmer with responsibility for analyzing the problem, preparing the computer solution and overseeing the actual computer production. Last was the installation which provided the computer itself along with ancillary equipment, supplies and services.
>
> (Painter 1964, 162–4)

Indeed, a review article published by Burton in the 1980s begins with what amounts to a roll call of major figures in early concordance-making in humanities computing, including Busa, Wisbey, Parrish and others, and discusses the work these scholars are implied to have personally executed so as to encode the texts they concordanced onto punched cards.[31] The keypunch operators who may have contributed to these projects remain utterly invisible in this discussion (Burton 1981b, 139–45).

On occasions when keypunching labour is brought visually or pictorially into view, no opportunity is lost to draw attention to the sex-disaggregation of scholars and keypunch operators, even in a text from the mid-1960s as demonstrated in Figure 1.1.

In the University of Toronto, whose press published the mid-1960s manual by Glickman whence Figure 1.1 is excerpted, the first women to be appointed to associate professor were in post by 1903 and the first to be appointed to full professor was in post by 1920. And while women faculty remained a minority among Canada's full-time faculty, by 1972 they represented 15% of assistant professors; 9% of associate professors and 4% of full professors (Samson and Shen 2018). Neither were women invisible in the international

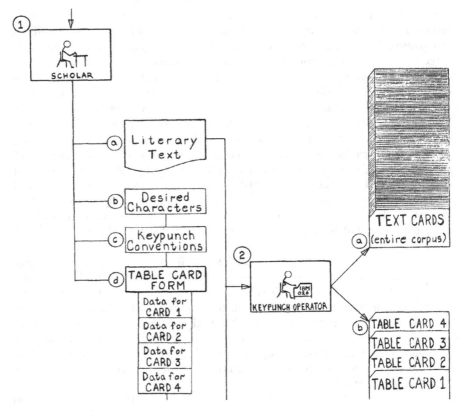

Figure 1.1 Excerpt from Robert Jay Glickman (1966)
Note: Manual for the printing of literary texts and concordances by computer University of Toronto Press.
Source: Prelim. ed edition (1966) (CC BY-NC-ND 4.0).

computing context. The Association for Computing Machinery had at least 27 women among 459 members by 1948, Ida Rhodes (with whom Busa was also in contact) among of them (Abbate 2012, 159).

Indeed, a comment of Wisbey suggests that the devaluation of the work of the keypunching "amanuenses" was not only epistemic but systemic and perpetuated, however unwillingly, by individual scholars and the institutions and academic system they worked for:

> The facilities of the Mathematical Laboratory [in Cambridge] were placed at my disposal with only one stipulation, namely that I should make my own arrangements for the tape punching. I stress the point, since this kind of practical difficulty will face anyone who embarks on such work. Eventually the Weiner Genesis was put on tape in the course

of six evening sessions of five hours each. The total punching time was about 20 hours. ... For this, and for a first reading of the "proofs", I am greatly indebted to my wife whose timely assistance prevented a delay of several months.

(Wisbey 1962, 169)

Nevertheless, in the above, Wisbey clearly attributes the agency of his wife and he does acknowledge her contributions to the practical work of making the concordance to the Weiner Genesis, suggesting that while such devalued portrayals may have been largely unintentional or unconscious, given the devalued status of keypunching, they were not inevitable.[32]

And while the *Index Thomisticus* was clearly not alone or unusual in segregating and devaluing feminised labour, it is not true that this was a universal reality of concordance projects. Other examples of male and female Principal Investigators, who acknowledged the input of the amanuenses on their team and who, moreover, gave credit also exist. Josephine Miles, another important figure in humanities computing,[33] who worked on a *Concordance to the Poetical Works of John Dryden* carefully credited in print and in interviews, the women and men who worked on her projects:

In her preface to the published volume, Miles thanked faculty from the English, French, and Speech Departments, but she especially singled out the female staff members from the computer lab who "worked under the guidance of Mr. Gordon Morrison and Mr. Boyd Judd at the Computer Laboratory," including Shirley Rice, Odette Carothers, and Penny Gee, who had punched each card in the Concordance with a single word, a symbol corresponding to the title of the poem in which it appeared, and a line number.

(Buurma and Heffernan 2018)

It would thus have been at least theoretically possible for the *Index Thomisticus* project to do things differently; however, as we shall see, gender segregation and the devaluing of women's contributions was to run all the way through the project, from its workplace organisation to its scholarly reporting.

The Rouses have connected thirteenth century reference tools to a new way of thinking about text, its authority and function. As such, indexes and concordances can be seen as reifications of a profound epistemological and ontological shift in definitions of knowledge and knowledge-makers. In contrast with the major works of the twelfth century, which sought to "assimilate and organise inherited written authority in systematic form", these reference tools allowed a text to be "used, rather than read" (Rouse and Rouse 1991, 221). They engendered the possibility to "search written authority afresh, to get at, to locate and to retrieve information" (Rouse and Rouse 1991, 221). Ramsay has described Busa's concordance as a "radically transformed, reordered, disassembled, and reassembled version of one of the world's most influential philosophies" (Ramsay 2011a, 1). And yet, few studies have sought to contextualise his intellectual contributions with regard to the *longue durée* of reference tool-making, or the attitudes to written authority and definitions of knowledge that his work reflected or disrupted as the Rouses and others have done for the earlier period.

Whatever it was that Busa's work did disrupt, it certainly was not the labour organisation that underpinned concordance projects. Busa's response to the problem of how to encode the *Index Thomisticus*' millions of words onto punched cards, so they could be manipulated to make all manner of indexes, was to devise a hybrid human-machine approach that "was at the pivot point (or was the pivot point) between handmade scholarly tools and machine-made scholarly tools" (Winter 1999, 16). Thus, in CAAL and the *Index Thomisticus*, as in earlier set ups, people remained at the heart of the operation. Despite Busa's, and indeed the later humanities computing community's emphasis on the role of automation in its work, individuals were required at every stage of the process: to parse and edit text, to encode punched cards, to operate project devices, to move stacks of cards from machine to machine and much more. From this perspective, we might say that the *Index Thomisticus* represents more than an automated continuation of the long-established operations of hand-concordancing. It also represents a continuation of, and indeed was a conduit for, the transferal from the analogue to the electro-mechanical and, in due course, to the digital of the long-established practice of engaging teams of largely unacknowledged workers to implement significant aspects of concordance making.

Indeed, with regard to the labour history of reference tool-making over the *longue durée*, and the specifically scholarly context, it seems that, for its female amanuenses, the *Index Thomisticus* represented a retrograde step. Busa's discussions of the benefits that technology would bring to concordance making verged on the techno-utopian. Yet keypunch operators were not only blocked from progressing through the ranks of the *Index Thomisticus*, instruction in tasks other than keypunching was blocked to them too. The *Index Thomisticus* seems to have shut out the possibilities that were at least notionally there in the earlier periods for some amanuenses to learn new skills and knowledge and to, perhaps, occasionally start on the road towards being scholars themselves.

Notes

1 Fr Roberto Busa S.J. was born in Vicenza, Italy, on November 28, 1913 and he joined the Jesuit order in 1933 (Passarotti 2013, 16).
2 In 1960, Busa wrote that "*Der Plan eines Index Thomisticus geht auf das Jahr 1946 zurück und die Arbeiten zur Automation begannen im Jahre 1949*" [The plan for the *Index Thomisticus* originated in the year 1946 and the automation work began in the year 1949] (Busa 1960a, 1, translation mine). Later, in 1992, he would place automation earlier in the timeline of his research activities: "In fact I started to explore how to automatize linguistic analysis in 1946. I started to play with IBM punched cards machines [sic] in 1949. I have punched and processed 6 million

cards." (Busa 1992, 125). Vanhoutte has concluded "the fact is that Busa's [published in 1949] dissertation ... was written without the use of or reference to any computer technology" (Vanhoutte 2013, 127).

3 These discussions are useful for what they implicitly reveal about Busa's ontological and epistemological viewpoints. For him, knowledge seemed to exist in an objective state that could be directly accessed by scholars. He refers to such tools as "aids to pure knowledge" (Busa 2019a[1951], 21).

4 The publication of the "definitive" editions of Aquinas was not completed at the time of writing this chapter in 2020 and continued to be worked on by the Leonine Commission which Pope Leo XIII set up in 1880. The edited editions that Busa would have had at his disposal when he began work include the 1882 Latin Leonine edition (Aquinas 1882) and prior publications including "the Parma edition (*Opera Omnia*, Parma: Fiaccadori, 1852–73) and the Vivès edition (*Opera Omnia*, Paris: Vivès, 1871–82)" (Davies 2012, 538). See (Busa and Associates 2005) for further bibliographic details of Aquinas' texts and editions used by the *Index Thomisticus* project.

5 According to Burrows, a key contribution of computing to the humanities lies in the possibilities it has opened for studying function words in all their abundance and in ways that would be impossible using analogue tools alone (see Nyhan and Flinn 2016, 43). Busa's contemporaries were naturally not all in agreement about the benefits of making all function words mechanically or computationally tractable. Daniel L. McGloin, Chair of Philosophy, Loyola University of Los Angeles, characterised Busa's work on this as a "fetish of scholarship gone wild", see (Rockwell and Sinclair 2020).

6 This mode of digital humanities does not usually position it as the instrumental pursuit of efficiencies of time, labour or scale but rather it seeks to understand how digital humanities gives rise to new forms of technologically-mediated interpretation (e.g. van Zundert 2015); new ways of thinking about the generative and social justice-oriented potential of a bi-directional social shaping of computing, for example, through the lens of postcolonial digital humanities (Risam 2018) and digital black feminism (Steele 2021). See also (Dobson 2019) for methodological approaches to critical humanities.

7 See, for example, Busa 1989, 130–31. The connections between Busa's and developments in Analytical Thomism, and Catholic intellectualism more broadly merit more attention.

8 Instead, he seems to reject its tenets obliquely: "The reader should not simply attach to the words he reads the significance they have in his mind but should try to find out what significance they had in the writer's mind" (Busa 1980, 83).

9 It was in the centuries after the invention of the printing press that indexes became a standard feature of scholarly texts (Pettegree 2010, 294). While this process was largely complete by the eighteenth century (Blair 2010, 144) it did not follow a continuously upward trajectory. Blair observed how in the sixteenth century there still existed many proto-indexes or "roughly alphabetised list[s] of entries based on summary statements printed in the margins of large books, without any or much attention to consolidating related entries" (Blair 2010, 142).

10 The alphabetical subject index also emerged around this time and "Numerous indexes employing a variety of techniques seem to have emerged spontaneously across Europe" (Rouse and Rouse 1991, 226). "In rapid succession there followed alphabetized subject indexes to major authors like Aristotle (indexed anonymously by 1250 in Paris), Augustine (by the Dominican Kilwardby at Oxford, 1256–61), or Aquinas (owner-indexed by Godfrey of Fontaines), then circulated more broadly" (Blair 2010, 40). Some scholars have centred the role of the printing press in the establishment and spread of the index (Eisenstein 1980, 90–94). Others have emphasised that thirteenth century reference tools were indeed devised in the

context of the manuscript book and pushed that technology to its limits (Rouse and Rouse 1991) and have considered the interconnections of these tools with medieval memory culture (Carruthers 2008, 129–30).

11 In discussing these teams, I range quite freely over references to and discussions of amanuenses from the early modern to modern period given that Blair, the authority in this area whose work is drawn on extensively in this section, observed "striking continuities" in how amanuenses are treated, portrayed and engaged over the longer term (Blair 2014)

12 Recent scholarship has cast doubt on the use of slips in the period that aligns with the earliest concordance projects. It seems more likely that work proceeded as in what is presumed to be a penultimate version of the Hugo of St Cher concordance where "each quire was written by a different copyist responsible only for a fixed portion of the alphabet, as one can see from the blank each left when he had finished his assigned task" (Rouse and Rouse 1991, 225; see also Blair 2010, 210). The earliest evidence for the use of paper slips in such contexts is traced by Considine to "the Swiss humanist Conrad Gessner's *Pandectae* (1548)" (Considine 2015, 490).

13 Considine discusses various approaches to the use of slips (Considine 2015, 488–9).

14 That so-called technological progress does not result in the obsolescence of earlier technologies, and that technological development entails mimesis as much, if not more so, than rupture see Edgerton 2019.

15 See Winter 1999, 9–10. Examples of individuals who sought to use punched cards in Humanistic contexts can be given, nonetheless. In 1948, in an article entitled "The Machine age in Historical Research", Lawson wrote of how punched card machines could be used by historians to prepare bibliographies for publication, noting that "By means of the alphabetical and numerical key punch the bibliographic item can be entered directly onto the punched card" (Lawson 1948, 146).

16 In 1949 Busa travelled to America in search of appropriate "mechanical devices" to assist in this work. Whilst there, he visited a number of universities and other institutions to view and appraise relevant technologies. For a detailed discussion of the trip and how it came about see (Jones 2016, 1–49).

17 The consumption junction is described by Cowan as "the place and time at which the consumer makes choices between competing technologies ... [this perspective is useful for] ascertain[ing] how the network may have looked when viewed from the inside out, which elements stood out as being more important, more determinative of choices, than the others, and which paths seemed wise to pursue and which too dangerous to contemplate" (Cowan 1992, 263).

18 See Jones discussion of the Rapid Selector (Jones 2016, 39–42); see also Busa's comments on the Rapid Selector (Busa 2019a[1951], 27). He rejected the Rapid Selector due to its lack of support for printing, use of photosensitive paper and its inability to encode alphanumeric characters directly (instead, the words of a given text had to be translated by hand into "numerical symbols" before input) (Busa 2019a[1951], 28).

19 As Busa himself points out in various letters, his knowledge of statistics and mathematics was not at a level that would have allowed him to pursue this work independently (e.g. Busa 1958a). It might be contended that in seeking to bring quantitative methods to bear on language Busa was operating entirely within the specialisation of unit record equipment, which was predominately used in calculations and quantitative routines in the private and public sectors. This points to as yet under-researched questions about the context in which Busa's interest in statistical approaches to language developed.

20 The work of the female operators resulted in a great magnitude of punched cards. By the 1960s, Busa's writings discuss the failure of punched card machines to scale to the processing of millions of words of text: "The first years we processed texts of 2,000,000 words using only punched card equipment. That experience has taught us that the processing of texts containing more than 100,000 words is not practical

without a computer. There are too many limitations in getting concordances this way" (Busa 1964, 66).

21 Ideas about OCR, or the extraction of machine-readable data from printed text, had been about for some time and had featured in US patents for technology to assist the blind in the early 1800s. It was in the early 1950s that prototypical yet promising OCR devices, like the Gismo device of David Shepard, gained traction, see Schantz 1982.

22 See Introduction, fn. 1.

23 These stereotypes not only limited employment prospects but were connected to agenda that advocated the confining of women to domestic roles. In the US, in the post-second world war context, the "trend toward working adult women was subverted by a powerful cultural reaction in the opposite reaction" (Carnes 2007, 117), as some intellectuals, child-care manual writers like Spock, and aspects of popular culture and the neo-Victorian revival portrayed women's purpose in life as a full time housewife and caregiver and emphasised their inherent unsuitability for participating in industrial or other paid employment (Carnes 2007, 117–20). For a sustained exploration of how gender stereotypes have been implicated in the practice, process and outcomes of science see e.g. (Keller and Longino 1996).

24 In the UK in 2011, 18% of computing science students were women (WISE 2012) and in 2012–13, 15.1% of ICT professionals were female, with only 10.6% of management roles in Science, Technology and Engineering being undertaken by women (WISE 2014). Across Europe in 2013, women represent around 33% of total graduates in science and technology and 32% of employees of the ICT sector (European Commission 2013). However, in 2007, the proportion of women working in ICT in Italy was found to be much lower than that, with 19.2% of the sector being female (European Commission 2009).

25 This was a stereotype that endured will into the mid 1960s. In a 1963 article, Valerie Rockmael describes her virtues as a female computer programmer "Women are less aggressive and more content ... and are more prone to stay on the job if they are content, regardless of a lack of advancement. They ... are less willing to travel or change job locations, particularly if they are married or engaged" (Rockmael 1963, 41).

26 The Electronic Numerical Integrator And Computer (ENIAC) was the world's first general purpose digital computing machine which could undertake the type of analysis done by Human computers, being reprogrammable, and with the potential of exceeding the calculation capacity of what those teams employed as scientific computers could manage. See Grier 1996 for an overview of its history.

27 See Grier 1996 for a further description of the hierarchical structures of workers employed to program the ENIAC.

28 See also Abbate 2012, 37 for similar testimonies from other female ENIAC programmers, and Light 1999 for a comparison of the contributions of these women with their media image.

29 The classic shot of the ENIAC computer at the Moore school (http://ftp.arl.army.mil/ftp/historic-computers/gif/eniac2.gif) contains a soldier at the foreground function table, named as CPL Irwin Goldstine. However, the woman behind the card punch equipment and the woman at background function table are unidentified. ("U.S. Army Photo", from 8x10 transparency, courtesy Harold Breaux, Historic Computing Images, n.d.).

30 Vanhoutte notes that "in 1957, and independently of the work of Busa or Ellison which hadn't appeared yet, Cornell university launched a program for a computer-produced series of concordances, with Stephen M. Parrish as general editor" (Vanhoutte 2013, 128, fn 30). On the significance of Parish's early concordance work, see also Burton 1981a, 7–9.

31 In this article, Burton seems to indicate that she personally punched the text of one of her scholarly projects: "When keypunching Kittredge's modern spelling edition to some plays of Shakespeare, I used a slash (/) to represent a proper name ..." (Burton 1981b, 139).
32 The twitter hashtag #thanksforthetyping draws attention to vast amount of labour that has been contributed by the (usually) wives of male authors in the typing and sometimes editing of their publications.
33 Recent scholarship has drawn attention to Miles previously looked contributions to early humanities computing. In addition to Buurma and Heffernan (2018) see Pasanek (2019) and Wimmer (2019).

2 Hidden tasks, hidden workers

Keypunching the *Index Thomisticus*

Introduction

With funding from the National Endowment for the humanities, Steven E. Jones led an international team in the research and building of an immersive 3D model of CAAL's laboratory workspace in via G. Ferraris 2, Gallarate (see Figure 2.1). The 3D model, which is freely accessible online, is informed by, among other sources, photos from October 1961, which show how the previously dispersed divisions of CAAL's workforce were brought together in this location, a former site of textile manufacturing in Gallarate.

As the 3D model communicates, the factory floor on which the *Index Thomisticus* was elaborated from 1961 does not appear to have had physical dividers, yet the work of keypunching and machine processing pursued in this space continued to be separated along gendered lines, just as it had been in other locations where the project was housed. While ostensibly an open-plan space, it seems that in via G. Ferraris the *Index Thomisticus'* workers were separated by dividers, some transparent, others invisible, which underscored the hierarchies that shaped the information spaces of the project and its workforce.

In March 2019, I had the opportunity of testing a beta version of this 3D model of CAAL. The experience was unforgettable, both haunting and compelling, akin, perhaps to seeing a shard of landscape reflected on the surface of a lake on a calm day, with all the points of uncertainty and clarity that such a reflection brings. Virtually exploring the 3D interpretation of CAAL, I encountered the ghost-like avatars that had been chosen to represent the staff of the *Index Thomisticus* (these avatars were chosen by Jones not only to obviate any sense of the uncanny valley that might arise from including likenesses of real people in the model, but also with regard to questions of digital ethics and the representation of identifiable individuals through such models). And I was also struck by how quiet and still the world conjured in the model was (the interviewees don't discuss much about the ambience and sonance of the locations they worked in yet other accounts of punched card operators' working conditions mention the word "noisy"; see, for example, Hicks 2017, 69).

Archival photographs and the 3D model show that glass dividers alone separated Busa's office from the workroom of the scholars and the factory

DOI: 10.4324/9781003138235-3

floor where the technical work was done (e.g. Busa Archive #0582). As I "stood" in the reconstruction of Busa's office, and looked towards the factory floor, I realised that, whilst in this space, Busa would have continually seen his technical staff, including the female keypunch operators, at work. And yet, to return to the sustained tension between "seeing" and "looking" that the metaphor of the blindfold evokes (see Introduction), Busa appears to have continually overlooked the keypunch operators as individuals who were making a valuable contribution to his project.

An expanding body of academic and gray literature has been drawing attention to the significant levels of devalued and precarious, and yet essential human labour upon which technoutopian narratives and performances of autonomous and artificial intelligence, and the many other kinds of automation that have long been promised us, are built. In their analysis of this, Mary L Gray and Siddharth Suri use the evocative term "ghost work" to refer to "the human labor powering many mobile phone apps, websites, and artificial intelligence systems [which] can be hard to see—in fact, it's often intentionally hidden. We call this opaque world of employment ghost work" (Gray and Suri 2019, 6).

Looking back to a time before apps, websites or artificial intelligence systems existed, this chapter seeks to bring the "ghost workers" of the *Index Thomisticus* back into view, and to explore the significant levels of "ghost work" that powered the incunabular period of digital humanities, and its use of electromechanical accounting machines, and in due course, digital computing. This chapter moreover contends that in this foundational project of the digital humanities, the recognition and definition of skill and expertise was socially constructed, gender-inflected and ultimately constitutive of a scholarly identity that was constructed in opposition to a technical one. Thus, despite what this chapter argues to be its indispensable utility, the work of the keypunching would remain largely invisible in publications about the *Index Thomisticus*, whether written by Busa himself or those in the humanities computing and digital humanities communities who seem to have taken its portrayal at face value. This not only contributed to the invisibilising of keypunching work (see Chapter 5), it also perpetuated the ironic situation that in a machine-centric field like the digital humanities it has often been those individuals who operate the machines on which the field depends that have been held in lower esteem than the scholars who interpret or make other uses of the outputs of those technical workers and their human-machine collaborations.

Before seeking to refocalise the "ghost work" of the *Index Thomisticus*, a note is necessary on the sources and the difficulties that beset the task of reanimation that this chapter undertakes.

A note on the sources

That science as process and praxis bears a fine-grained resemblance to science as publication is not guaranteed (Mahoney 1980). Many who do creative work, including academics, "keep the arduous process of preparation for public display well behind the scenes. Thus, the process of trial-and-error in science is less visible than the final published results" (Star and Strauss 1999, 21). With regard to Busa's oeuvre, accounts of praxis and process, including that of trial and error and the distribution of labour is arguably more obfuscated than has tended to be appreciated so far.

This may have been, to a large extent, unavoidable and is arguably indicative of the shifting technological and financial bedrock of the *Index Thomisticus* (see Chapters 3 and 4). The technologies available to the project changed dramatically and sometimes rapidly with the ebbs and flows of technological change. Busa's team used electromechanical accounting machines, digital computers and:

> Autocoder, Fortran, PL1, the languages in which the indexing programs were written; the algorithms from general-purpose sorts to automatic lemmatization were designed; data storage moved from punched cards to magnetic disk; output devices moved from noisy line printers to silent lasers; print from unpunctuated capitals to elegant photocomposition.
>
> (Burton 1984a, 109)

Other contingences were in play too, for example, the patterns of supply and demand that shaped IBM's commercial activities and thus the machines that were available to Busa at various times. They could be cutting edge machines, seemingly too specialised for IBM customers (Jones 2016, 39) or far less cutting edge, like the "outdated or surplus machines freed up after 1945" (Jones 2016, 37) that may also have been put at the *Index Thomisticus'* disposal. Accordingly, Busa had to iteratively adapt his working methods to changing technologies, workflows, workforces and circumstances. His archive does contain some documents that help to elaborate our understanding of certain moments in this trajectory, like the flowchart that was prepared in IBM World Trade Engineering, New York in 1952, almost certainly by Tasman.[1] This depicts 45 manoeuvres, some multistage, that underpinned the *Index Thomisticus'* technical realisation. For the most part, however, this "bootstrap process" (Jones 2016, 39) was not recorded in high fidelity in either archival or published materials know to be extant.

Moreover, and this is crucial, what is recorded manifests discrepancies, omissions and unhelpful simplifications. For example, in 1951 Busa boasted of the level of mechanisation his process delivered: with the "sole work done by human eyes and fingers directly and responsibly" executed, humans would thereafter be required in a merely supervisory capacity, to ensure that the machines ran as they should (Busa 2019a[1951], 28). Yet a volte-face follows:

> I must confess that in actual practice this was not so simple as I endeavoured to make it in the description: ... The result was attained by exploring the cards, column by column, in order to identify by the nonpunched columns, the end of the previous word and the commencement of

the following one; thus, operating with the Sorter and Reproducer together, were reproduced only those words commencing and finishing in the same columns.

(Busa 2019a[1951], 28–9)

In fact, we learn that the "exploring" of the cards had to be done by humans (Busa 2019a[1951], 29), indicating this process to be less automated than initially claimed. What is more, the extent and intensity of human intervention that was required across this process is difficult to ascertain even from the more qualified discussion that follows. The suggestion that this muddling of the level of human and machine interaction and intervention in the project may not have been a one-off finds some corroboration in the oral history interviews, as interviewees recall performing manual tasks when the requisite IBM machines for verification or segmentation of phrases were occasionally unavailable to the project (see The Operator et al. 2014). One wonders, then, about other "confessions" that may have been silently omitted from Busa's publications? And about the balance in Busa's publications between reporting on what should have been possible were certain machines and other dependencies available to the project versus what was actually done by the project on a day-to-day basis?

Further difficulty also arises from Busa's anachronistic use of technical vocabulary. For example, writing in 1997, he described the capture of the text of the *Index Thomisticus* as its "digitisation". One might conclude from this terminology that he was, in fact, referring to its later publication on CD-ROM (Busa 2019m[1990]). Yet, the timeline of proof reading and lemmatising in which he sets the "digitisation" does not support this interpretation:

In digitizing the text we inserted references, typology codes, and "eol" (end of line) markers. We performed three 100 per cent proof readings. Later on, when lemmatizing, we discovered that 1,200 mistaken characters had escaped our notice ... Of course, I have shortened and simplified its description.

(Busa 1998, 6–9)

In the quote above, then, Busa is very likely referring to the initial capture of the *Index Thomisticus* on punched cards despite his use of a term from a much later period, and a rather different technical lineage. Again, one can appreciate why Busa wrote in this way, and sympathise with the difficulty of the communicative task that faced him. Had he not communicated in this way it would have been necessary for him to explain to readers the technical details of processes that had become obsolete or decisively estranged from them. But this decision is not without consequence. It matters because it limits our ability to understand, and to derive post-hoc interpretations of the human and machine configurations and technical processes that really gave rise to the *Index Thomisticus*. And this, in turn, complicates efforts to understand the context of the *Index Thomisticus* within wider drives to automation, which is:

> often far less impressive than the puffery and propaganda surrounding them imply—and sometimes they are nowhere to be seen. Jobs may be eliminated and salaries slashed but people are often still laboring alongside or behind the machines, even if the work they perform has been deskilled or goes unpaid.

(Taylor 2018)

Indeed, this reminds us that the story of the invisibilising of the work of the keypunch operators is not merely a story of unfair working conditions. This story has consequences to this day because it continues to cast a shadow over our understanding of the nature, distribution and extent of the human and machine intervention that gave rise to the *Index Thomisticus*, and indeed, computing in the humanities.

The high-level reconstruction set out below of the technical processes and human intervention that underpinned the *Index Thomisticus* covers the period from the inception of the project until c.1967. It is reassembled from Busa's publications and some secondary sources, supplemented with oral history interviews and archival materials. It can be read with reference to the online project "Reconstructing the first humanities Computing Centre", where readers will find 3D models of many of the accounting machines mentioned below, and can take a virtual reality tour (see Figure 2.1) through a reconstruction of the industrial

Figure 2.1 An image of the navigable 3D model of CAAL devised by the RECALL project
Source: See http://www.recaal.org/pages/walkthrough.html.

hall where the *Index Thomisticus* staff worked for a significant part of the time that the project was based in Gallarate (see Jones et al. 2017).

The high-level reconstruction set out below is, perhaps, the most substantial extant of the processes, technologies and human labour that underpinned the *Index Thomisticus* during the years in focus. Yet, considering the previous caveats, it is put forward with acknowledgement that it may imply a fixity of approach that was unobtainable for the *Index Thomisticus* on account of its frequently-changing circumstances, not only technical and financial, but also due to its shifting work locations and indeed, the unfurling consequences of its uneven treatment of project staff. What follows brings into view the substantial level of human intervention, much of it arduous, repetitive and mundane (and that must have been as true for those who keypunched the text as those who parsed and lemmatised it) that was required for the execution of the project in the years under focus. Writing in 1990, Busa made an incisive observation whose implications for the way he acknowledged his workforce were apparently not fully grasped by him:

> … there is always someone who, in wonder at the novelty and the unexpected, ends up by attributing the result to the machine's own magic, as if it were the machine itself that produces the result and not the people who enable it to do so.
>
> (Busa 2019m[1990], 146)

While we might wish to be able to read this comment as evidence of an individual who is reassessing his project with the benefit of hindsight, an acknowledgement of the keypunching work upon which the *Index Thomisticus* was built does not follow in that text.

The methodology of the Index Thomisticus c.1954–67

The methodology of the *Index Thomisticus* is here discussed according to six stages: pre-editing; sentence cards and verification of accuracy; word cards; form cards; entry cards; and printing of information eypunching.

Stage 1: Pre-editing

The work of keypunching transformed the documents that were available to CAAL in facsimile or printed-book form into a galaxy of perforations, constellated across the rows and columns of IBM issued, 7⅜ by 3¼ inch punch cards.[2] To minimise the degree of information entropy and distortion that occurred during this textual migration, a "pre-editing" stage was executed by CAAL's "scholars". They parsed the respective texts of Aquinas and related authors and annotated salient semantic, structural and lexical textual components. Annotations, or markup, that categorised and labelled those components was applied to some documents directly, with pencil or ink. Markup could also be applied indirectly, with washable inks on superimposed sheets of cellophane (Busa 2019b[1958], 43). One keypunch operator recalled that at the beginning of their working day:

TO: We would start to look for, in fact, we had all the pages there ...
MP: ... These pages would be of St. Thomas' text?
TO: St. Thomas. They had cut it in a way that all the pages were loose.

(The Operator et al. 2014)

As reported by Busa, the scholar's markup functioned to: delineate the beginnings and endings of paragraphs and sentences (Busa 2019b[1958], 43); distinguish quotations and paraphrases from surrounding narrative content (Tasman 1957, 254) and determine them to be *ad litteram* (a direct quotation from an external source) or *ad sensum* (a paraphrase) (Busa 1964, 68); disambiguate dashes, hyphens (a "diabolical" distinction; Busa 2019j[1968], 121) and full stops from elision markers (Busa 1964, 68). Maximum sentence lengths were established to avoid words being truncated across two or more punched cards. Scholars could indicate certainty with "the addition of special signs [to] show, *inter alia*, to what extent the expression can be attributed to [Aquinas]" (Busa 2019j[1968], 120–21). Until at least 1968, *ad litteram* quotations were underlined in green (Busa 2019j[1968], 120–21). *Ad sensum*, or "those phrases in which it is believed that there is a mixture of thought, or of vocabulary, or both, when the author summarizes, outlines, interprets, or refutes the ideas of another," were underlined in red (Busa 2019j[1968], 120–21).

Busa described how:

The pre-editing phase inserts special marks which define the borders of the two coding systems we use: one for the "text": i.e. words, punctuation, special marks, the other for "formulae" i.e. formulae, figures, and other special sequences of symbols.

(Busa 1964, 68)

The "formulae" to be marked up included "dates and chemical formulae, which must be punched in different codes from those of the words" (Busa 2019j[1968], 121). So called "introductory formula", for example, were marked in blue (de Tollenaere 1963a, 4).

Thus, the output of stage 1 was a text that was marked up with symbols, colours (Busa 2019j[1968], 120–21) and other annotations. This annotated document was then given to keypunch operators to guide their work: "And then I remember we punched things in Latin, if I can recall, they were St. Thomas' works" (Brogioli et al. 2014).

The practice of giving annotated texts directly to keypunch operators (see Figure 2.2), without having first transformed them into the intermediate formats that had been shown to improve the precision and alacrity of keypunch work seems to have been at variance with IBM recommendations.

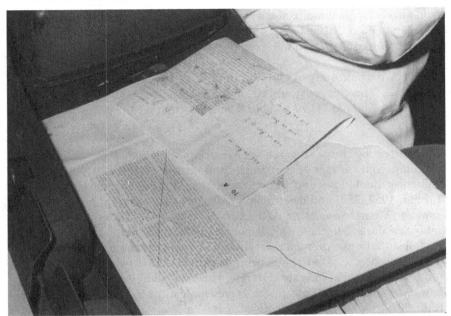

Figure 2.2 An example of the hand-annotated texts given to keypunch operators for
punching.
Source: Busa Archive #0088.

Instruments like "transcription forms or alignment sheets" (IBM Corporation
1949, 5) were recommended by IBM for marshalling the data to be punched
into the same line-by-line arrangement as it should appear on the punched
cards: "Because the card moves automatically through the keypunch as each
column is punched, the operator must read the data from the document in the
same sequence in which they are to be punched" (IBM Corporation 1949, 5).
These instruments were also flagged as useful when base documents were
difficult to read and were recommended for jobs that required frequent shifting between alphanumeric and numeric text encoding (IBM Corporation
1949, 5–6). That marked up texts were given directly to keypunchers, and not
represented in intermediary forms, must have further increased the cognitive
load of a task that was in any case demanding and tedious.

Whether this was a processual blind spot of the male-dominated culture of
the *Index Thomisticus* project that was structurally compounded by the dis-
couragement of female worker's feedback when it pertained to error (see
Chapter 4) or whether this was an implicit commentary on the perceived
completeness of the scholar's work or, indeed, an implicit commentary on the
perceived simplicity of the keypuncher's work, such that they were thought
not to require instruments that could be read as acknowledging the inherent
complexity of their work, is unknown. Perhaps all of these factors were in
play, and further inflected by widely held attitudes towards women's work,

also in the context of computing, which estimated it as inherently less demanding than that of men (e.g. Abbate 2012, 22).

Stage 2: Sentence cards

Female keypunch operators' work was rarely attributed to them in discussions of the *Index Thomisticus'* methodology. When brought into view, these workers were designated with terms that seem to dismiss or undermine the usefulness of their contributions to the project. They are briefly referred to as "clerks" (Tasman 1957, 254), "girls" (Busa 1964, 67) "female operators" (Busa 2019j[1968], 124) and with the more professional term of "keypunch operators" (Busa 1980, 85). Collectively, the keypunch operators populated the *Index Thomisticus'* dataset. They did this by encoding onto punched cards

> natural texts containing 12,000,000 words in 9 different languages in the Latin, Hebrew, Greek, and Cyrillic alphabets, which deal with different, subjects, periods, and cultures: such as the Qumran manuscripts, the works of St Thomas Aquinas, and abstracts of nuclear physics.
> (Busa 2019j[1968], 120)

At the following rate: "Last year we punched an average of 135 fully punched cards per man-hour" (Busa 1964, 69). Cervini recalled that she and her colleagues punched: "MC [Marinella Cervini] ... on and on ...sitting by the machines, and we had these cards, the text next to us, and we never looked at the keyboard because by then we knew it by heart. ...". Within the *Index Thomisticus* project, the cards the keypunch operators punched were called "text cards" (Busa 2019j [1968], 122), "sentence cards" (Busa 2019b[1958], 44), "pericope" or "coherent unit of thought" (Rockwell and Passarotti 2019, 19). It is the nomenclature "phrase cards" (Tasman 1957, 254) that best conveys how they wrangled the phrases of text that had been marked by the scholars for further processing. The cards they punched listed a sentence or phrase from a hardcopy text, a serial number for that phrase and metadata categorising or describing that phrase was added too (Rockwell and Sinclair 2020).

The keypunch operators are known to have used IBM 024, 026 and 131 card punches (Rockwell and Sinclair 2017; Busa 1952, 14). The IBM 026 Printing Card punch was one of the most commonly used punches at the time (see IBM Corporation 1961; see Busa's discussion of it 2019b[1958]). Its input mechanism was similar in appearance to that of a typewriter, the difference being that when the keypunch operator pressed a key one or more holes, rather than inked letters, resulted (IBM Corporation 1961, 6). Other fundamental elements of the card punch with which operators would have been familiar included a hopper, which fed cards for punching and was located on the upper right of the machine, and a card stacker, located on the upper left. Both held about 500 cards. Cards were initially fed from the hopper, from there they passed through the punching and reading stations and on to the card stacker (IBM Corporation 1961, 6–11).

The punched cards they worked with (see Figure 2.3) corresponded to the:

> IBM card format. This had been developed in 1928 and had become a *de facto* standard. Each card was 7⅜ inches wide by 3¼ inches tall. They were made of stiff paper with a notch in the upper left for orientation. The arrangement of holes was standardized so that all relevant machines could process them.
>
> (Rockwell and Sinclair 2020)

IBM cards had 80 columns and every column had 12 possible punch locations: "12, 11 (sometimes referred to as X), O, 1, 2, 3, 4, 5, 6, 7, 8 and 9" (IBM Corporation 1961, 2) from top to bottom. Digits were recorded as perforations in locations 0 to 9; a combination of the digit locations 0 to 9 and the zone punching positions 12,11, and 0 were used to encode:

> any of the 26 letters [of the English alphabet] in one column … The various combination of punches which represent the alphabet follow a simple pattern. The first nine letters of the alphabet, A to I, are coded by the combination of a 12 punch and the digit punches 1 to 9. Letters J through R are coded by an 11 punch and the digits 1 through 9. S through Z, the last eight letters, are the combinations of the 0 zone punch and the digit punches 2 through 9. The eleven special characters are recoded by one, two or three punches in a column.
>
> (IBM Corporation 1961, 3)

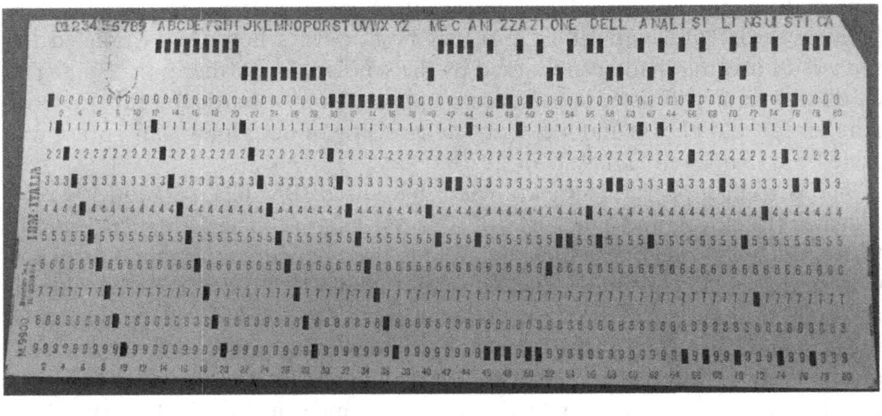

Figure 2.3 Extant *Index Thomisticus* punched card
Note: The card shown here is in the IBM card format, also known as type 5081 or general-purpose cards. That this particular card was issued before 1964 is indicated by its square corners (see IBM Corporation 2003b).
Source: Jones et al. 2017.

A 1968 article by Busa, which does not name the keypunch operators as co-authors, relays detailed discussions of the key combinations they were required to know and execute. A single letter (or "univocal code" in the project terminology) was input simply by pressing the corresponding letter on the keyboard (Busa 2019j[1968], 121). When operators encountered a "simple dicode", or a phrase underlined in green, they were required to render it as a quotation *ad litteram*:

> at the beginning of each phrase underlined in green, you punch three times: 3–8, 12–1, 12–3–8. At the end of the same phrase underlined in green, you punch 3–8, 0–3–8, if no other colour follows; if another colour does follow, you punch the sign proper to it: 3–8, 12–2, 12–3–8 for red etc.
>
> (Busa 2019j[1968], 121)

From these key combinations resulted the symbols used to annotate the cards in the zone the *Index Thomisticus* called "nota". For example, "# means: These are the words of another author whom St. Thomas quotes here literally" (Tasman 1957, 254).

When operators encountered a "complex dicode" they were required to disambiguate it and render it appropriately:

> For example: if you come across the Latin word AB printed like most other words, you punch it using the codes for "words" (it is in fact a preposition). If, however, it is printed in another way, for example as the geometrical expression AB, you punch it as a "formula": if you are undecided, ask the head of the department.
>
> (Busa 2019j[1968], 121)

The benefit of punching text in this way was "not only for statistical but also for lexicographical purposes, it allows automatic excluding or including in the indices of the words contained in these special parts of the text" (de Tollenaere 1963a, 5). References to the way that at least one keypunch operator contributed to the elaboration of key combinations can be found in the archive (see Chapter 3).

Keypunches, like the 026, could represent alphanumeric text and 11 special characters. The machines' default special characters were, unsurprisingly, those required in office-based settings but they could "with moderate cost be substituted by signs used in linguistic or philologic studies" (Busa 2019b [1958], 53). The problem of accents, and other special characters proved thorny and made punching more complex:

> When special characters for symbols of punctuation, diacritical marks and accents are required at the same time, the top space of a column is not sufficient, except for certain kinds of work and for some languages, for example English, Italian, or Latin. It is necessary then to consider

IBM machines which use codes of punches consisting of combinations of two or more columns.

(Busa 2019b[1958], 53)

Neither were these symbols and characters rare occurrences: "[b]esides words *per se* the Thomistic corpus contains Arabic and Roman numerals, notes of music, non-Latin words, logical symbols, cancelled words, and many special characters" (Burton 1984b, 891). Keypunch operators punched texts in languages like Hebrew too, where requirements could not be met through key combinations alone. Clever modifications were made to the physical setup of the operator's machines so they worked with a "punch bed ... [that had been] turned around and we left everything normal so the cards actually fed in the opposite direction" (Tasman 1968).

Adding to this complexity, keypunch operators were trained to interpret texts and mark up in an entirely procedural way.[3] Instruction neither in the languages they were punching (see Chapter 4), nor the function of the mark-up they were encoding was conveyed to them. This gave rise to what seems to have been a byzantine and absurd level of complexity. And it became, in any case, necessary for keypunch operators to engage in some interpretative decision-making processes so as to cut a pathway through the tangled and briared information landscape they were required to traverse:

> The dot is another case in point. It is sometimes used as a decimal point, and so has its own code within the "formulas". It can also be a punctuation mark indicating the end of a sentence, or the end of a group of phrases making up one long single sentence. If you are sure that it is a punctuation mark, punch it as such. The dot will be a punctuation mark when the following word, which would otherwise begin with a small letter, begins with a capital. (This must be checked for each book, for it is not a universal printing convention). But if you think that the following word should always begin with a capital, ask the head of the department. However, the dot is also used as a sort of last letter in a word that has been abbreviated: in such a case use punch 11: in fact, it must be treated in a completely different way. And if the first letter of the following word is a capital and the word is not a proper noun, punch the dot as a punctuation mark: many printers use only one dot for both these functions, i.e. full points in abbreviations and punctuation marks. Do the same if you find two consecutive dots, also if you find three consecutives, such as suspension points ... if however, it is printed in another way, for example as the geometrical expression AB, you punch it as a "formula": if you are undecided, ask the head of the department.

(Busa 2019j[1968], 121–2)

In addition to the procedural complexity signalled by the above passage, it raises the question: why did the scholars not disambiguate the dots? As we have seen, this was reported by Busa to be part of the work of the scholars. Discussions like this suggest that the scholar's work may not have been as self-contained and thorough as Busa tended to indicate in public. Moreover, it suggests that the boundary between the interpretative work of the scholar and supposedly merely mechanical work of the keypunch operator was more porous, and their knowledge jurisdictions less distinct, than is otherwise acknowledged.

As discussed in the Introduction, what counts as labour can depend more on context than content (Star and Strauss 1999: 12–14). In the *Index Thomisticus* project, as elsewhere, expertise was not immutably tied to the nature or complexity of the work. Work was not valued with reference to its internal composition or contributions to achieving the aims of the project overall but questions of scholarly versus technical identity played an unhelpful and ultimately obfuscating role in determinations of the value of project work and workers. Testament to this is that, just as the keypunch operators went beyond mere mechanical punching and necessarily engaged in some of the parsing work that was deemed scholarly when done by scholars, so too some interviews show that they grasped aspects of the textual mark-up that went beyond what was intended for them.

MP: What kind of work did you do?

…

NR [Nadia Re]: And so, from the specific phrases the Jesuit priests would give us – they would stand at the right of the punched card machines …

MP: … What do you mean by specific phrases?

NR: Specific phrases because they were highlighted in different colours, or between two asterisks, or in quotation marks, or with particular markings.

MP: Did you know what these markings corresponded to, their meaning?

NR: No.

MM [Mirella Mainardi]: No.

MP: You didn't know?

MM: No, no. Our job was to copy it, just like …

NR: … Because afterwards they were extracted and worked on by the computer, depending on whether they were, for example, between two asterisks, in quotation marks, between … and they distinguished the argument.

(Mainardi et al 2014)

As Re's comments reveal, she did indeed understand what the mark-up corresponded to.

Recalling Bray's discussion of the technopolitics that portray women as "passive beneficiaries of the inventive flame" (Bray 2007, 38), stage 2 was thus determined, and portrayed as one where the female keypunch workforce would execute the learned instructions of male scholars in an almost mindless way, in the sense that they were not to have any understanding of what they were punching or of the project itself. This was communicated not only to the keypunchers themselves, but to the wider scholarly community in myriad ways (see Chapter 5). Suggesting that this portrayal was not "natural", but one that came to further the scholar-centered rhetoric of the *Index Thomisticus*, the pre-editing stage was not presented as a distinctive stage of the work in Busa's *Varia* (1951). The corralling of "stage 1" followed in Busa's publications from 1952, and by the 1957 publication of Tasman's "Literary Data Processing", which reported on the work of the *Index Thomisticus*, the data preparation and input stages were treated as quite distinct:

> Instead of one step for "transcription of text" he has two steps, that of the scholar who marks up the text and that of the keypunch operator who copies it onto cards. This more clearly separates the scholarly from the data entry work.
>
> (Rockwell and Sinclair 2020)

Despite the blurring of the correlativity of the work of the scholars and keypunch operators, their roles in the data entry process did exist in a state of contingent connection. While the punched card operators relied on the input of the scholars to guide the transposition of the text from container to container, so the scholars relied on the keypunch operators to reify the *Index Thomisticus* and related texts as scalable, computable artefacts. One could not properly do their work without the other; both played fundamental roles in the process of data capture and dataset elaboration. Yet, the techno-social context of the *Index Thomisticus* constructed keypunch labour as subordinate and largely ancillary.

It may be relevant to understanding the efforts that were made both to control and diminish the work of the keypunch operators that, in the context of their day, it was they and not the scholar who possessed the rarer and more specialised skill. It was the keypunch operators' work that output "the first or fundamental group of cards ... With this first and only data transcription, it is possible to accomplish mechanically, speedily, and accurately all of the most diverse and complex analyses" (Busa 2019b[1958], 44). The work that was a precursor to this (the pre-editing) required the ability to read and parse Latin and related Classical and European languages. This really would have been quite common in Jesuit and ecclesiastical circles at this time. In the Pontifical Gregorian University in Rome, for example, teaching was delivered in Latin (Di Giovanni 2020) and the Catholic Mass continued to be celebrated in Latin until 1962 (Hardiman 2005). It is hardly surprising, then, that no training school needed to be set up by Busa for the scholars.

The ability to devise, learn and to consistently and accurately execute the multikey combinations required to encode heterogeneous and complex multilingual texts on punched cards (using what appear to have been unsatisfactory working materials) was not, however, anything like as common as the scholar's expertise. Across Italy, and despite the requirements of industry, young people (male and female) were predominately taking humanities degrees and the numbers of those taking scientific degrees decreased between 1950 and 1962 from "30.1% to 26%" (Bison 2013b, 267).

Indeed, though it would have resulted in a less-categorically manipulatable output, when necessary, it was possible to do without the pre-editing work of the Scholars and even some models of accounting machines:

> MP: ... The task always consisted of typing the text?
> TO: Typing, transliterating the text, and then, these punched cards, since over there in Gallarate we didn't have the mach ... there, instead, we typed the text in one punched card, one word.
> MP: Ahh, which text? The one in Occitan?
> TO: In Occitan.
> MP: So, the *Index Thomisticus*, one punched card, one phrase.
> TO: One phrase, whatever could fit on the punched card. And meanwhile, on that one ...
> MP: ... On the Occitan, one punched card, one word.
> TO: One word.

> (The Operator et al. 2014)

Keypunch operators' work was often diminished, but this work was consequential and the skills it required were not commonly available. In addition to the key punching of stage 2 (and aspects of subsequent stages probably too, as will be discussed below) keypunch operators' work also comprised the verification of the accuracy of the punched text.

Stage 2.1 Verification of accuracy

Currently, it is recommended that the accuracy level of texts transcribed for scholarly work should be at least 99.5% (Deutsche Forschungsgemeinschaft 2016, 37). For the *Index Thomisticus*, as much as for current digital humanities, data science, collections as data and other data-driven research, the project-compiled dataset became the locus of subsequent textual and computational transformations. So, accuracy was "an indispensable condition" of the *Index Thomisticus* (Busa 2019a[1951], 31) and of computational work in the humanities, and beyond, today.

For the *Index Thomisticus*, accuracy was not only a proxy for reliability. It vouched for the project's transferability and mobility beyond CAAL, establishing the *Index Thomisticus* as a reference work that was fit for scholarly work, irrespective of the location, disciplinary specialism or computational routine that utilised it. Perhaps more than any other quality, it was accuracy that established the *Index Thomisticus* as the "right tool for the job" (see Clarke and Fujimura 1992) of scholarly research. Despite the breezy

portrayals of the process of validating accuracy that are given in earlier publications on the *Index Thomisticus*, this process would prove to be among the
most laborious, frustrating and yet rhetorically productive aspects of the project.

Various methods of verifying punched text were deployed by the *Index Thomisticus*.[4] The ideal scenario was portrayed to hinge on a machine like the IBM 056 Alphabetic Verifier.[5] Similar to an IBM 24 Card Punch (IBM Corporation 1961, 22), it required a human "verifier operator" to retype the material prepared by an initial operator in a process broadly similar to that known as "double keying" in current text capture workflows. Rather than perforating a new set of punched cards, the verifier machine had

> a sensing mechanism consisting of twelve pins [that] replaced the twelve punch dies ... If a verifier operator depresses the same key which the keypunch operator selected in making the original hold, the card proceeds to the next column to be checked. If, however, she depresses a different key, the verifier "lights up". This was a signal that the hole pattern detected by the sensing mechanism did not agree with the depressed key.
>
> (IBM Corporation 1961, 22)

Interviewees do seem to obliquely refer to using a verifier machine, for example, Segatto recalled how "We punched and we verified. One would punch and the other would verify if the holes were precise." (Lombardi et al. 2014) Of the process, Tasman wrote that "the accuracy of the text cards is rigorously checked and cards containing transcription errors are replaced" (Tasman 1957, 254). That the task was straightforward, and largely automated was also echoed by Busa (2019a[1951], 31).

However, the contentedness of the earlier portrayals would soon give way. Writing in 1968, Busa's communicates his exasperation with the checking process:

> 41,888 text cards were punched in 470 man-hours. 2,185 mistakes, i.e. 5%, were found and corrected during punching. The first IBM 056 check revealed a further 682 mistakes, i.e. 1.6%. I had another IBM 056 check done on the same cards, and I was rewarded by the discovery of another 245 mistakes, i.e. 0.5%. These cards were then printed and checked against the original document. Would you believe me if I told you that another 37 mistakes were discovered only at that moment? We totalled up 3,149 mistakes, i.e. 7.18%.
>
> (Busa 2019j[1968], 122)

Though the *Index Thomisticus* is held to have processed alphabetic text on an unprecedented scale, it is interesting that by 1949 IBM was already in a position to advise its customers on the processing of alphabetic text at scale. Indeed, that the Verifier machine would not have been applicative to the *Index Thomisticus* material was readily discoverable in IBM literature. There it is observed the Verifier is well suited to those situations: "when a small amount of alphabetic information is found with the numerical data …. When there is a large amount of descriptive alphabetic information, however, one of the visual verification methods may be more effective" (IBM Corporation 1949, 14). As archival photographs suggest, and interviews corroborate, the *Index Thomisticus* text was, in fact, often checked with visual verification methods but out of necessity, it seems, rather than design, because Verifier machines[6] were not consistently at the project's disposal:

> TO: The fact is that after a year or two we had all these punched cards in the card file, and then later the machine arrived, the checking machine.
> MP: How did the checking machine work?
> TO: We would insert the punched cards in the machine, retype the same text and if there happened to be a mistake, it would point out there was a mistake.
> …
> MP: So, if I understand the sequence correctly it goes punched card machine, verifying machine …
> TO: We didn't have the verifying machine.
> MP: You didn't have it from the start?
> TO: We didn't have it. Therefore, we went straight to the sorting machine, from the sorting machine to the tabulating machine and then we checked for mistakes by hand.
>
> (The Operator et al. 2014)

Might it again have been the association of the female keypunch operators with the work of verifying, an association also made in the IBM literature, along with stereotypes like women's supposed propensity for accuracy that caused Busa and Tasman to so underestimate in their earlier publications the complexities of verifying the text through automated means? And might this also explain why the *Index Thomisticus'* division of labour with regard to accuracy verification diverged quite markedly from earlier, mechanically assisted projects that also pursued what we would now call data-driven research?

Notwithstanding their different numerical versus textual focus, the segmented and distributed labour design of the *Index Thomisticus* mirrors, to some extent, the labour organisation of the computing bureaus that calculated astronomical and nautical tables in Europe and the United Kingdom during the eighteenth and nineteenth centuries as told by Grier (2005). Inspired by Adam Smith's *The Wealth of Nations*, it was Gaspard Clair François Marie Riche de Prony (1755–1839) who first implemented this way of working when he was Director of the Bureau du Cadastre, and his team was undertaking difficult calculations for "the standardization of weights and measures that produced the metric system" (Grier 2005, 33). De Prony divided the staff who executed this work into two groups: computers and planners. The computers, who were economic casualties of the French Revolution and had lost their jobs as "servants or wig dressers" (Grier 2005, 36), executed the arithmetic. Their work was choreographed by planners who:

took the basic equations for the trigonometric functions and reduced them to the fundamental operations of addition and subtraction. From this reduction, they prepared worksheets for the computers ... these sheets identified every operation of the calculation and left nothing for the workers to interpret. ... Once the computers had completed their sheets, they returned their results to the planners [who checked them].

(Grier 2005, 36–7)

De Prony's approach to labour distribution influenced early makers of computing machines, like Babbage, whose machines sought to automate the work of planners and computers alike (Grier 2005, 38–45). This approach also became associated with influential and proven models for computing bureaus, like the British Nautical Almanac and the Royal Greenwich Observatory, which had: "a central computing room, an active manager, pre-printed computing forms, standard methods of calculation, and a common means of checking results" (Grier 2005, 54). It is not only that the conceptual affinities between the labour and spatial organisation of the computing bureaus, recommended in the wider IBM literature and the broad setup of the *Index Thomisticus* are notable, so too punched card machines came to be used in computing bureaus, sometimes replacing but more often, it seems, augmenting older technologies like comptometer machines (e.g. Gutzwiller 1999).

Working in a rather different textual tradition, even if Busa was aware of the finer points of the labour distribution of these settings only in so far as some of their elements became enfolded in IBM setups, the *Index Thomisticus* does appear to have represented at least a partial regression from this model. De Prony's planners communicated their instructions to computers in a standardised way that was apparently cognisant of the demands of calculating work and of how the material forms in which instructions were communicated could aid or hinder the execution of a task. It is not only, as already observed, that in the *Index Thomisticus* project we find keypunch operators being handed guillotined leaves, teeming with annotations and coloured inks, and unresolved textual features to interpret. During the years in Gallarate, the *Index Thomisticus* broke De Prony's circular approach to data preparation, capture, manipulation and checking. The *Index Thomisticus'* scholars completed pre-editing or preparation only. It was the keypunch operators who did the work of verification, to the detriment, perhaps, of the progress and delivery of the project over the longer term? Later, we shall consider how this can nevertheless be read as rhetorically advantageous for Busa and the *Index Thomisticus* project.

Stage 3: Word cards

This third stage has been identified as delivering a "crucial innovation that showed how systems designed for accounting could be used for unstructured text" (Rockwell and Sinclair 2020). Refining the data captured in the previous stages, "Each Word Cards" (Flow chart 1952) or "Word Cards" (Tasman 1957,

254; Busa 2019b[1958], 44) could now be extracted. Each and every individual word listed on sentence cards could be duplicated on another set of punched cards, one word per card. This stage multiplied the number of cards hugely, resulting in a file that contained "as many cards as there are words in the text" (Busa 2019b[1958], 44). This process, writ large, is now known as "tokenising" and it is a fundamental stage of many if not all computationally-executed text analysis routines to this day (see e.g. Rockwell and Sinclair 2016)

Once the word cards had been extracted there followed an iterative process of gang punching[7] each card forwards and backwards through the punch with information that could tether the word to its original documentary location and initial punched-card capture (Flow chart 1952). Annotations added to the word cards included[8] a word's sequence in the text from which it had been excerpted and a reference to its phrase card. A unique identifier was also supplied along with the first letter of the preceding and succeeding word and the reference of the following sentence (de Tollenaere 1963a, 5; Flowchart 1952; Tasman 1957, 254). The textual context of the word was also printed on the reverse side of the card "in the horizontal spaces between the punched lines – with a maximum of 12 lines or 64 strokes or an average of 100–120 words" (Tasman 1957, 254). This textual content was printed to aid humans, as they engaged in the subsequent lemmatisation of the corpus, and it must also have facilitated the keypunch operators in their verification work. Though not readily apparent from Busa's or Tasman's descriptions, the human labour involved in moving millions of cards along the human-machine sequence that formed the assembly line of the *Index Thomisticus* cannot be underestimated (see e.g. Haigh 2001). As Rockwell and Sinclair observe:

> Many of the processes from keypunching to sorting involved physically manipulating the cards themselves, not data in memory. The human was also part of the sequence of operations as someone would have to load cards, move stacks from machine to machine, and cards would actually be consulted by humans at certain points.
>
> (Rockwell and Sinclair 2020)

In 1958, Busa wrote of the three approaches to the process now known as tokenising that were known to him. Option 1 was to have keypunch operators directly punch one word per card, as discussed in the excerpt above regarding the punching of Occitan. Option 2, also discussed above, was achieved via a combination of the Sorter and Reproducer machines and human intervention (Busa 2019a[1951], 29). Option 3 entailed the Cardatype 858 accounting machine. Released by IBM in 1955, this machine that could be augmented with other machines (like electric typewriters, a card punch, a tape perforating machine and an auxiliary keyboard) to maximise its range of automatic and manual operations and forms of output (IBM Corporation 1955c). Of it Busa wrote: "The use of the Cardatype offers the advantage of preparing typed copy of the text while punching the individual word cards. Thus, the context of the word is printed on the reverse side of each card" (Busa 2019b [1958], 44).

The Cardatype could also accept the sentence cards that had been punched by the operators as input, convert the information on the cards into continuous text on punched tape for serial processing, segment the individual words and then output them as word cards (Tasman 1968). As such, the boon of the Cardatype was that it allowed the project to process the text of Aquinas serially on tape rather than with the parallel, column by column approach on which punched card processing was based. de Tollenaere described how the IBM 858 Cardatype was used to atomise the text of the sentence cards in 1961,[9] now as part of a workflow that enfolded a non-IBM machine:

> Now on feeding the sentence cards into the IBM 858 Cardatype Accounting Machine, the IBM 866 Cardatype Typewriter makes masters of the different contexts, while at the same time, the IBM 536 Cardatype Printing Card Punch is punching and interpreting each different word of the sentence cards on separate word cards, together with [supplementary information] …. With the help of the master, each word card is provided with twelve to thirteen lines of context printed on the reverse side of the card by a Davidson 816 Litho Duplicating Machine.
>
> (de Tollenaere 1963a, 5)

de Tollenaere's notes on the process raise the possibility that the keypunch operators augmented this stage too. It is difficult to establishing whether he is referring to keypunch operators in what follows, though we have seen this particular use of the passive voice to be entailed in the devaluing of their work: "The portions of context are automatically delimited, just as they were staked out by special marks x … x while pre-editing the text: these marks are also punched in the sentence cards" (de Tollenaere 1963a, 5).

Once the word cards had been created, they were arranged in alphabetical order and identical words were grouped together and given the same sequence number.[10] This was done to aid the lemmatisation that would follow in the next stage. In 1951, Busa wrote that alphabetisation was "a trifle" that involved the use of the Sorter which "proceeding backwards, from the last letter, sorts and groups gradually, column by column, all the identical letters; in a few minutes the words are aligned and the card file, in alphabetical order, is already compiled" (Busa 2019a[1951], 29). However, the sorter fed cards row by row and, as discussed above, alphabetic letters were recorded with two holes and so alphabetic sorting required two rounds of sorting of each column:

MP: And what did the sorting machine do?
TO: I sorted everything in alphabetical order.
MP: Would you be able to recall how long a sorting machine would take to sort the words in alphabetical order?

TO: Who knows, it was fast (laughs). One time I remember it took two days. And, for ...
MP: For what? Two days for what?
TO: For sorting all of it, all those punched cards in Occitan.

(The Operator et al. 2014)

By 1958, when the number of cards that the *Index Thomisticus* was working with had grown exponentially, it was necessary to investigate various means of speeding up the work of the sorter. One strategy was to pre-sort words into different lengths before alphabetisation:

> The operation can be shortened by several means, e.g., by separating first the shortest (one- and two-letter) words, then the next shortest words, and so forth. The shorter sets so divided are then inserted into the alphabetically sorted sets of longer words. The final result will be that all the words of the text are alphabetized and all identical words are grouped together.
>
> (Busa 2019b[1958], 45)

In interviews it is recalled that the sorter was used for alphabetisation, with human augmentation:

> MP: And organizing them in alphabetical order?
> TO: I sorted by alphabetical order but most of all by the first [letter].
> MP: Yes.
> TO: So that I could then separate them all, the words that started with A, then those with B, then C, so that it could do the complete task. And then, these punched cards were inserted into the tabulating machine.
>
> (The Operator et al. 2014)

This suggests that human intervention was again required to pre-sort words, though it may have been possible to re-wire the machines for this at a later stage. Once again, the level of human intervention required in the technical work is discovered indirectly, and the scope and duration of it across the project over time remains unclear. Based on de Tollenaere's description, it seems that it was possible to fully automate alphabetical sorting by 1961: when he visited CAAL, sorting was implemented with the IBM 082 sorter and its output was further checked by the IBM 101 Electronic Statistical Machine (de Tollenaere 1963a, 6). According to one of Busa's publications from around this period, around 1,190,580 words can be calculated as having been punched by 1960 (see Busa 1960a). Presumably the project was sorting words on a text-by-text basis, rather than seeking to sort the entire corpus of words that had been punched from a number of texts and Busa accordingly presents quantitative summaries of capture on a text-by-text basis. For example, he states that 325,894 words had been punched from Aquinas' *Summa contra Gentiles,* which included 17,943 word forms. He also notes that the work of lemmatising could be done in a most limited way only with the machines (Busa 1960, 1).

The word cards alphabetised and sorted, it was now possible to print an abridged list of the words that had been punched. The list was abridged in the sense that it listed each word form just once, irrespective of how many times it appeared in a given text. Word frequency was also supplied, Busa reported (Busa 2019b[1958], 46).

Rockwell and Sinclair have emphasised the practical importance of Busa's and Tasman's success in automating the process of tokenisation (or perhaps semi-automating given the continued necessity of human intervention in stages 1 and 2 and in the lemmatisation to follow in stage 4) (Rockwell and Sinclair 2020). Yet it is difficult to see how this stage represented a technological paradigm-change in the sense of using a technology to deliver a process that would otherwise have been impossible to implement or was radically new. For all the usefulness of Busa's and Tasman's automation of the process of tokenisation, in this stage, as in others, the contribution of the *Index Thomisticus* was in determining how to deliver the ato-misation of texts that the concordance tradition had always delivered, with what may have been less human input but still relying on considerable human input. They were, as Haigh has observed of the use of unit record equipment across this period doing "the same things, faster" (Haigh 2001, 81).

Stage 4: Form cards

While the aforementioned abridged list was being printed, the "summary punch" was connected to the "accounting machine" so that another set of punched cards could simultaneously be output (Tasman 1957, 254). In 1961, an IBM 441 accounting machine was used to list words and an IBM 519 Endprinting Reproducer was used to punch corresponding form cards (de Tollenaere 1963a, 5–6). The "form cards" (Tasman 1957, 254) or "different word cards" comprised "only one card for each graphically different word" (Tasman 1957, 254). Form cards came about by the machine printing "the first word. If the following word is different from it, it prints it. If it is iden-tical, it does not print it, but counts it" (Tasman 1957, 255). As such, form cards seem to be analogous with the individual rows of word-frequency tables familiar to digital humanities today.[11] Busa noted that:

> Such a group of cards is not necessary for ordinary concordance work but it may open up the possibility of different and new investigations. Such cards, in fact, contain the summary of the author's vocabulary and can be analyzed indefinitely.
>
> (Busa 2019b[1958], 45)

Not being stored-programme machines, accounting machines could process data on a graphical level only. To move beyond this, to a semantic differ-entiation of words, it was necessary to, for example, distinguish between homographs and to group inflected words under their respective lemmata. Significant human intervention was again required.

Stage 5: Entry cards

During the years under examination, this phase appears to have remained predominately manual. The significant role played by scholars in this stage is acknowledged in Busa's publications, the keypunch operators' contributions to it almost not at all. The cards that resulted from this stage were called "entry cards" (Tasman 1957, 255), "entry word cards" (Flow chart 1952) or "main cards" (Busa 2019b[1958], 42). The term "entry card" is the most meaningful of those terms in the way it recalls how a lexical entry in a scholarly dictionary often presents a headword, and information about that headword like its inflected forms, examples of its textual usage and indicators of the frequency or register of its use (e.g. Merkin 1983).

In the *Index Thomisticus*, entry cards formed "a second summary list of the author's lexicon, based on the structure of the words he uses, but on a basis which is no longer purely graphic, but graphic-semantic" (Tasman 1957, 255). It was the staff members whom Busa referred to as scholars who worked through the word forms to separate homographs, lemmatise inflected forms and then write a list of entry words (Flow chart 1952; see also Busa 1960a, 3). This list was once again given to keypunch operators so that entry cards could be punched. As in the stages described above, the work must have been achieved through various sub-routines that involved the punching and verifying of the entry cards and the use of augmenting machines, like the gang punch, to assign metadata to the cards.[12] As is frequently the case, reports of this stage acknowledge the work of the scholars and obscure the collective reality of the keypunch operators' input:

> The scholar examines the list of the form cards and groups all the different forms of one and the same graphic-semantic unit under the single expression or word which will serve as an entry listing. ... In addition, the scholar separates all the homographs in their various uses. ... The scholar in this way compiles a list of the entry words for the complete word index. A card is then punched for each of these, and these cards are arranged alphabetically and numbered sequentially.
>
> (Tasman 1957, 255)

It should be noted that the chronology of lemmatising is difficult to establish in the timeline of the *Index Thomisticus*. Busa's publications from the late 1950s portray it as ongoing. He describes the work the scholars are doing as that which involves parsing and separating

> cases of homographs, which turn out to be quite frequent; dismember [ing] words that comprise prefixes and suffixes each having a proper

function also when isolated (such words may be considered as two words rather than one); assembl[ing] the separate words that are in reality just one verb form; and finally, regroup[ing] under the functional semantic unit all the diverse forms a word assumes according to case, tense, mode, etc.

(Busa 2019b[1958], 45)

However, the oral history interviews indicate that the process began later than this:

MP: What was your idea of the overall project? This transferring Saint Thomas' text from the print version to the machines – you knew the reason why it was carried out?

TO: Yes, because they had to find all the lemmas.

MP: That's it.

TO: Every word, then every lemma. Then, for example, in the work I did for Zampolli, they had all the phonemes, graphemes and all that stuff.

MP: However, you weren't involved in lemmatization?

TO: No, I wasn't there in time because by '63 they hadn't started, all that time – lemmatization or that – was done exclusively for Zampolli's project. With that too, I had starts amongst other things and it was later passed on ...

MP: On which data?

TO: On a book, they chose a book that had non-academic language, but, however, was well written.

MP: In Italian?

TO: In Italian.

MP: I see.

TO: It was by Diego Fabbri.

(The Operator et al. 2014)

In any case, from what Busa described as "one initial punching of the text" (Busa 2019b[1958], 45), an interweaving of human-machine operations, some prominently discussed in publications, others not, gave rise to four sets of cards:

the text cards and the word cards, that contain all the words of the text and represent two new editions of the entire text; and the form cards and the main cards, which constitute two summary indexes of the vocabulary used in the text. The first lists the words grouped according to graphic form, the other lists the same words arranged according to graphic-semantic units.

(Busa 2019b[1958], 45)

Stage 6: Printing of information

Throughout the period under scrutiny, it was envisaged that the *Index Thomisticus* would be output in hardcopy, as most concordances, even machine-assisted, continued to be until at least the wide-spread take-up of personal computing in universities. This is evoked by John Bradley's recollections of the generation of a concordance to a Diodorus Siculus text with Oxford Concordance Program (OCP) software in the "very probably" late 1970s. The process was run on a time-shared machine at the University of Toronto Computer Services Department. And the expectation, even in the late 1970s, seems still to have been that the concordance would be output as hardcopy text. Bradley recalled that the work was difficult and time consuming and:

> they got so many boxes of paper that they filled up the back of a station wagon. Because they didn't ever want to run it again it was printed on paper with carbon copies attached, so you got two copies. They had this big machine to pull the paper all apart, so it was really an industrial-strength type of computing.
>
> (Nyhan and Flinn 2016, 211)

Unsurprisingly, then, the assumption of a material output underpins many of Busa's and Tasman's earlier discussions of the new opportunities opened by the transmediation of the *Index Thomisticus*.[13] They approvingly noted that, for example, the captured information could be printed "on sheets, in brochures or books or on other cards. Valuable tools in philological research like an *index verborum* or concordance are available without further scholarly effort" (Tasman 1957, 255).

For all this, it is testament to their foresight that neither Busa nor Tasman discussed the *Index Thomisticus* in a way that constrained it to the fixity of a printed, scholarly edition. They both emphasised the captured data's manipulability and reproducibility, discussing how the sorting of word cards and form cards into various combinations, together with respective entry cards, could lead to the printing of numerous indexes, lists and concordances. These included, for example, the *Laterculum Verborum*, "an alphabetical listing of words as they appeared in the text" together with frequency counts and other identifiers (Busa 2019b[1958], 48). The *Rationarium Verborum*, "the diagram, systematized and with frequencies, of all the same words regrouped according to their meaning, or more exactly, according to the identity of their functional ele- ments." (Busa 2019b[1958], 47). Other forms of index that could be derived included lists of prefixes, lists of suffixes, a reverse index, an index according to length of words and so on (see Burton 1984a, 1984b).

These research primitives, and the dataset whence they were derived (which had been encoded by the keypunch operators) were used by Busa to conduct subsequent team-driven scholarship on the "semantic heterogeneity" of words included in the *Index Thomisticus* (Busa 1994). Suggesting that the importance Busa attached, or felt compelled to attach to ostensible sole-authorship did not wane even in the later years of his life, it is Busa who is named as sole-author of this later, book-length work. Yet he does include a section on "collaborators and dates" and he makes clear the substantial input his (later) collaborators provided to the research, perhaps suggesting that he became more aware of the necessity of giving credit to collaborators and co-workers in his later years. It may also have become more conceivable for him to do so, since co-authorship has been rising in many scientific disciplines since the second world war (e.g. Wuchty, Benjamin and Uzzi 2007).

Move to computer

Though punched cards played a central role in the *Index Thomisticus*, their limitations became manifest to Busa already at an early stage of the project, as the words of Aquinas and related authors that the keypunch operators had captured, and the machines had duplicated, became a teeming mass. Aside from the difficulties of seeking to process natural text with a technology that did not process it as a continuous stream of input, the cards had material limitations. The logistics of actually storing and moving millions of cards from machine to machine were troublesome (Busa 2019b[1958], 56) and cards could break and fray from frequent use, creating more situations that demanded the verification of the punched text (Busa 1964, 66–7).

Thus, the project moved to using punched paper tape around 1958. In due course it used magnetic tape and many other storage media. Yet paper and magnetic tape seem to have been used as intermediate media in the processing workflow, while punched cards remained preeminent largely because the process of verifying the accuracy of what had been punched was too difficult on tape (Busa 1964, 67). Text on tape was represented as notches, while the text that was encoded on punched cards could be printed on their reverse side in one pass, and read by humans. By 1958,[14] Busa had also declared:

> in the near future I intend to occupy myself with the new electronic calculators with magnetic tapes (the Electronic Data Processing Machines, EDPM, of the IBM of the 600/700 group) in order to examine precisely how far such machines represent a saving, given that they eliminate the mechanical passage of the cards through the machines.
>
> (Busa 2019c[1958], 66)

The integration of EDPM machines would take longer than envisaged, and it is from around 1964 that Busa makes more regular reference to the incorporation of computers in the workflow of the *Index Thomisticus* project, following experiments that he and Tasman had already executed in the context of the Dead Sea Scrolls project (see Busa 1958b; 1959a). However, far from obviating the project's reliance on punched cards, in many ways this incorporation fortified and reemphasised the centrality of punched cards, and accordingly keypunch operators, to the project, while arguably further destabilising the position of the scholar.

In the above discussion of the methodology and technical elaboration of the *Index Thomisticus* we have seen how punched cards and accounting machines effectively bridged scholars and keypunch operators in a process that required input from both and crystallised in the eventual encoding of the *Index Thomisticus* as punched cards. Yet, their contingent connection was arguably destabilised by the introduction of the computer to the workflow of the *Index Thomisticus*, where it made inroads into what had previously been the sovereign domain of the scholar. Though Busa was careful to state that "Lemmatizing is a human operation ..." (Busa 1964, 71), from discussions of the computing programs for a Latin machine dictionary that the *Index Thomisticus* project staff worked on, it is difficult to conclude anything other than that the dictionary would have automated significant portions of the lemmatisation work.

Discussing this Latin machine dictionary, Busa described how "we punched" the c. 90,000 entries of an authoritative Latin dictionary, Forcellini's *Lexicon Totius Latinitatis* (Busa 1964, 72–73). The word forms that had been captured by the *Index Thomisticus* up to that point (50,000 unique word forms extracted from the 2,000,000 million words of Aquinas' *Summa Theologiae* and *Contra Gentiles*) were then cross-checked against the Forcellini lemmas, and the captured forms were mapped to one or more lemma. The scholars are not specified as having done this work but Busa states that "Ten persons, for six months, worked on it full-time", and so it is presumed that they did (Busa 1964, 73).

The point of this work was to semi-automate the work of lemmatisation, previously done by the scholars. Semi-automate seems to be the case as the process would output, among other things, lists of homographs that could not be automatically disambiguated, so scholars were still required but surely in a fewer number (Busa 1964, 73). In addition to the scholars and keypunch operators, this work would also require the input of programmers (Busa 1964, 74). And while Busa does attribute programmer's work (Busa 1964, 74–5), his subsequent discussion of the programme evokes the "ghost work" with which computing would go to become implicated, as it is the machine aspects of the routine that are focalised, along with statements of the intention that the programs written should be transferrable to other projects, that special characters should be represented adequately, that the work should be divided into several separated sub-programs and that the time needed for processing should be minimised (Busa 1964, 74–5). Discussions of the machine dictionary in the secondary literature invisibilise all but the input of Busa:

> Busa's method of determining his list of lemmata is among the special features of the Index. After keypunching the ... lemmata from [Forcellini] ..., he listed the 130,000 graphically different words found in the Thomistic corpus, comparing each of them with the list of lemmata to determine which forms belonged to which lemma.
>
> (Burton 1984b, 892)

Across and beyond all of this, the "ghost work" of the keypunch operators would continue to be utilised by the *Index Thomisticus*, either directly, as the keypunch operators continued to punch text, or more indirectly, as the punched cards their work output continued to be used long after its workplace in Gallarate was closed in the late 1960s. Like many other information processing setups (e.g. Nyhan and Flinn 2016, 99–121, 123–36), the *Index Thomisticus* continued to use punched cards until at least the 1970s. Aspray's work indicates that the continued use of the cards into the 1970s might be seen as unusual:

> traditional punched-card machines had effectively gone out of production ... punched cards themselves continued to be the dominant input-output medium for electronic computers. IBM flirted briefly with a new 96-column card in 1969 for its small System range of computers, and included an off-line sorting machine, but it was not a commercial success. During the 1970s even this vestigial use of punched cards declined with the increasing use of direct data entry on visual display units.
>
> (Campbell-Kelly 1990, 151)

Yet, more recent journalistic work has explored the use of punched cards even in 1990s corporate America (Dyson 1999).

In any case, punched cards would prove crucial to the *Index Thomisticus* right up until its publication in hard copy from the 1970s. This is captured in an oral history interview conducted with Righetti, who recalled how his work entailed, from the early to mid 1970s, moving the text of the *Index Thomisticus* from punched cards and tapes in preparation for its output as printed hard copy.

JN: How did you begin to work with Busa?
DR: Father Busa was working in the United States [in Boulder, Colorado]. In 1966, there was a big flood in Venice and the whole of Venice went under water. So, IBM decided to study the flow of the tides in the lagoon and created a research center in Venice. They rented a big building on the Canal Grande in Venice and there they began to study the lagoon. Father Busa, who was working in the United States, decided to come back to Italy and join this research center. Because he was near his family home and near his clerical order.
...
JN: And he was going to work in the research center?
DR: In Venice.
JN: Studying the lagoon?
DR: No, there was two projects in this research center: the lagoon and the *Index Thomisticus* ... He didn't have much money and so he payed some students to help him ...
MP: ... students from the University of Venice?

DR: Yes, students and other people, young people ... When the study of the lagoon was finished, IBM decided to close the center and so Father Busa had no more help from IBM.

MP: Which year? Roughly?

DR: The end of the seventies ... About ... they began to lose this around 1977–78. And so, he had no more programmers. Father Busa (PB to the team) wasn't a computer scientist; he didn't know how to program a computer, but he was a great architect of information systems. When he explained his idea to me, I remember I thought "This one is half crazy". It took me a long time to realize the greatness of his project. He tried to find some computer companies, but they asked for a lot of money for this job, about two hundred million lire at that time. At the actual level of euro, that was about two million euros to do this work.

MP: You could buy ten flats with that!

DR: And so we searched for some people who ...

MP: Volunteers?

DR: Volunteers who could program and he knew a friend of mine who worked with me, the other programmer, who died last year. He was more than 80 years old and this friend of mine asked me to help him to program. He, Father Busa, had some young programmers but they weren't able to ... he needed a word processor. Something like the Word program of the PC, a word processor to program a prototype laser printer of the IBM 2686. I searched for this device on the Internet but I didn't find anything; it's very, very difficult to program. When Father Busa asked how much money we wanted, the friend told him, "a bless from you (*la sua benedizione*)" [laughter].

...

JN: What kind of work did you do?

DR: My friend (the other collaborator) and I, we had to make a word processor. This word processor was not based on the keyboard but had to read a lot of punch cards, and build pages of printed text.

MP: The task of the co-workers was to move the data from the punch cards to printed paper.

...

DR: We initially worked from punch cards, then, a second time ... for tapes ....

[DR proceeds to produce, and discuss, an exemplar of the printed output of the *Index Thomisticus* that resulted from his work]

MP: [scanning the printed page] ... this is the reference, so this is the first work of the *Index Thomisticus*, the first book of the *Sentenze di Pietro Lombardo* and the second *Distinctio,* third *Quaestio,* fourth, fifth *Ethica.* And this is the opening, first argument, second argument, third argument and so on. And each sentence in the punch card was assigned a reference in the text and so, as far as I understand, the work of this processor was to read the punch cards, and later the tapes, and to assemble the information in the right place. So the text here was in bold and [to DR] you told me that this was not easy.

DR: No, no, this was very difficult. You can see that the justification is not correct here.

MP: Ah. It was not correct yet [in this exemplar], because in the final print it was correct.

(Righetti, Nyhan and Passarotti 2014)

Thus, the "ghost work" implemented by the keypunch operators of the *Index Thomisticus* gave rise not only to the data foundations of the computational humanities in the form of the *Index Thomisticus*, but it also, via the millions of punched cards their work created, acted as the weft that threaded together the warp of interchanging technologies, processes and even workers that gave rise to the *Index Thomisticus* in ways often unseen.

Notes

1 The chart is signed: "6–17–1952 New York IBM World Trade Sales Engineering PT-J[E?]G". The PT initials are presumably those of Paul Tasman (Flow chart 1952).
2 In the earlier years of the project, Busa's work was constrained by the punched cards that were available to him. When working on the hymns of Aquinas he "had at his disposal an IBM card punch 131, with 38 characters only (based on one or two holes per column). In 1949, IBM had announced a card punch of 48 standard codes, i.e., the 024 and the 026; both, however, seem not to have been on the European market until about 1951–1952" (de Tollenaere 1972, 147–48). Rockwell and Sinclair's humanistic fabrication research has also concluded that the encoding system used by *Index Thomisticus* was something like the 48-character BCDIC (Binary-Coded Decimal Interchange Code) (Sinclair 2016).
3 The IBM literature states that manuals should be drawn up and made available to staff of an IBM machine accounting installation. These manuals set out the task to be implemented, assisting staff with their work and informing those in executive management roles about the fine-grained processes implemented by operators and other staff (IBM Corporation 1955, 3–4). So far, I have not managed to locate CAAL's manuals or references to them.
4 The description that Busa gives in the *Varia* of the project's approach to verification in its earlier years emphasises the role of the collator machine: "Two separate typists punch the same text, each on his own; the collator compares the two series of cards, perceiving the discrepancies: of the cards not coinciding, at least one is wrong" (Busa 2019a[1951], 31). His discussion makes much of how he perceived his method to be superior to that recommended by IBM, which made use of a Verifier machine, but the grounds on which he is proposing the superiority of this method are unclear..
5 The coeval IBM literature states that few projects output cards in quantities sufficient to justify the use of a verifier, underscoring how different the *Index Thomisticus* project was from the type of project IBM usually supported (IBM Corporation 1961, 22).
6 The 1952 flowchart mentions the use of a verifier (Flow chart 1952). In 1961 an IBM 56 Verifier was in use. Errors that the verifier did not detect were found by "listing the sentence cards on either the IBM 866 Cardatype typewriter, or on the IBM 441 Accounting machine" (de Tollenaere 1963a, 5) and presumably checking by hand.

7 Gang punching involved a source card which passed through a reproducing punch so that the information it contained was ganged or duplicated from one card to another (see e.g. Aspray 1990, 125).

8 Busa certainly drew on the established referencing systems of the analogue concordance tradition in his work. The question of how, or whether it was necessary for him to extend these systems given the scale of text with which he was working deserves further attention. See Nyhan and Passarotti 2019, 12–14.

9 As Jones notes, "The Busa Archive contains a brief typescript of a chapter for a book in progress during 1961–1962 by the Dutch linguist, Félicien de Tollenaere (1912–2009), telling the story of CAAL in detail" (Jones 2016, 121). Among other sources, the 1963 typescript draws on observations made by de Tollenaere during his visit to CAAL in 1961.

10 De Tollenaere goes on to discuss other machines in use in Busa's lab, for example, the "IBM 441 Accounting Machine ... counts [the word cards] and checks them for the right sequence and for their having been punched in the proper columns" (de Tollenaere 1963a, 5).

11 See, for example, the online text analysis platform Voyant Tools (Sinclair and Rockwell 2021).

12 After the entry cards had been punched and alphabetised they were "provided with a punched and endprinted number on the left front side of the card, together with their form frequency and word frequency. By gang punching the form cards and the word cards are now provided with their lemma number" (de Tollenaere 1963a, 6).

13 As ever greater numbers of words were marshalled, we find evidence of Busa's concerns about the practicalities and cost of hardcopy printing. In 1964, for example, he wrote of how the work was expected to occupy "500 volumes of 500 pages each. We are making an experiment for adopting a kind of microprint readable by means of a magnifying glass to be placed on a book and to be moved only downwards" (Busa 1964, 77).

14 He and Tasman had already experimented with this approach during work on the non-biblical Dead Sea Scrolls, see Busa 2019b [1958], 57.

3 Situating the *Index Thomisticus*
Views from inside

Introduction

The previous chapter reconstructed and explored the detail of the work
that was executed by the staff of the *Index Thomisticus* on a day-to-day
basis. But what must it have been like for the *Index Thomisticus'* staff, and
the keypunch operators in particular, to work on what would become one
of the foundational projects of the digital humanities? And what about the
distribution of tasks to the various groups of individuals who worked on
the *Index Thomisticus*, and the *de facto* invisibilising of one of those
groups, the female keypunch operators? To what extent was the *Index
Thomisticus'* workflow and staff organisation entirely "natural" (as in the
natural order of things), objective and inevitable in conceptualisation and
execution? And was its organisation without consequence? To explore
these questions further, this chapter sets about retro-engineering the technical design of the *Index Thomisticus* to the social and situated contexts of
its making.

Attention to "big picture" historical dynamics is useful when seeking to
examine how the technical implementation of the *Index Thomisticus* may
have been shaped by the social contexts that gave rise to it. By attending
to the significance of the *Index Thomisticus'* historical inheritance we can,
for example, readily understand why it was the work of keypunching, in
particular, that could be devalued in reporting on it. This inheritance has
been interpreted elegantly by Jones in his discussion of photographs of
project staff and apprentices at work when they were stationed in a former
textile factory. He noted how:

> The industrial model for CAAL's work is vividly illustrated by the location
> and layout [of the former factory]. Instead of textiles, texts; instead of
> weaving and sewing, punching and sorting of cards; the reality in this case
> poetically invokes the historical connection between mechanised looms,
> which had in the nineteenth century often been controlled by punched
> cards, and mechanised linguistic processing using decks of punched cards
> that were directly descended (via Holleriths's inventions) from those

DOI: 10.4324/9781003138235-4

Jaquard-loom punched cards, versions of which had surely been used in Gallarate's historical textile manufacturing.

(Jones 2016, 122–3)

Scholarship that historicises the themes of Jones' discussion: gender, light manufacturing and information processing has emphasised the significance and tenaciousness of those dynamics' conjuncture in the second industrial revolution. Nineteenth-century women were employed in light-manufacturing roles in industries like textiles and paper-making, which "helped pave the way for their hiring in new manufacturing sectors like the electrical industry in the twentieth century, and contributed to the notion that they would be suited to 'light manufacturing' in the office" (Hartman Strom 1989, 60). With the advent of typewriters, comptometers and even accounting machines such as those used by CAAL:

> … the association between women and light manufacturing was already an acceptable image upon which advertisers and employers could draw in establishing the widespread use of new machines in offices. The nineteenth century had implanted firm notions of men and women in the industrial world: native-born men were associated with artisanry and craftsmanship; native-born women with light factory work; and immigrants and blacks with manual labor. The new office found it desirable to appropriate these notions in familiar forms.
>
> (Hartman Strom 1989, 60)

Thus, we understand that gender (and other modes of difference), technology and labour were articulated, within and outside CAAL in the automation of data processing in complex, socially-inflected and sometimes practically invisible ways. And we are reminded, moreover, that the *Index Thomisticus* is not only a story of cutting-edge technological application, it is also a story of how a formative project drew on the hegemonic nature of computerisation (e.g. Hicks 2017, 6), industrial manufacturing and the feminisation of the office to confine women to the "light manufacturing" of emergent literary and linguistic computing.

But for all the "big picture" historical and sociocultural trends and practices that the *Index Thomisticus* invoked or rejected, it was first and foremost a highly situated project. Scholars of the history of science have argued that "all scientific work is situated – done in particular spaces, times and locations, with particular material practices. Nothing is predetermined" (Clarke and Fujimura 1992, 5). Thus, neither the *Index Thomisticus'* trajectory nor the form of its day-to-day realisation was inevitable or predetermined. It was actively enabled and constrained by decisions that were made by Busa and others, by the cultural circumstances in which it was pursued and by particulars like the "materials, techniques, instruments, models and the funding work and arrangements" (Clarke and Fujimura 1992, 3) that it could harness, as this and the next chapter shall explore.

As Bucher observed of algorithms in particular but as is also true from broader ontological perspectives: "'Conditions of possibility are not given' but shaped in and through situated practices" (Bucher 2018, 39, citing Mol 1999). Thus, while acknowledging that CAAL and the *Index Thomisticus* were shaped by, and that they conversed with big-picture historical and sociocultural themes and dynamics, this and the next chapters will examine the locations, processes, practices, workflows, workforce and funding arrangements of the *Index Thomisticus*, with a particular focus on those that pertained to or impinged on the construction of the role of the female keypunch operators. This will include situating this study more within the historical context of women and labour in Italy in the post-war period, to explain what can currently be surmised about both the similarities and differences between this and Busa's setup.

In other words, this and the next chapter will explore aspects of the historical contingencies and subjectivities of the *Index Thomisticus'* making, which are rarely detectable in formal reporting on it (or, indeed, in reporting of research findings more generally). The point of this highly situated examination is to challenge the dominant portrayal of the *Index Thomisticus* as a "singular, generalizable primacy" (Clarke and Fujimura 1992, 4), pursued in a context where dominant views about determinative aspects of its elaboration, like the role of gender and labour force organisation, were so uncontroversial and inevitable as to be invisible to those who held them and thus incontestable. In the place of this primacy, these chapters will build a more problematised, fragmented, provisional, contingent and sometimes even contested view of the elaboration of the *Index Thomisticus*. In this way, this and the next chapter might be understood as seeking to build a view "from the inside", a view that seeks to contextualise the technical elaboration of the project with regard to the operational and very human circumstances and constraints in which it was pursued by a large team of staff.

Founding and funding

Regarding the founding of CAAL and the training school, Busa wrote, for example, that "In 1954 I started my own punching and verifying department; two years later I established my own processing department, but employing large computers always in IBM premises. That year I started a training school for keypunch operators" (Busa 1980, 85). As this quote suggests, Busa's references to the setting up of CAAL and the training school can be a bit opaque, and leave mentions of "IBM premises", for example, unglossed. But Busa spent various stints in IBM headquarters in Milan and New York between c.1949–1954 (Jones 2016, 85–6), where he received significant assistance from IBM employees, especially Paul Tasman, in devising the technical implementation of what would become the *Index Thomisticus*. Working in a "proof of concept mode" with IBM, Busa selected hymns of Thomas Aquinas and the third canto of Dante's Inferno as microcosms of inquiry into mechanically-assisted means of concordance extraction and compilation

(Busa 2019a[1951], 28, 33). It was following this period that he founded CAAL in Gallarate around 1954, and, shortly thereafter, the training school where the *Index Thomisticus*, and the other projects that CAAL worked on, would be punched.

CAAL was the "first independent center devoted entirely to the analysis of literary and linguistic data" (Zampolli 1973, 343). Its foundation and period of activity had a synchronicity with the international ascendency of data processing and analysis as a central activity of government, commercial enterprise, research and education, military and defence outfits across the world. CAAL's mission was both service and research-orientated and Jones has emphasised its internationalist orientation and multisectoral connectedness. Indicative of this, in 1961, Busa hoped that CAAL would become "a node in a network of linguistic data processing centres" that were forming around the world (Jones 2019, xi). Indeed, this internationalist orientation may itself be seen as a node of connection between Busa and a chronologically earlier generation of European information scientists, theorists and writers, including, inter alia, Paul Otlet, Albert Robida, Jules Verne and H.G. Wells, who were active in the late nineteenth and early twentieth century (see Wright 2014, 63). Their writings valorised not only technoutopianism but internationalist orientations too. The

> internationalist movement, coupled with—and enabled by—new communications technologies and a spirit of cultural progress, imbued many learned Europeans with a new way of thinking about world affairs, one less rooted in traditional national concerns and more concerned with building a futuristic, postnationalist global society.
>
> (Wright 2014, 67)

The impact of the world wars on this internationalist outlook notwithstanding, future studies of the history of computing in the humanities in the context of the rhetoric of internationalism may prove interesting.

The "training school" set up by Busa for machine operators does not seem to have been an entity that was substantively distinct from CAAL. This is suggested by Cervini's oral history interview, when she recalls that after completing her keypunching training "... I should have started working. My mom, a bit protective, said, 'but how can she start working at sixteen?' So, then we asked Father Busa and he hired me" (Cervini et al. 2014).

Those who were hired by CAAL after completing their training received an employment card and a modest wage that was around 2/3s of the industrial average:[1] GB: "The pay was poor, maybe 20,000 *lire* per month" (Cervini et al. 2014). As such, interviewees seem to have perceived the difference between CAAL and the training school in terms of their employment status, and the prospect of a wage, rather than any material difference in the nature of the labour they executed there, or the space where they executed it.

Both CAAL and the training school seem to have been wonderfully protean entities, the training school perhaps most of all. This is suggested by the malleability that can be observed in the training school's naming conventions, which were not fixed but could be adapted to shifting rhetorical agenda and publication contexts. So, in formal academic and humanistic publications, Busa refers to a "training school", the mention of a school emphasising the educative dimension and balancing the decidedly applied and vocational dimension of "training". Or he refers to a laboratory:[2] "The Centre consists today of 30 units: 6 for philological work; 2 for the secretariat; 22 for the laboratory. We are setting out to achieve 40 to 45 units" (Busa 2019d[1972], 72). In project-internal documentation, its title is rendered quite differently: "*Centro Addestramento Professionale Operatori Servizi Automazione Contabilità Aziendali*" (The Professional training centre of operators of automated services for business accounting).[3] This framing is echoed in Italian media reporting on the school,[4] where the training school's male trainees, vocational dimensions, industrial and commercial connections tend to be foregrounded. The adaptability of the naming conventions of the training school must have been useful given the economic backdrop of the *Index Thomisticus* during the years under review and the fundraising demands that were made on Busa in the execution of the project.

Why Busa could not or did not house CAAL and the training school in IBM headquarters in Milan, or in the Jesuit Aloisianum College in Gallarate, where he was a faculty member, is currently unknown. The explanation may be quite prosaic, and centre on issues like funding agreements, space constraints and overheads. And yet the import of CAAL's institutional, fiscal and physical instability would prove anything but prosaic. It is arguably crucial to understanding the rationale for the labour arrangements of the *Index Thomisticus*. Burton has referred to Busa's early activities as "the heady mixture of idealism and hustle that fostered so many early computer projects" (Burton 1981a, 1). This approach was required by the difficulties of pursuing digital humanities research in this incunabular period, before the field really existed in the sense of being an institutionalised entity supported by agents for stability, strategy and foresight, including now-familiar funding bodies (like, for example, the National Endowment for the Humanities Office of Digital Humanities) or scholarly associations like the European Association for Digital Humanities.

With Busa's ambition for the *Index Thomisticus*, and the extramural setting up of CAAL and the training school, came the need for workplaces that could accommodate, and funds that could maintain an expanding complex of humans, machines and material objects enlisted in the core tasks of data preparation, capture, verification, processing and transformation, output and storage. This empire building would require resources far greater than IBM and the Jesuits' in-kind contributions of machinery and labour.[5] In 1962, Ida Rhodes wrote how Busa had "to devote practically all of his time and energy to the task of collecting his annual budget requirements of $65,000. This leaves him no opportunity for scientific research ..." (Rhodes 1962).

The consequence of this for *Index Thomisticus* workers was that Busa remained a largely absent figure whose time and focus were greatly taken up by external activities. This is recalled in oral history interviews, where interviewees nevertheless indicate their awareness of his status in the project:

> BV: I mean, we saw very little of him.
> GB: Very little.
> BV: But, when we saw him, he gave off an intimidating aura, the few times he would show up [makes the sound of a typewriter, they laugh].
> MP: Oh yes, you would work …
> BV: No, were always working …
> MP: Yes, yes, I can imagine.
> BV: Anyways, when he would show up … [they laugh]
> GB: … we worked in a particular way.
>
> (Brogioli et al. 2014)

That keypunch operators had little opportunity to interact with Busa is also recalled by another interviewee. When asked about her memories of Busa from the years in Gallarate she responded:

> [sigh] What can I say? What should I say? When I did punched card work, nothing. No, there was no dialogue, nothing. Yes, I did speak to him when he hired me, he knew I had arrived thanks to my uncle, "Great, welcome, ciao" but nothing else".
>
> (Crosta et al. 2014)

That he could seem mentally detached, or bad-tempered when he was present, perhaps signalling the immense pressure he was under, was further recalled too: "He certainly wasn't the easy-going priest who trusts everyone" (Mainardi et al. 2014; see also Barras and Nyhan 2019, 226). Many of the keypunch operators' recollections of the Busa they encountered during the Gallarate period stand in contrast to the Busa who is recalled by many in the field of digital humanities, and beyond, as a charismatic and kind man.[6] Yet this figure is not completely absent from the interviews and Cervini recalled a lovely interaction with Busa during her time in the training school:

> MP: … Could you read to me what Father Busa wrote you [in 1966]? Mrs Marinella Cervini is reading the message Father Busa wrote to her on her journal when she left the center to start working.
> MC: Since my last name is Cervini (the Matterhorn) …
> MP: … Yes.
> MC: And my first name Marinella (from Marine) …
> MP: … Yes.
> MC: He referred to the Matterhorn and the sea. And he wrote, "May the most beautiful part of your soul lay ever immersed in the heavens, like the

Matterhorn's peak. And may the goodness of your heart grow ever vast like the sea".

(Cervini et al. 2014)

Jones has discussed Busa's energetic transatlantic travel and fund-raising efforts during these years, as he courted the IBM World Trade Corporation, the Catholic Church, industrialists of Gallarate and the Military-Industrial complex (see Jones 2016).[7] Yet, relatively little attention has been paid, thus far, to how Busa sought to ignite CAAL and the training school's momentum with the touch paper of the opportunities that were being opened in Italy for employers to access cheap labour, for extended periods, during the post-war years and later.

From the macroeconomic and aggregate perspective, the years 1945–1970, including those of the "Italian economic miracle" (1958–63) were harbingers of expanded access to education, employment and economic gain. Italy became one of the most industrialised countries in the world (Bison 2013b, 261) and "per-capita output growth rose to double its long-term average, exceed[ing] that of any comparably large area elsewhere in the world" (Nardozzi 2003, 139).

In a succession of articles carried in Italian newspapers like *La Prealpina* and *L'Italia,* [8] Busa's efforts to leverage the economic miracle in the service of literary and linguistic computing are depicted with aplomb.[9] Sometimes camouflaging, sometimes de-accentuating CAAL and the training school's academic stripes, narratives about its services to regional industry and commerce intermesh it with discussions of innovation, employment and economic growth. Its name is variously given as the "Centre for the professional training of computer operators and business accountants" (L'Italia 1961a); the "Centre for Professional Training of computer operators in business accountancy" (*La Prealpina* 1961b); and "Centre for professional training" (L'Italia 1961b).

One such report portrays the school as having been the first in Italy to provide training for female keypunch operators and male machine operators. It was carried under a somewhat nationalistic headline that positioned the school as a first in Italy: "For the first time in Italy". And it called on readers to support the school and "the course for mechanographic accounting" it offered[10] (*La Prealpina* 1957). Positioning it as a benefactor of the local area, the article claims that CAAL is poised to bring about "the elevation of the working masses" and the "modernization of industry". The theme was not a one off, and in other articles the school is connected with the inroads that computing was making into local industry, with its take-up by workers and senior management (e.g. *La Prealpina* 1961a; 1962). The immediate purpose of the articles was surely two-fold: to convince local entrepreneurs of the longer-term returns of investing in CAAL and to court the interest of readers who might send their students or children to work on the *Index Thomisticus* as a stepping stone to their participation in the wider economic miracle.

Wider political and economic contexts, of European Integration, the Cold War and the Communist threat to the Catholic Church seem detectable in the framing of the training school in these articles too. The European Economic Community's Treaty of Rome, which was signed in 1957, established the common market and its free movement of "people, goods, services and capital" (Ewers 2022). Vocational training, such as that offered by the *Index Thomisticus* training school, was directly mentioned in the treaty and recognised as important for "the harmonious development both of the national economies and of the common market" (Article 128), which would be furthered through the "productive re-employment of workers" from other sectors and the free movement of labour (Addison and Siebert 1994, 696). Italy was actively in favour of the common policy for vocational training envisaged by the Treaty, which the Commission attempted to accelerate in 1960 (Petrini 2004, 45). It was expected the policy could foment employment and economic growth in Italy and could likewise enhance Italy's vocational training sector, moving it, perhaps, towards parity with Germany and France (Petrini 2004, 45). However, despite Italy's concerted support of the policy, it was not taken-up, and Petrini has argued that self-interested opposition from France and Germany played a role in this (Petrini 2004, 53–4). In the somewhat nationalistic headline mentioned above, and the interconnection of the training school with economic growth and expansion, the wider international debates on European vocational development, which Italy sought to influence can be detected.

The articles under discussion might also suggest that Busa, and perhaps others in Gallarate, might have conceptualised the training school as part of the machinery of the Catholic Church's opposition to Communism in post-war Italy and Eastern Europe, which was not only understood by the Church as a threat to Western democracy but as a threat to the Church itself (see Saresella 2020). Such was the perceived threat of Communism to the Catholic Church in Italy in the post-war period, writes Carillo, that it resulted in the Catholic Church becoming "deeply involved in the political life of post-war Italy" (Carillo 1991, 647). The emphasis in the media articles discussed above on the economic mobility through education that the training school could open to its trainees, male in particular, may speak to this by positioning the training school as a bulwark against the allure or economic imperative of Communism. The threat apparently posed by Communism does feature in Busa's writings, as he tries to grapple with the ideological consequences of how opposing Cold War players used largely identical technologies, some of which were, moreover, identical to those being used by CAAL. Thus, in a 1966 essay, for example, Busa sought to repudiate the view of Leonid Il'ichev, the "secretary of the Central Committee of the Russian Communist Party" (Busa 2019g[1966], 95) on the compelling case that cybernetics made for atheism, instead arguing that cybernetics opened new paths to God.

Perhaps also suggesting Busa's hand in shaping some media articles, some are furthermore notable for the careful political acumen they manifest. Ensuring that CAAL's exceptionalist portrayal does not overstep the mark, the articles co-locate local Catholic business men (whose resources and favour Busa both sought and was reliant on) in the inner circle of those "in the know". This is evident, for example, in a report on a CAAL graduation ceremony that emphasises how it was not CAAL alone that awarded the grants. CAAL's conferring is instead presented as having been given further approval by a cast of local businessmen and governmental entities including: industrialists of Gallarate, the City Council of Gallarate, the oil and gas company ENI, and the Executive Committee of the CAAL (*La Prealpina* 1962). Other reports suggest that Busa's plans to court industry were more ambitious still. An article directed to the business men of the region and their sons (the "heirs of industry") announced Busa's plans for setting up a new school to train those young men in bringing computing to small and mid-dling-sized firms (*L'Italia* 1963).

Locating

Busa's publications state that CAAL occupied workplaces in Italy and the USA: New York (1949); Milan (c.1949–1967); Pisa (1967–69); Boulder, Colorado (1969–71); and Venice (1971) (see e.g. Busa 1980). Oral history interviews, enriched with archival materials, work to destabilise the apparent fixity of these geographical locations, giving way to a view of the spatiality of the *Index Thomisticus* that is shifting, sometimes precarious, yet embedded in its locality and dependent on Busa's connections with entrepreneurs and other socially powerful people in Gallarate.

During CAAL and the training school's years in Gallarate, the different arms of the project reached into at least six different individual spaces, ranging from private, semi-public, religio-educative to industrial in nature. Indeed, as CAAL and the training school peregrinated from locations like an industrial basement to a former factory, they remained very much outside of the typical sites of intellectual exchange—the library, archive, seminar, office and perhaps documentation centre—of the institutional humanities. Whether in terms of the locations where it was housed, or the programmes of study its training school delivered, CAAL had little formal connection with authorised locations of Humanistic teaching, learning and research. Connections that were built between the work of CAAL and the training school and the wider Academy were thus not forged on site or in praxis. Rather, they were forged by Busa, through the sole-authored publications and lectures he disseminated to an international audience, usually far from the spaces where the *Index Thomisticus* was actually executed.

The earliest of CAAL's keypunching locations to feature in the oral history interviews is the refectory that the Canossian nuns of Gallarate may have granted Busa use of, perhaps as early as 1954. Two female keypunch operators are said to have worked there temporarily. Mirroring the status of the *Index Thomisticus* project itself at this time, this location is depicted as unsatisfactory and unsecured. Due to its semi-public nature, there existed the possibility of young people, school children presumably, gaining unsupervised access to equipment:

> MP: Could you please explain to us: what did the job consist of? You would arrive there each morning and what would you do?
> TO: In the morning, I turned on (laughs) because, as I said, after all, it was a refectory, which meant we had to unplug the transformers ... to prevent ...
> MP: ... A blackout?
> TO: No, because perhaps some young girl might go there to try to touch ...
> MP: Oh, I see. Therefore, you would turn them off and then turn them back on again in the morning.
>
> (The Operator et al. 2014)

The suggestion of domesticity evoked by the mention of the refectory is amplified when we next catch glimpse of the project in June 1956, at "Casa Sironi" or the home of the Sironi family (see Busa Archives #0025, 6, 7, 8). This was probably "the Via Novara 12 laboratory, Gallarate" that Busa refers to in letters around this time. My presumption is that space in Casa Sironi was temporarily put at Busa's disposal. The archival picture is even more fragmented than usual on this, but it does seem that keypunching work was carried out in Casa Sironi while the machine operating work was carried out in a separate premise in Gallarate.[11]

While Busa's refers to the keypunching setup in Casa Sironi as a "laboratory", its domestic referent recalls how

> Amid the proliferation of academic laboratories by the early twentieth century, and given the tenacious exclusion of women from those new spaces, homes increasingly became retreats where men of science still carried out private researches and yet received the "hidden" assistance of wives and other family members.
>
> (Opitz 2016, 254)

Keypunch operators did not have a personal or familial relationship with Busa but their otherwise "hidden" and feminised assistance is captured in archival pictures from this domestic location, suggesting not only the weight of historical precedent in the devaluing of their labour but the diversity of the spaces in which data-driven research has been carried out over the longer term.

Photos taken in Casa Sironi in June 1956 show two unnamed female operators sitting at their punches in white coats, fingers poised, faces turned away from the camera (Busa Archive #0025). The machines they are using look aged and scuffed. They contrast strongly with the state-of-the-art machines, like the Cardatype, that featured in the high-profile demonstrations in which Busa had participated, for example, in Brussels in 1953 (e.g. Busa

Archive #0015). In the foreground of one photo from Casa Sironi is an IBM type 31 punch from around 1933. The machine behind it is a slightly later model, perhaps an 036 from 1936. It appears to have the same keyboard as the 026 (which was announced in 1949). This may be because the operators were using a later card punch, one between the 036 and 026, or they may have been working with some kind of composite machine (Short 2019). These photos, staged in one of an iteration of CAAL and the training school's provisional locations, where generations of punched card machines, some Former keypunch operators perhaps experimental, and a local, temporary workforce were brought together frame the *Index Thomisticus* as an ongoing instance of Knorr-Cetina's concept of tinkering or "constant engagement in producing and reproducing some kind of workable object which successfully meets the purpose ... temporarily settled on" (Knorr-Cetina 1981, 34).

The *Index Thomisticus* as a "workable object" would continue to be "produced and reproduced" in locations across Gallarate in the years before late 1961. It is possible, though uncertain, that some keypunching was ongoing at the Aloisianum.[12] Former keypunch operators also recalled working in: the Valentini Electromechanical workshop[13]; the firm of Cuccirelli[14] (MC: "We worked on the machines, all of us in these big halls over in Cuccirelli" (Cervini et al. 2014)); and at the laboratory in via G. Ferraris 2 (also referred to as Lab Valentini, after its benefactor (Jones 2016, 122)). That the project occupied some of these locations simultaneously is indicated in de Tollenaere's description of CAAL's setup in 1961, which he describes as:

> still physically dispersed over three localities: 1° the Aloisianum, where the philological work of hands and brains, (preparing the texts, lemmatizing of the punching [sic] cards) is going on; 2° a locality in a factory for the machines with which the text cards and [sic?] punched and controlled; 3° a cellar in another factory where the remaining machines and administration are.
>
> (de Tollenaere 1963a, 6)

These temporary workplaces were located near the Aloisianum and were rented or otherwise put at Busa's disposal by entrepreneurs of Gallarate.[15] Late in 1961, the previously dispersed scholarly and technical sections of CAAL were brought together in a former textile factory on via G. Ferraris 2, Gallarate. There the operation would remain until 1967, when IBM closed CAAL and the training school and Busa and a few continuing staff departed for Pisa.

Thus, an enduring feature of the *Index Thomisticus*' setup in the years before 1961 was that the scholarly work of the project was housed separately from the technical work. Moreover, it seems that the key punching and machine operating were done in separate locations or spaces for much of this time too. One might accordingly wonder whether the sex-segregated labour distribution was a side effect of the project's pre-1961 physical dispersion, itself seemingly linked to issues of local contingency, like the workplaces that could be put at the *Index Thomisticus* disposal in Gallarate along with the international and commercial contingencies that influenced the IBM machines that could be put at Busa's disposal?

The practice was, however, continued even after the staff of the project, and its material infrastructure was united under one roof in via G. Ferraris. There the work continued to be sex-segregated, with photographs showing young women seated at keypunch machines, or engaged in manually-led verifying activities, while young men are shown standing at tabulating and sorting machines.[16] Though the set-up of the lab at via G. Ferraris was ostensibly open-plan, even when the project was housed in one location, the possibilities the *Index Thomisticus* afforded for human interaction between Busa and staff members, between humans and machines and with the emerging field of textual data processing was stunted and disaggregated. "Space ... is not ... simply the stage on which the real action takes place. Rather, it is itself constitutive of systems of human interaction" (Livingstone 2003, 7). Indeed, the gendering of space has been argued to play a fundamental yet often invisible role in facilitating or impeding the acquisition of knowledge, often associated with status and power in wider society and thus seen as the preserve of men:

> Women's position within society, whether measured as power, prestige, economic position, or social rank, is related to spatial segregation insofar as existing physical arrangements facilitate or inhibit the exchange of knowledge between those with greater and those with lesser status.
>
> (Spain 1993, 137)

No longer separated by physical walls, as they had been in earlier phases of the project, in the laboratory at via G. Ferraris, workers were instead separated by the hierarchies that structured the gender-, praxis- and knowledge-based *wissensraum*, or knowledge space, of the *Index Thomisticus*, and to some extent, the humanities computing and digital humanities that would follow.

Labour organisation

As Busa became an indefatigable fundraiser for the *Index Thomisticus* project (e.g. Passarotti 2013), his workforce played a crucial role in the execution of the *Index Thomisticus* and the other projects being undertaken by CAAL. CAAL's workforce was taxonomised into three hierarchically incommensurate divisions: scholars, technical staff and administrative staff (Busa, n.d.).

The post of scholar was depicted by Busa and others as most esteemed (see Chapter 5). The scholars were "graduated collaborators (dr. phil. or litt.)" (de Tollenaere 1963a, 8), usually Jesuit or religious brothers. Ordination was not a pre-requisite of admission to the post of scholar in CAAL. The lay Antonio Zampolli, for example, was responsible for the "enlisting, training and guidance of the scientifical [sic] members of the staff, with the planning, coordinating and supervision on [sic] the different works that have to be executed, and with the sorting of the homographs and the lemmatizing" (de Tollenaere 1963a, 8). Being male does, however, seem to have been a de facto prerequisite for admission even against the international backdrop of Jesuit universities and colleges continuing their somewhat uneven progress towards full co-education (e.g. Higgins 2004). So too, a suitably qualified female workforce for the role was emerging. In Italy, from 1959 to 1977, the percentage of women between 19 and 24 who were studying at university rose from 2.5% to 18.3% (their male counterparts accounted for 25.1% by 1977) (Bison 2013b, 267) and the majority of those women chose humanities subjects (Govoni 2009, 233–35) This increase notwithstanding, in the academic year 1960–1961, just 1.7% of Italian women and 3.7% of Italian men had a degree, which does indicate that for a substantial part of the training school's operation university-qualified staff members of either gender cannot have been available to hire in abundance.

Staff of CAAL's administrative division included a "secretary-bookkeeper" (de Tollenaere 1963a, 8) and individuals like Gerolamo Passarotti (Busa 1993), who performed tasks such as moving punched cards around. That female keypunch operators do not seem to have participated in this work may be linked to the Italian laws that prohibited employers from requiring women to engage in strenuous physical labour.[17] Some material traces of administrative staff remain in archival materials, for example, in a 1958 letter that was sent on Busa's behalf by an individual named Alice Walsh (Walsh 1958). With the exception of female typists, men only were admitted to the administrative department.

Otherwise, staff were part of the technical division, which was further subclassified according to sex, the machines that individuals were thus permitted to use, and concomitantly, the esteem accorded to their work. Women technologists were admitted to the machine department alone; other technical roles, including those of operators and programmers were open to men only at this time.

As mentioned above, in the context of keypunching, apprentices and employees of CAAL seem to have done very similar work. That this was not anomalous in post-war Italy attests to how the experiences of the *Index Thomisticus'* keypunch operators also shed light on wider questions about the experiences of female workers in Italy during the years of accelerated economic growth. Across the *piste*, accounts of female apprentices of the period emphasise their frustration at the unfairness of achieving a proficiency that was comparable with qualified workers without being given a comparable salary or benefits (Betti 2020, 173). Not that employees necessarily had it much better than apprentices: "The success of the economic boom has to be measured against the sacrifices faced by Italian workers, many of whom endured low pay and forwent basic rights to job security" (Dunnage 2002, 152). And while those sacrifices were made by men as well as women (Betti 2010b, 192), gender disaggregated analysis shows that women had significantly worse terms, conditions and tenure, and fewer employment opportunities than men (see e.g. Betti, 2010a). Female labour in Italy, concluded

Betti, "has been employed on different and nearly always inferior terms to male labour, whether quantitatively or qualitatively. In most cases pay scales have been lower, periods of qualification and dequalification more unfavourable, and contract terms generally less secure than for male workers" (Betti, 2010b, 175).

In the industrial sector during this time, while levels of male employment rose significantly and rapidly, there occurred a "massive decline of female employment ... that was especially marked from the late 1950s to the early 1970s, a time at which more than a million women lost or quit their jobs and vanished from the labour market" (Betti 2010b, 184). Women who entered this labour market were predominately "young, unmarried, and childless women" (Betti 2016, 69; see also Betti 2020, 34), often hired on exploitative and discriminatory terms (Betti 2016, 69). Women's wages in the industrial sector were 30% less than men's, and the gender pay gap could widen to 50% "when one threw in the variable items on the pay packet (cost of living index, seniority, piece-work, etc.)" (Betti 2010b, 193).

Reform of this situation, which flouted the 1948 Italian constitution (Suk 2018, 126) was pursued through the 1960 equal pay agreement, which sought to end sex-based wage discrimination for blue- and white-collar workers by tethering levels of remuneration to workers' qualifications and levels of seniority (Betti 2010b, 193). Employers, however, found ways of enacting self-serving, discriminatory practices by reclassifying or consigning women to the lowest levels of the organisational matrix, concomitantly forcing through a de-professionalisation of the female workforce over the longer term (Betti 2013, 17–45). As women workers were perceived to be innately less competent, intelligent, effective and committed than their male counterparts, they could be classified in lower grades than men who did the same work.

Technosocial, cultural and, to some extent, constitutional factors bolstered this framing of women workers too. It was not only that women in the textile industry were often deemed replaceable by the new machines that were brought in with the modernisation of industry (Fornaciari 1956, 230), thus positioning them as temporary intruders to a workforce that would ultimately dispense with them. The 1948 Italian constitution, as intimated above, unequivocally guaranteed equal pay for equal work, and rejected sex, and other protected characteristics as grounds for discrimination. And yet, while its ostensibly patriarchal intent has been convincingly questioned (Suk 2018, 126), "The Italian Constitution included an article which, in the same breath, guaranteed equal pay for women workers, while also proclaiming women's traditional role as mother within the family" (Suk 2018, 125). This emphasis on the domestic sphere as the natural place of women was amplified by the Catholic Church too, which "played a key role in encouraging women not to go to work, on the grounds that this would mean sacrificing the family, while greater contact with the outside world would make them turn to 'sinister' pleasures" (Dunnage 2002, 160). Such was the strength of the heteronormative identification of women with the domestic realm that the post-war trend in Italy has been summarised as understanding "women's issues—specifically childcare and education—as issues of motherhood" (Pojmann 2011).

Interlocking religious and political dimensions may be relevant too: Catholic teaching, such as that delivered through the training school may have been perceived as an ideological bulwark against communism given the potential for economic uplift it might create in communities like Gallarate for the average worker. The training school may also have been associated with future-focused hopes for the role of vocational training and the prosperity this could help to leverage for Italy through European integration. Yet it was not only that the Catholic Church deemed the woman's place to be in the home, it furthermore saw the family as the site of formation in democratic life.[18] Indeed, both Italian Catholic and Communist women's organisations active during this Cold War period "counted on women from their traditional bases to help them make inroads into more homes" (Pojmann 2011).

With regards to the international stage, Cronin has analysed religious commentators' rhetorical mobilisations of "the family", understanding it as a political springboard whence discursive interventions into national and international politics could be launched: "the American family became a site of rhetorical politics through the malleable metaphor of the home fallout shelter as a domestic response to the fear of Soviet nuclear attack in the context of the Berlin crisis in 1961" (Cronin 2021, 73). Discourses on the family, and the positioning of the role of women in the home and workplace can similarly be understood as having been mobilised performatively in this incunabular period of digital humanities, as the keypunch operators' posts may have been understood by Busa as being of practical necessity (the keypunch operators were needed to execute the work that technologies for text capture could not) but ideological complexity that could perhaps be resolved by positioning their posts as transitory. This would have allowed those who executed keypunching temporarily to return to what was otherwise considered their rightful domestic setting. And from which may have followed the rather predicable human tendency to devalue and overlook that which is perceived as transitory and temporary. Thus, the complex tapestry of national and international political, social, economic and ideological entanglements of the cold war, technology, gender and organised religion that contributed to the overlooking of those who contributed to the take-up of computing in the humanities are called into view.

Historians have emphasised that some feminist gains were made in Italy during the immediate post-war period. Women were granted suffrage in 1945, a development brought about by those feminists who had also helped to defeat fascism (Malagreca 2013, 77). Yet the 1948 election resulted in an election landslide for the Christian Democrats (Dunnage 2002, 139–44), a party that was closely linked with the Catholic Church and its highly conservative social agenda (Caldwell 1991, 14). Over the following years, "Italian women continued to live as a minority group in a situation of serious inferiority, not unlike that reserved for them by the Fascist regime that had just passed" (de Clementi 2002, 333, cited in Malagrenca 2013) Excluded from government, the Italian Communist Party (PCI) did attach to a feminist agenda, yet their

> views on women and work focused on the emancipation thesis ... i.e. that participation in work, political life and social relations outside the home would produce a series of effects which were positive and generally unproblematic. Such an account left the general signification of woman as subordinate unexamined.
>
> (Caldwell 1991, 37)

Likewise, feminist groups like the *Unione Donne Italiane* (Union of Italian Women), while achieving much that was positive like helping to increase the visibility of women in "universities, magazines, working spaces and journals" (Caldwell 1991, 78–9) did not tackle the pervasive, heteronormative identification of women with familial procreation and domesticity. Thus, when the waning of the economic miracle was made to coincide with the sacking of some 283,000 female workers between 1963 and 1964 (Betti 2013, 39), this was viewed by many as unproblematic as women could return to their domestic and caring responsibilities (Betti 2013, 20).

During the same period in Italy the white-collar or tertiary sector, which included office staff and typists, almost doubled as a percentage of the total workforce (Dunnage 2002, 152). Women who chose to move away from, or were rejected from the agricultural and industrial sectors also found employment there (Fornaciari 1956, 226), yet the increase in office jobs held by women was proportionally modest, rising from 27.7% to 31.8% of all office staff (Betti 2010b, 186). Here too women were clustered in the lower rungs of clerical jobs: "first category and executive women were barely more than 5% in 1951 and only 6.5% in 1971" (Betti 2010b, 186). Again, social and cultural attitudes were in play. In Italy and beyond, "Women were usually perceived as not having the emotional makeup, the judgement, the analytical reasoning, or the long-term commitment to the job that was required for a manager ..." (Wootton and Kemmerer 2007, 586). Neither was it usually deemed acceptable for women to be seen to control even junior men in public.

Thus, in CAAL and elsewhere keypunch operator positions, like other feminised roles, did not tend to offer possibilities for promotion. Rather, it was the male machine operators who could progress to supervisor and then department head (Haigh 2010, 52). Haigh discusses a 1958 survey of forty-two punched card installations in Oklahoma City (or a survey that covered most of the punched card installations in what was then a major economic hub of the USA) conveys the socio-structural implications of this in practice:

> At the bottom, punch workers accounted for around thirty seven percent of the workforce in the punched card installations. They were all women. Twenty four percent of the punched card machine operators were women,

and ten percent of the supervisors. Key punch work was a dead-end job. Although the average key punch operator had more experience in punched card work than the average machine operator she could hold little hope of advancement with the department. Only three per cent of the punched card machine operators had originally been hired as key punch operators. No department supervisor had worked as a key punch operator.

(Haigh 2010, 53)

Regarding remuneration across this sector in Italy at this stage, it seems that between 1959 and 1963 the wage gap between men and women was lessening. And yet, Betti has concluded that "In general it is fair to say that both blue- and white-collar staff were caught up in a process of 'dequalification' too" (Betti, 2010b, 194). At the aggregate level, the gender pay gap was shrinking during this period, but it seems that wages overall were shrinking too (Betti 2010b, 193–4).

Apprentice status

Today, formal, credit-bearing apprenticeships and internships are often understood to offer digital humanities students valuable "real world" training opportunities in the many contexts and institutions in which this work is undertaken. Some institutions have even integrated apprenticeship and internship modules into the core curriculum of their digital humanities undergraduate and postgraduate degrees.[19] Still, whether through critiques of the role of internships in the neo-liberalisation of universities (e.g. Johnston 2011) or the status of student labour in digital humanities projects (Anderson et al. 2016), the power dynamics that can be operationalised through this form of labour are understood to be complex.

The female keypunch operators of the *Index Thomisticus* appear to have been engaged on terms that were even less secure than those of the average female employee of the Italian economic miracle, as sketched above. Though the word apprentice does not, to the best of my knowledge, occur in documentation pertaining to the *Index Thomisticus*, it was very much in this context that the young keypunch operators were engaged in the training school. Legislation regulating apprenticeships was introduced in Italy in 1955,[20] defining them as a special category of work relationship in which employers were obliged to provide individuals with the training necessary to become qualified workers (see Betti 2020, 108). Between 1951 and 1971, as increasing numbers of women younger than 20 entered the job market, female apprentice posts more than doubled and reached 13.6% of the female workforce in industry (Betti 2020, 55). The *Index Thomisticus* training school was, then, one among many: in Milan in 1956, 313 professional courses were run, with another 188 in the wider province and this was in addition to those already offered by professional schools (Commissione 1959, 459–60).

Some employers were abusing apprenticeship status so as to hire young people with modest levels of formal education or applied training to positions where they did the work of qualified employees, for meagre wages, over an extended time-period, with little in the way of job security. A Commission was constituted in 1955 by Parliament, proposed by two MPs, Alessandro Buttè (Christian Dem ocrats) and Ettore Calvi (Catholic Action) to inquire into this. The subsequent report, published in 1962, found that female apprentices earned less than their male colleagues for the same work and that they were frequently victims of breaches of contract. The treatment and conditions of female apprentices also showed a marked disparity with qualified workers (Commissione 1959, 299). Such was the ill-treatment of apprentices that in 1955 an investigation had to be called in Bologna into work-related deaths (Betti 2020, 109). Perhaps it was with implicit reference to this context that one interviewee was careful to emphasise that even if she was frustrated by the inequality she encountered in CAAL:

I have to say that in my case, I was never treated poorly, and when it was possible, [Busa] also made me travel a lot. For example, I went to Rome for a month, right away, for several things. But I was interested in women there being able to do the same tasks as men.

(The Operator et al. 2014)

Many similarities can be noticed between the 1955 legislation on apprenticeships and a typed, undated document that, on internal and external evidence, was created in CAAL during or prior to 1959. It sets out what may have remained the aspirational "Regulations" of the *Index Thomisticus* training school for two named courses: "One for trainee operators [male] of data-processing calculating departments and one for trainee perforators and verifiers [female] of these departments" (CAAL, n.d.). Cross-references to the Regulations suggest it was drawn up in connection with the Italian Ministry of Labour's oversight of training schools and Busa may have been its author.[21] Irrespective of place and time, neither legislation nor regulations necessarily reflect life as it is actually lived, in all its complexity and unpredictability. One archival document, apparently authored by a fellow priest, which will be explored later, is highly critical of how CAAL and the training school were being run. As we shall see, it claims that the Regulations were not being adhered to even by CAAL itself (Unknown 1960).

In any case, the 1955 legislation on apprenticeships states that this relationship could last no longer than five years and young people between the ages of 14 and 20 only could be hired as apprentices. It was made compulsory for employers to provide apprentices with vocational training, of an unspecified duration, which should count as work time. Apprenticeship training was to be regulated by various bodies, including the Ministry of Labour and

Social Security, who we shall see mentioned in connection with the training school again. To assist in the determination of candidates' aptitude, employment agencies could arrange psychophysiological assessments but the outcome of these assessments did not necessarily prevent them from being hired. Apprentices were also entitled to a fixed allotment of annual leave and could not work for more than eight hours per day or 44 hours per week. Wages should be commensurate with apprentices' level of seniority. After completing their vocational training (or if they were 18 and had completed two years of training), apprentices who passed a summative test could obtain the relevant qualifications. They could also be kept in service with a new title and a new seniority level, unless the apprenticeship-employer relationship was terminated with advance notice.

Seeming to push–even if it may have been largely on paper—against the informality that shaped many amanuenses' relationships as set out in Chapter 1, CAAL's Regulations seem to correspond to the 1955 law on apprentices in matters like recompense, working hours and hiring conditions. The Regulations stipulate that to become a trainee keypunch operator, a young woman should be "not less than 15 and no more than 18 years of age" (CAAL n.d.). As corroborated by oral history interviews, the entry age for the training school's keypunch operators was in practice lowered to 14, as permitted by the relevant legislation.

That Busa could hire, depending on the historical perspective, girls either as young or as old as 14 years to apprenticeship roles was due not only to the expanding labour market in Northern Italy, it was also linked to educational reforms.

During the 1960s, various educational reforms were made in Italy, including, in 1963, the extension of the compulsory age for school attendance to 14 years (Shavit and Westerbeek 1998). Obligatory education thence required a five-year cycle of primary education followed by a middle school cycle covering grades 6 to 8. This obligatory schooling complete, students could continue to one of 4 upper secondary institutes. Those who successfully completed the upper secondary institute that specialised in general education were eligible for admission to university. Other institutes specialised in technical, vocational, artistic (*liceo artistico*) and teacher training-related education (Shavit and Westerbeek 1998, 34). As such, keypunch operators attended Busa's training school instead of attending one of the institutes mentioned above, which is not to imply that the duration or quality of the training provisioned by CAAL was on par with that of an upper secondary institute. Yet there certainly was a sense that keypunch operator training in CAAL constituted a form of continuing vocational training and education.

The Italy in which the *Index Thomisticus'* training school was set up was thus delivering rapidly expanding access to education (Shavit and Westerbeek 1998, 37). Individuals born between 1930 and 1959, a cohort that includes a number of the individuals who were hired to keypunch the *Index Thomisticus*, benefited from enhanced access to education and had a higher probability of completing that education. Rates of completion of middle and secondary school increased significantly among this cohort: "The number of Italians with middle-school diplomas increased from 5.9 per cent in 1951 to 14.7 per cent in 1971, while those completing secondary school education increased from 3.3 per cent to 6.9 per cent" (Dunnage 2002, 160–61; see also Shavit and Westerbeek 1998, 38–41). As mentioned, numbers entering university increased too. Overall, the impact of gender and socioeconomic inequality on educational attainment declined (Shavit and Westerbeek 1998, 41).

Yet, there remained "significant and large gender differences in the long odds of success" in favour of men (Shavit and Westerbeek 1998, 45). Progress was unevenly distributed, with levels of educational attainment increasing earlier for men than women, disregarding those born during the second world war (Shavit and Westerbeek 1998, 38). And in the post-war period, even when a woman had a secondary school diploma or degree, the fact of having this qualification didn't make a great difference to her ability to secure a job (Bison 2013a, 175–6). These dynamics can be detected in the *Index Thomisticus* too. One interviewee recalled that the training she and her fellow keypunch operators received in the training school was "absolutely innovative". Yet, CAAL was run not as a meritocracy but in a way that furthered the careers and knowledge of its male employees predominately. Promotion prospects within CAAL were extended to male employees only, as were career development activities. For example, de Tollenaere noted that the men who became machine operators were "able to assist the lectures at the technical school for Industry" (de Tollenaere 1963a, 8) while no comparable external opportunities for female trainees are recorded or recalled. CAAL can accordingly be viewed as a microcosm of the wider Italian situation, where the education and training opportunities that were being opened to the population were not transmuting into gains that were equally distributed across a population where the patriarchal gender-order continued to hold sway. In fact, apprenticeship schemes, when they were abused, seem to have been one of the ways that Italian employers shut down some of the opportunities that were notionally being opened for women through expanding access to education, training and some sections of the labour market. The question of whether Busa used the apprenticeship scheme in exactly this way is a difficult to answer with a simple "yes" or "no".

Despite having completed their obligatory education, the young women who were admitted to the training school were minors, as evoked by the requirement for their parents or guardians, rather than they themselves, to sign a statement confirming that they accepted the Regulations. The Regulations pre-empt any expectation that their working hours would accord with the state educational system: "The courses do not follow the usual terms of state schools. In particular, they do not allow for long periods of holidays except in summer. Normally they allow one whole day free in addition to

Sunday" (CAAL n.d.). Attendance was mandatory for a minimum of four hours a day, five days a week for ten months of the year; daily timetable and attendance requirements were subject to change. Perhaps implicitly referring to the external contracts that the keypunch operators also worked on during their time in CAAL, it is specified:

> The Directorate may require more hours of attendance. These will not be obligatory except for short periods, or for particular courses of theory whether at Gallarate or elsewhere; such courses will not last for more than a month and will not involve the trainee in any expense.
>
> (CAAL, n.d.)

In a 1967 letter to Tasman, Busa indicates that some staff of the centre had spent "week-ends [sic] in Milan IBM premises" (Busa 1967), perhaps availing of facilities during down-time.

The Regulations also specify that apprentices should not previously have been employed elsewhere. The rationale for this may be linked to the decree of the Ministry of Labor and Social Security that applied to the training school from at least 1960.[22] Despite a concerted and repeated search in relevant archives, online databases and with assistance from a legal professional in Milan, the text of this decree is still not located at the time of writing. A letter from Busa to Tasman, discussing IBM's then recent closure of CAAL[23], may cast light on what it contained. Busa writes that he was not troubled by the closure of CAAL except in two particulars, one being:

> ... it seems to me that it would have been reasonable to keep alive the Gallarate centre (in Gallarate or elsewhere, e.g. in Rome): as a punching section specialised for literary punching: as many universitarian [sic] projects do not go into realisation because of the problems of getting an extremely clean input, and because our costs are more than half cheeper [sic], being non-profit, no salary for me, and a training school *without social security burdens*.
>
> (Busa 1967; emphasis mine)

Employers in Italy were permitted to pay low rates of social security on behalf of apprentices (Commissione 1959, 417). Busa's correspondence to Tasman raises the possibility that a full social security exemption from the Ministry of Labour and Social Security may have been obtained for the training school. The existence of such an exemption, whether partial or complete, raises various unanswered questions: would the government have covered apprentices' social security contributions? Could such an exemption have meant that they were potentially left two years short of payments towards benefits like old age pension if they joined the training school towards the later points of the specified age range?

The Regulations also proposed that, "On completing the course and passing the practical tests the trainees will receive a regular certificate" (CAAL n.d.). Students of the centre, both male and female, were also to receive, for the unspecified year in which the document was written, not wages as such, but a study grant or bursary of 120,000 lire.

Additional "Prizes for encouragement" were also to be dispensed. To put the bursary amount in context, Busa invoiced the *instituto di Biologia e Zoologia Generale della Facoltà di Medicina dell'Università* on 27 June 1959, 12,600 lire for the punching of about 3200 cards (Busa 1959b). Based on his estimation elsewhere that in 1961 "we punched an average of 135 fully punched cards per man-hour" (Busa 1964, 69), and not taking time for verifying into account, this means that the services of the key-punch operators could be sub-contracted for about 525 lire per hour. With enough external contracts, keypunch operators could return their yearly bursary sum to CAAL within about three months of work (based on a 20-hour week). Their work may have been low-paid but for CAAL it was far from low-value. For an extended period of a given year trainees could essentially provide CAAL with free labour.

Today, the availability to undertake an unpaid or meagrely paid internship is often associated with pre-existing economic stability and a class position that enables individuals to forego, or to be able to tolerate being required to forgo, recompense in lieu of training or another factor that employers can package as value-laden (e.g. Crain 2016). The Regulations can be read as assuming a similar socioeconomic profile of applicants, in that it states that bursaries would be given to students at the end of the academic year only, implying that apprentices were to be engaged without ongoing recompense. A note is included to the effect that "Bi-monthly advances will be granted on the written request of parents or guardians only in cases of exceptional poverty and at the discretion of the Course Director" (CAAL n.d.). It is difficult, however, to imagine how students who faced financial hardship could participate in such a course in the first instance.

The Regulations do not make a commitment to maintaining the grant amount or to distributing it yearly; some newspaper reports may be read as indicating that bursaries were not distributed to every student, but rather to "deserving" students (*La Prealpina* 1962). The bursary amount, then, was very far from handsome, and the suggestion that some trainees may have worked for long periods without remuneration, or indeed, may even have worked without any remuneration is troubling though hardly unheard of in internship arrangements. Indeed, the Regulations offer the bursary next to a commitment that students would receive theoretical and practical instruction throughout the two years that their courses lasted. The usefulness and longer-term economic value-creation potential of this would have been significant, were it to be delivered. It seems that students were essentially being asked to make a "trade-off" between, on the one hand, the opportunity to undertake "free courses of technical instruction" (CAAL n.d.) that would ultimately improve their prospects with symbolic capital and, on the other hand, regular remuneration.

The final aspect of the Regulations to be brought out here is the warning that students could be excluded from CAAL if they "fail to fulfil their obligations or ... [if their] behaviour is seriously undisciplined or immoral". Presumably with a view to reducing opportunities for "immoral behaviour" (CAAL n.d.), when CAAL was located in via G. Ferraris, its staff seem to have been required to use sex-separated entrances.[24] One interviewee recalled that male and female students had separate cloakrooms. They recalled how respective cloakrooms each had a door that opened onto the technical work floor of CAAL, providing a sex-separated entrance and exit routes for staff. A generous way of understanding the morality requirement, and the efforts made to monitor it, is that CAAL was *in loco parentis* of its young charges, and it was taking seriously its duty of care towards them. And surely it cannot be faulted for this. Yet the particularly Catholic context of the school is relevant to too. As Caldwell writes:

> Any examination of the corpus of statements from the Church fathers reveals a profound preoccupation with the question of the relations between the two sexes and the idea of the body, the place of marriage and virginity and the intractability of sexual desire.
>
> (Caldwell 1991, 16)

Those preoccupations were actively mobilised by the Church in the Italy of the *Index Thomisticus* and "its positions have had substantial effect in debates about the place of women and the family in Italy" (Caldwell 1991, 8). Through the *Index Thomisticus*, then, we encounter a fascinating conjuncture as dynamics like the Catholic Church's attitudes to women, to sexuality, the precarious labour arrangements of the Italian economic miracle and indeed wider cultural stereotypes of women framed the nature and limits of the gendered encounter with technology in this early and influential digital humanities project.

Regulations

That the "Document of Regulations" (CAAL n.d.) might best be read as an aspirational document, an imaginary of the training school that Busa would have wished to create, is suggested by a series of complaints raised by the technical staff of CAAL and the training school from late 1959 through to early 1960.

In late 1959, documentation records the "general psychological situation" of male trainees as one of "a continuous deep discontent" (CAAL 1959). Their discontent stemmed from their perception of being engaged in work that they felt to be repetitive and mechanical. They claimed that neither the theoretical instruction nor recompense they had been promised had been discharged.[25] In Busa's short reply to the 1959 complaints, he seems to reject their validity but indicates that new staff members would join the team (to deliver the theoretical instruction, perhaps). He also calls for the "collaboration of the trainees; at the moment their discipline is somewhat lacking" (Busa 1959f).

Though male technicians are mentioned all through the 1959 document of complaint, it closes by positioning the issue in a way that this book interprets as extending beyond male technical staff. Notably, the male operators ask for CAAL to institute "an absolute equality of treatment in everything that does not depend exclusively on length of service or the intrinsic ability of the individual, i. e. in relation to the specific tasks carried out by each person within the Centre" (CAAL 1959). That the male machine operators' call for equality of treatment can reasonably be read as pertaining to all members of the training school and CAAL, male and female alike, is further bolstered by documents from the early 1960s, showing that male and female staff alike were perceived to have been treated unfairly (and so a call for all staff to be treated equitably is plausible). Discontent was very much in the air. According to the archival traces that remain of these events, the complaints that were submitted and documented in early 1960 were initiated or synthesised following some kind of a fact-finding intervention by a person who seems to have been a fellow priest.[26] How this individual came to act in this intermediary capacity is currently unclear. The tone and manner in which this individual recorded some staff complaints does, however, suggest his exasperation at how the school was then being run:

> ... the Italian Ministry of Labour "officially recognizes the Centre and acknowledges [?*illegible*] it as 'a Centre for Professional Training for operators [male] of Automation Service for Business Accounting'";
> –not even Padre Busa would be completely convinced of this pre-valently disciplinary aim (he is afraid of inspection visits, he does not publish the Regulations of the Centre, which he does not give even to [a staff member who appears to have had a supervisory function], nor does he let the operators [male] and their families have them) ...
>
> (Unknown 1960)

That this discontent was not limited to male employees of the school is indicated in a letter that is quite unique because it is one of the few currently known to be extant that records the experiences of a keypunch operator in her own voice, close to the time when the events the letter discusses actually occurred. The female member of staff emphasises in the letter that she wrote it only on the suggestion of the Intermediary (thereby presumably communicating the matter more formally) (Lettera Della Sig.Na. 1960). Echoing the complaints made by the male operators mentioned above, this letter further suggests that the terms promised, what this book refers to as the "apprenticeship trade-off" were not being met. Training was not being delivered to all staff as had been promised; gender was a factor in decisions about who could use which machines. Clarifying the nature of this latter objection, the letter-writer explained: "if the [male] Head of Department were to change often, it would be the case that I should have to teach them while being under their authority" (Lettera Della Sig.Na. 1960). This asymmetry was not limited to the *Index Thomisticus* but has been foregrounded in histories of computing where it is understood as being part and parcel of "attempts to shape the newly developing digital economy" along gendered lines (Hicks 2017, 1).

In a slightly later publication, CAAL was noted to have had just one permanent technical employee, a young woman who was described as being in a position of responsibility "supervis[ing] permanently the punching and the other mechanical work" (de Tollenaere 1963a, 8). That a young woman was the only member of staff to be permanently employed by CAAL looks, on the surface, to be a progressive step. However, this may be read as having been linked to the (however short-term) economic gains that could be won by employers who instituted sex-segregated workflows and workplaces, paying some groups of individuals less than another irrespective of the content of their work. That the *Index Thomisticus* benefited from this, and that, in fact, some trainees seem even to have gone financially unpaid[27] for their work is claimed in these documents of complaint.

The early 1960 letter composed by the Intermediary poses to Busa a "request for clarification" in relation to a detailed list of complaints pertaining to male and female technical staff alike. We read of the severe underemployment of one individual who worked, "solely on operations of mainly manual correction, so much so that ... [there exist] fears that she is losing the skill she acquired as a card-puncher" (Unknown 1960). The problem of remuneration is raised, and emphasis is placed on the grossly inadequate basic recompense of one female staff member, and the overlooking of her decisive contributions to the project: her "personal gifts and merits ... and her essential functions in the Centre in the specific area of punching, new punching, codes and traced [?][28] cards)" (Unknown 1960).

It is claimed that study grants had not been disbursed to some male and female staff; where remuneration had been distributed it seems to have been to young men. A complaint is made about the inconsistently generous remuneration given to two young men "who, after requesting a certain increase in the study grant, receive an "extraordinary" reward (i.e. not the one of "encouragement" normally recognised by the Regulations) of 30,000 lire each in "recognition of their continuous excellent work and serious approach" (Unknown 1960). This one-off reward was well in excess of the entire monthly pay of some young women in the centre. Elsewhere, the treatment of a young woman whose work also merited a reward, is recalled:

Padre Busa, having to pay a perforator [female] of the Centre ... for extraordinary and meritorious work, promised to do so the next time. The next time was when this lady retired from the Centre: Padre Busa made this payment coincide with her severance payment.

(Lettera Della Sig.Na. 1960)

Looked at together, these incidents also seem to suggest that while, on paper, the Regulations of the school propose that female keypunch operators and male machine operators would be remunerated equally, in the practice of the day-to-day execution of the *Index Thomisticus*, this did not always prove to be the case.

The 1960 letter of complaint compiled by the Intermediary likewise refers to how a female member of the training school had been removed from a supervisory role, referring to "the less than convincing way in which the [female head of department] was put to one side" (Unknown 1960). From oral history interviews and archival documents there is indeed reasonable grounds to infer that female members of staff did, at various times, hold posts in the training school that were managerial or supervisory in nature if not in name.

One former keypunch operator recalled her time in a supervisory role, though in a somewhat disjunctured way, making it difficult to extract a linear narrative of her recollections from the interview. The fundamentals of the account are that when the man who had previously been Head of Department left CAAL, Busa asked a female member of staff to take on this role: "Father Busa said, "Since this man here is leaving, you are now supervisor in charge" ... Because, in fact, all those women depended on me [laughter]" (The Operator et al. 2014). At some later date, Busa attempted to replace her in that role with a man, even though that particular man was less experienced and less knowledgeable than she: "I don't know if under Jesuit influence or so, he didn't—because I was in charge of the group—he tried to substitute me with a man" (The Operator et al. 2014).

The Operator recalled that the staff of the project rebelled, because it was known that she was highly skilled. It seems that she could deliver the training in house, presumably obviating the need for students to spend time and money traveling to Milan for training:

> Exactly, just that more or less everyone – we also had men who arrived later for the sorting and tabulating machines – even the men revolted because the men's course, the one on the sorting machines etc. would have then been in Milan. But I had learned on my own.
>
> (The Operator et al. 2014)

This talk of revolt does seem to suggest that the events recalled here represented some kind of redemptive narrative for the interviewee (e.g. Schiff, McKim and Patron 2017). That this incident occurred is, however, probable, based on the internal evidence of the 1959 and 1960 documents of complaint and external inference.

For much of the period under examination, beliefs about the inherent unsuitability of women for management roles were widely held. In contemporaneous literature, for example, it was observed that while other variations were possible, "A natural path of promotion is from equipment operator to analyst to supervisor" (Van Ness 1963, 153). Thus, it was usually male machine (or equipment) operators only who could be promoted as possibilities for promotion beyond the keypunching department were not usually open to women. Haigh has observed that within the keypunch department, for female keypunch operators "As in most other white-collar jobs, their most realistic avenue of advancement from this position was to over-see other women, in this case as a supervisor of keypunch operations" (Haigh 2001, 83).

Busa appears, then, to have been on the exceptionally conservative end of the spectrum in not countenancing that female keypunch operators could formally supervise other women. Yet, this woman does indeed seem to have performed a management role, which extended into the male machine operator domain too, at least for a time. Perhaps, then, Busa was content for The Operator to perform the duties of a supervisor in an unofficial way only. Perhaps the presumption underlying the decision to initially allocate the work to her, before replacing her in that role with a less knowledgeable man ("the other one didn't know anything", she recalled) was that this could be done without detriment to the wider project. She could, it seems, be required to continue to perform the role *de facto*, without recognition, recompense or even a rightful claim to continue in the role. Given the complaints set out above regarding the unfairness of remuneration and the overlooking of individuals contributions to the project the suggested scenario does not seem outlandish.

Keypunch operators may have been framed in their hiring and training, and in the communication of their work, as women who executed undemanding posts that required little education or training, and as being without the capacity to progress to more senior roles. But this is once more belied by the events that surrounded the putting aside of the female manager, which involved a highly competent young woman being expected to compensate for the deficiencies of some of her hierarchically senior male colleagues. Despite The Operator's recollection that "even the men revolted" (The Operator et al. 2014) when Busa sought to replace her, from her oral history interview, it does indeed seem to have been the case that she was replaced with a male supervisor.

This experience of thwarted progression and gender discrimination may not have been a one off. Cervini does not portray her experiences regarding progression in a way that corresponds with The Operator, but the state of affairs alluded to in her testimony may be similar. She recalls that she was "sort of the boss for the new, young girls" (Cervini et al. 2014). The qualifier "sort of" may again point to how a role was executed in function if not in name. This suggestion is also plausible from the perspective of the timeline, as the periods these individuals spent working on the *Index Thomisticus* was not co-terminus. Female punched card operators of the *Index Thomisticus* could not, it seems, hold more senior roles in Busa's centre that were also recognised as such.

Yet, what is most fascinating about these examples of inequality is not the fact that they occurred, for as has been intimated in the techno-social and historical contextualisation of CAAL already set out, these were practices that were adopted by employers of the day on a scale that prompted government intervention in an attempt to ameliorate them.[29] Rather, what is most interesting is how some staff of CAAL and the training school pushed against this unequal treatment and called for a fairer workplace.

Even if the Regulations may have been written to meet the stipulations and procedural requirements of apprenticeship regulation, they may also be understood as capturing Busa's imaginary of CAAL and the training school. The Regulations present the training school as an orderly and predictable place of training and data capture, where students and their parents should conform to stated rules and behave according to Catholic stipulations of moral rectitude, with Busa as arbiter of cases of extreme poverty. That the *Index Thomisticus* would, as portrayed in the documents of complaint, become a place of contestation and discontent, where the power dynamic between management and staff, and even Busa's own authority would be challenged, is certainly not envisaged in the Regulations. Yet, in the space of contestation that emerged between the Regulations of the school, and the day-to-day execution of the *Index Thomisticus* as the school's staff experienced it, Busa and the wider Directorate of the school were arguably offered valuable lenses that could have assisted in the acknowledgement and redress of the unequal treatment of the *Index Thomisticus'* staff. These were lenses onto the *Index Thomisticus*, that were not, however, to be peered through during this stage of computing in the humanities.

Contestation and discontent

The above episodes of crisis and contestation evoke the troublesome relationships that could exist between amanuenses and scholars, as set out in Chapter 1. They also allow us to look beyond the exceptionalist reports on CAAL that have appeared in the media and academic literature, revealing the radically different narratives that can be foregrounded when the perspectives and experiences of those who actually executed the *Index Thomisticus* on a day-to-day basis are attended to. This suggests new ways of narrativising the "deep history" of present-day digital humanities, looking beyond those stories that portray it as a place of technological advancement, to explore it as a space of contestation and debate, to which many voices, some well-known, some lesser known, can be shown to have contributed.

In the episodes recalled in this chapter, we catch sight of CAAL as a locus of dissent, where male technicians felt obliged to call for the school to be run in a way that actually corresponded with its own document of Regulations. We also see them challenge the inconsistent, unpredictable and unequal treatment of the technical workforce as a whole. And when the documents relating to this period of discontent are read together, the details they contain do attest to how the project's female keypunch staff were particularly constrained. Female staff were prevented from operating machinery used by male operators, from participating in training that was open to male operators, from holding managerial positions even when they were qualified to do so and would otherwise be managed by men with less knowledge and experience than they. Female members of staff were paid the lowest wages of all, despite their valuable contributions to the work of the *Index Thomisticus*.

Yet, most crucially of all, far from seeing the treatment of CAAL's staff as an inevitable instance of how things had to be, the project's male operators notably called for the above-cited "equality of treatment" for each person in the centre.

In their calls for equality of treatment for the staff of CAAL, the male technicians arguably signalled that they too understood that workflows, definitions of skill and expertise, and their interlinking with gender were and are neither inevitable, objective nor immutable. Abbate has written how "Gender categories are not fixed; they must be constantly maintained through the actions and interactions of individual people, and in the process, they may be modified, strengthened, or challenged" (Abbate 2012, 4). One way that they are strengthened, is through "vertical segregation" where women (along with minorities and lower-class males) are relegated to positions of lower esteem and apparently lower ability, while processes of "horizontal segregation" demarcate areas of endeavour and inquiry as those of women or men (Harding 1986, 58). It follows that narratives which position gender as determinative of professional roles and prospects may become entrenched in organisations, through multiple pathways, but they are neither immutable nor inviolable. Neither are those narratives invisible to all those around them, as the complaints of the male staff, and the apparent exasperation of the Intermediary, himself a priest, who communicated them, indicate. Even when such narratives are given structural significance and purchase within an organisation, it is not inevitable that they will be met with absolute assent, as the complaints of the' *Index Thomisticus*' male operators also attest.

This is an important rejoinder to the objection that historical actors like Busa were, to quote a peer reviewer of the original proposal for this book "simply acting as many then did" and that "it is wrong to apply current attitudes and beliefs to the past, however strongly we may hold them". This critique seems to imply that Busa was a thoughtless prisoner of his times, a man whose actions effortlessly corresponded with a static and monolithic arrangement of external circumstances, against which no resistance of any form was exerted. This critique is explicitly challenged by the events recounted above, which suggest that Busa's staff did not interpret their circumstances as a neutral, natural and, above all, an inevitable instance of "what [was] going on". Rather, Busa's staff pushed against their treatment and brought their dissatisfaction to his attention, suggesting that the aforementioned "current attitudes and beliefs" are not, in fact, unique to this present day and neither was just one set of beliefs in circulation in Busa's day.

In other words, this book explicitly rejects the suggestion that Busa was "simply acting as many then did" because it disempowers Busa and his staff and presents the past as though it were homogeneous in the sense of being dominated by one ideology that eclipsed all others and was uncritically accepted by all. Rather, this book argues that Busa's stance was neither unthinking nor inevitable, but came about as a result of a series of choices, made by individuals, groups and wider society, which did benefit from the wider realities of social and gender-based inequality. Yet, in examining the technological, economic, knowledge-based, social and disciplinary factors that contributed to the diminishing of women's contributions to the *Index Thomisticus*, the point is not to judge Busa as an individual, or to suggest that he acted with malice (see Introduction). As we have seen, Busa was very far from a lone operator in this arena and he was working in difficult circumstances which may have served to focalise "the product" over and above critical reflection on the process. Nevertheless, this book argues that it is important to recognise that this foundational project of the digital humanities sought to constrain and limit female workers in particular (and, some male technicians too) and to learn from how and why this came about, so that the possibility, at least, of a more equal future for digital humanities workers can be opened.

Bridge

In the course of this chapter and book, we encounter CAAL and the training school in multiple formations and guises. Recalling the variety of the amanuensis tradition (see Chapter 1), CAAL and the training school show a propensity to shapeshift to the gaze of internal, external and imagined audiences. Like an origami artwork, CAAL could be, and can be, assembled and told, *inter alia*, as a story of automation in the humanities; as a space of boundary setting and gatekeeping; as a social space where wider gender relations and inequalities were both reanimated and contested; and as a place of political engagement and even revenue generation, where photoshoots and technical demonstrations were staged to impress visiting dignitaries and win keypunching contracts.[30] CAAL also had a deeply protective and personal resonance for some who encountered it. Above, we have seen that for one operator's mother, CAAL and the training school were places where her daughter could be protected from the external world for a time.

Not unlike his scientific colleagues, then, Busa was working in the midst of variety and, for a significant proportion of his time in Gallarate, locational impermanence. Thus, Busa arguably had to work to create for CAAL and the emerging field of humanities computing "'the same' conditions and techniques in different places in order to render it, like a laboratory, a 'placeless place' in which scientists might successfully replicate results and thus create empirically based assent" (Nyhart 2016, 14). Indeed, discussions of how computing might make the Humanities more empiricist are often taken up in Busa's writings (see Passarotti and Nyhan 2019). And within this "placeless place", a constant feature of the *Index Thomisticus* was its strict bifurcation into scholarly and technical, and the distribution of its tasks according to gender rather than expertise, experience or knowledge in the first instance. Among the most enduring features of the *Index Thomisticus*, features that were replicated from location to location, were segregation and inequality.

This chapter has explored some of the very real difficulties that Busa encountered when he sought to pursue humanities computing in post-war Italy at the scale he desired. In the extant literature, the fundraising activities of Busa have often been discussed with reference to large, multinational corporations like IBM, his connections with Italian businessmen and the Catholic Church and more recently, the geopolitical dynamics of the cold war (see e.g. Jones 2016, 113). This chapter has suggested that a crucial facet of the "fundraising" for the *Index Thomisticus* was raised through the cheap labour that was extracted from trainees through what seem to have been positioned as a series of apprenticeship arrangements. By hiring young women, without prior experience or recourse to the most basic of employment benefits like social security, it was possible to dramatically reduce costs and, of course, wages, which remain one of the costliest outlays of digital humanities projects to this day. Through the *Index Thomisticus*, the field of digital humanities is in some ways a downstream beneficiary of a project that leveraged an Italian labour market that in turn profited from positioning women, in particular, as a cheap and transient labour force.

Yet, as we shall see, positioning the work of keypunch operators as transient, interchangeable, low-skilled and outside scholarship proper was arguably a poor response to the issues that the *Index Thomisticus* faced. It was 5 to have detrimental consequences in terms of the retainment of highly trained staff and, more speculatively, for the timely completion of the *Index Thomisticus*. Signs of the negative consequences of the *Index Thomisticus'* labour force organisation were already apparent in early 1961, when a visitor to Busa's lab observed of the staff of the centre:

> The personnel neither was altogether satisfactory. … the running of the machines by pupils, who after a course of two years leave the CAAL for the industry, is not ideal. For such a center a professional staff, not an accidental one, is necessary.
>
> (de Tollenaere 1963a, 28)

In the next chapter, we will zoom in on the experiences, context and narratives of the female keypunch operators themselves.

Notes

1 Around the end of the 1950s and the beginning of the 1960s, the average industrial wage in factories in Bologna (among all workers, at all levels including apprentices, regardless of gender) was between 25,000 and 28,000 lire per month (Betti 2020, 111).

2 Jackson has observed: "The association between the laboratory and science, moreover, remains distinctly Anglophone: in Italy, for example, the word *laboratorio* continues to refer generically to workshops in a wide range of artisanal and artistic as well as scientific settings" (Jackson 2016, 297). A study into Busa's use of words for laboratory in his Italian, French and English-language publications

might be instructive as to the interactions between emergent humanities computing and industry more generally considering the "laboratory turn" in the humanities that would follow later (see Pawlicka-Deger 2020).

3 It is recorded in this way on headed notepaper used in 1961. Slight variations of this name can also be found. For example, on the 1961 certificate that was awarded to students upon completion of their training, the name of the school is given as "*Centro Di Addestramento Professionale Per Operatori Di Servizi Automazione Contabilità Aziendali*" (see Chapter 3).

4 Busa seems to have sought to maintain control over the information about CAAL that was put into the public domain by voices other than his own. This is suggested by the anecdotal comments that were made to me by a former colleague of Busa about the input that Busa sought to provide to articles about CAAL that were published in *La Prealpina*. Hints of this may be detectable elsewhere too, for example, a 1966 *U.S. Catholic* article includes unattributed quotations and paraphrasing from another of Busa's published articles (Nyhan and Passarotti 2019, 93), perhaps implying that Busa had input to the writing of that newspaper article? Likewise in a letter that de Tollenaere wrote to Busa, de Tollenaere mentioned "… you made me swear an oath, that I should not publish a single letter about the CAAL without your <u>imprimatur</u>" [underlining in original] (de Tollenaere 1962).

5 IBM subsidiaries sometimes paid for staff to pursue short-term projects using IBM machinery in CAAL's premises, with Busa's input. For example, in March 1959, Busa wrote how "Mr Wieland Schmidt, a student of Prof Schadewaldt of Tübingen University has been appointed by IBM Deutschland (Dr. E. Aikele Boeblingen) and by Goethe-Woerterbuch (through Prof. Schadewaldt) to work out in my Laboratory the Index of Goethe's *Farbenlehre*. He is now with me in Gallarate and we together we work [sic] to the above said Index …" (Busa 1959c). In April of that year, in a letter to Allen Kent, Busa mentioned that the student was paid for by "IBM Germany" (Busa 1959d). The short publication that followed, and was related to this work is: Busa 1960b. Elsewhere in Busa's publications, the work on the *Farbenlehre* is described as being among "selected works useful for obtaining a method [for the *Index Thomisticus*] (Texts of the *Qumran*, Kant's *Prolegomena*, Goethe's *Farbenlehre* b.3, St Bernard's *De Diligendo Deo*, and some others)" (Busa 2019f[1964], 88). This episode evokes the contingency that shaped the *Index Thomisticus* and of Busa's skill in portraying the contingent or serendipitous as intentional.

6 For example, Ott recalled Busa's kindness. When Ott was supporting Father Bonifatius Fischer's work on a concordance to the Vulgate, Busa shared a copy of his *Lexicon Electronicum Latinum* (LEL) with them and they used it as a basis for lemmatisation (Nyhan and Flinn 2016, 59).

7 To advance this, he set up fund raising committees, which included, for a time, the Cardinal who would go on to become Pope Paul VI see (e.g. Ubell 1964).

8 *La Prealpina* is an independent daily newspaper that was founded in the city of Varese on December 1888 with the intention of reporting on regional events, news and entrepreneurial endeavour. Its newsroom in Gallarate was founded in 1947 (La Prealpina 2020). *L'Italia* was a Catholic and political daily newspaper founded in 1912 by Cardinal Andrea Ferrari, who was archbishop of Milan at the time (Treccani 2020).

9 Busa's work was covered in media outlets in Europe, the USA, Israel and beyond. In this way, he performed a significant service to the public communication of the field that later came to be known as digital humanities, an aspect of his career that is under-researched.

10 "For the first time in Italy. [The] School of automation at the centre for literary analysis: the course for mechanographic accounting must be supported and helped" (*La Prealpina* 1957).

11 This is suggested by a letter that Busa sent to Rev. P. Angelo Serra: "As regards the perforating and the checking, you may contact … the Laboratory in Via

Novara 12, Gallarate, the telephone of which is now only in the [house of] the Sironi family: ... (between 9–12 and 14–17). For the successive operations, however, it will be necessary to meet at Gallarate in the other Laboratory on a date to be decided" (Busa 1959b).

12   Photos and videos taken during the inauguration and blessing of CAAL at the Aloisianum in 1956 suggest this by showing young women seated at punched card machines (Busa Archive #0077; #0084; #0085). In March 1959, a young woman is again pictured keypunching in the Aloisianum (Busa Archive #0154). Some secondary reports also claim that the *Index Thomisticus* was based in the Aloisianum at an early stage (e.g. O'Neill 1964). Present-day inhabitants of the Aloisianum whom I asked about this seemed doubtful, however, and suggested that the machines had been brought to the Aloisianum for the purposes of publicity and staged photographs only.

13   About the Valentini workshop we currently know little, just that Sr. Valentini did own a mechanics firm (Jones 2016, 122) and that the building's owner was a textile manufacturer, Sr. Dragone (Jones 2016, 122).

14   In March and June 1959, pictures were taken in the location given by Busa as "Cuccirelli" or "Ditta Cuccirelli" [the firm of Cuccirelli] (Handlist n.d.). Based on the appearance of the space captured in those photos, and keypunch operators' mention of having worked in a "basement underneath some Cuccirelli place" (Brogioli et al. 2014), it is possible that this is the cellar location that de Tollenaere referred to (1963a, cited above). The 1959 photos of the operations in the Cuccirelli firm feature mostly young, male technical workers. Clerics, some senior, clearly on some kind of a visit, are pictured too (e.g. Busa Archive #0147). Like the female operators who are also shown in a few of the photos from this location, the male operators wear white coats. Unlike the female operators, the names of some of the male operators are given by Busa, including Ing. L. Galdabini and Ing. DeAngelis Ercole. The photos in which they appear require further research, as those named individuals appear in some accounts to have held more senior roles in the project than that of machine operator, see e.g. (La Prealpina 1958). In any case, male workers are mostly shown standing, and engaged in machine operator duties (Busa Archive #0166). In some photos the male operators interact with Busa and his visiting guests (Busa Archive #0149). A few photos show men and women sitting together at accounting machines (e.g. Busa Archive #0167). Women invariably sit at the IBM 536 Printing Card Punch while men sit next to them at the IBM 858 Cardatypes. An IBM Electric Typewriter is placed next to each Cardatype. These machines were identified with the help of Max Campbell and IBM Corporate Archives (Campbell 2019). In contrast with the photos from Casa Sironi, then, it seems that at this stage the project may have had fairly state of the art equipment at its disposal (the Cardatype having been released just a few years earlier). IBM Corporate Archives hold pictures from 1959 that appear very similar to those that Busa labelled as having been taken in Ditta Cuccirelli. IBM Corporate Archives, however, refers to the location of their taking as the IBM Cucirelli [sic] Plant in Italy, suggesting that the photos may have been taken in the context of some kind of promotional or informational visit to this IBM plant. Thus they cannot be assumed to cast light on the machines that the *Index Thomisticus* had available to it in locations where CAAL was regularly housed.

15   Some are thanked on the Acknowledgement page of the *Index Thomisticus*, for example, Aldo Luigi Cuccirelli and Mario Valentini are thanked under the heading "*in re Oeconomica.*" Valentini also appears in numerous photographs in Busa's archive.

16   This was in line with setups elsewhere: "Tabulator and collator operators would work standing, sometimes overseen by multiple supervisors who might be men or women. Meanwhile, the women performing data input generally worked seated in large pools, overseen by a woman supervisor" (Hicks 2017, 65).

17 See, for example, Legge n. 25 del 19 gennaio 1955, "Gazzetta Ufficiale", n. 36, 14 February 1955. Available at: https://www.normattiva.it/uri-res/N2Ls?urn:nir:stato: legge:1955-01-19;25!vig=-01-19;25!vig.

18 On the longer history of the Catholic Church's shifting responses to liberal democracy, see Sigmund 1987.

19 For example, the MA/MSc programme in UCL, of which the author was Programme Director from 2017-2021.

20 *Legge n. 25 del 19 gennaio 1955*, "Gazzetta Ufficiale", n. 36, 14 February 1955. Available at: https://www.normattiva.it/uri-res/N2Ls?urn:nir:stato:legge:1955-01-19; 25!vig=.

21 I suggest this because of external and internal aspects of the document. External include that this document found its way into Busa's archive in the context of a tranche of papers that were later added to it, as discussed in the Introduction. Internal include the structure of the document, with its list of numbered state- ments, which is similar to the structure of many documents authored by Busa in the archive, along with the typeface of the document, which is similar to other letters and documents drawn up for Busa at this time.

22 On the certificates distributed to students who had completed their training is specified: "*decr. n. 9843/N del 4–2-1960 del Ministero del Lavoro e della Previdenza Sociale*" (decree ... of the Ministry of Labor and Social Security).

23 When CAAL was shut down by IBM in late 1967, the *Index Thomisticus* project was transferred to the "*Centro Nazionale Universitario di Calcolo Elettronico* (National University Computing Center) in Pisa" (Busa and Zampolli 1968). There it could avail of IBM computers in the next iteration of its work. After about two years in Pisa it moved to IBM in Boulder, Colorado, and in 1971 it moved to Venice. Busa later described the reasons for the moves as being driven by IBM's provision of computer time (Busa 1980, 85).

24 This phenomenon has also been observed in connection with women's entry in to the clerical workforce in England in the early twentieth century by Zimmeck (1986). Caldwell has discussed the segregation of men and women in the domestic and devo- tional realms in some parts of Italian society around this time (Caldwell 1991, 41).

25 De Tollenaere's account of his visit to CAAL, which occurred about 1,5 years after this period of discontent, suggests that the substantive issues had by then been resolved. His typescript records that students were following courses at IBM in addition to their work in the centre (though he does query whether this was indeed the case in notes that are attached to the main typescript). It also states that stu- dents were in receipt of scholarships (de Tollenaere 1963a, 8). The question of how closely de Tollenaere's summary reflects the day-to-day experiences of the technical staff is an open one, however. Archival correspondence indicates that de Tollenaere wrote to Busa in English or French, possibly indicating that his command of Ita- lian may not have been at a level that would have allowed him to converse freely with trainees of the school?

26 The document summarising these complaints bears a signature that seems to read "I Caniato". Busa's move to appoint Fr Caniato as Director of the Scientific divi- sion of CAAL was approved in April 1960, some months after the events explored in this section (Aggiornamento 1960).

27 Diego Righetti recalled the non-financial payment that he received from Busa during a later stage of the *Index Thomisticus* project: "Father Busa ... I had a big surprise at the end [of the work]. We didn't ask money for this and Father Busa was very, very generous and ... I was called by the ... priest of our ... Diocese. And he told me ... that ... the Pope ... conferred ... upon me, the honor of the knighthood of the Vatican, the knighthood of Saint Sylvester. I am: *sono cavaliere di San Silvestro al Vaticano.* ... And last year I discovered that my name is on ... *www.vatican.va* ... on the acts of the Holy Seal" (Righetti et al. 2014).

28 The translation of the Italian word given here remains unclear and is suggested to be "traced" or "sketched" or "outlined".

29 For example, *Legge n. 25 del 19 gennaio 1955*, "Gazzetta Ufficiale", n. 36, 14 February 1955. Available at: https://www.normattiva.it/uri-res/N2Ls?urn:nir:stato: legge:1955-01-19;25!vig= (accessed: 10 October 2020) sought to regulate apprenticeship contracts. The report Commissione parlamentare d'inchiesta sulle condizioni dei lavoratori in Italia, *Relazioni della Commissione parlamentare di inchiesta sulle condizioni dei lavoratori in Italia*, VIII, *Rapporti particolari di lavoro: contratto a termine, lavoro in appalto, lavoro a domicilio, apprendistato*, Segretariati generali della Camera dei deputati e del Senato della Repubblica, Roma 1959, delivers the results of a parliamentary inquiry (1953–1958) that investigated the conditions of industrial workers and sought to improve and better enforce the rules protecting them. Moreover, Commissione parlamentare d'inchiesta sulle condizioni dei lavoratori in Italia, *Relazioni della Commissione parlamentare di inchiesta sulle condizioni dei lavoratori in Italia*, VII, Tomo III, *Indagini sul rapporto di lavoro: qualifiche e carriera del lavoratore e trattamento e tutela delle lavoratrici*, Segretariati generali della Camera dei deputati e del Senato della Repubblica, Roma 1962 is another instalment of the above-mentioned inquiry, with a focus on the possibilities of professional development and the treatment of female workers.

30 The importance of creating a positive impression on potential clients and collaborators is indicated, for example, in a letter that Busa received from a representative of the Department of the Air Force, Department of Defence, USA. The author wrote of his and his colleagues visit to CAAL that "the operation seems to be the best controlled, most carefully studied text preparation group I have ever seen", before going on to ask Busa to send a quote for the keypunching work they wanted done (Pankowicz 1966). Photos and reports of those visits, including that of the first Minister for Science in Italy, Prof. Carlo Arnaudi, were carried in newspapers (e.g. La Prealpina 1964, 1965a) and so were crucial for courting support for the project in Italy and beyond.

4 On the "willingness to acknowledge mistakes"

Constructing the role of the keypunch operator

Introduction

Mahoney has argued:

> Whatever one wants to say about such abstractions as the Turing machine, it is hard to known how physical computers and the systems running on them could be anything other than socially constructed. Computing has no nature. It is what it is because people have made it so.
>
> (Mahoney 2011, 109)

Perhaps Mahoney did not intend unit record equipment, like accounting machines, in this discussion of computing. Accounting machines were neither universal nor stored programme computers. They were physical, modular, specialised machines—interlinked by the humans who used them and the punched cards they processed—that executed a series of tasks, in a particular order, to achieve the desired output. Still, this chapter will argue that Mahoney's observation holds largely true for the "computing" of the *Index Thomisticus*, which was made "so" by humans not only as they conceptualised and executed the computing of the *Index Thomisticus*, but also as they assigned subjective value assessments to the human-executed stages of that computing, judgements that were intertwined with socially-situated power differentials, including that of gender.

The previous chapters have looked at feminised keypunching labour and the circumstances in which it was done. They have accordingly explored pertinent historical, local and disciplinary perspectives that help explain why it was the work of the keypunch operators in particular that could be devalued despite the importance of this work to the *Index Thomisticus*. This chapter seeks to zoom in on the role of keypunch labour further, asking: how was the role of the keypunch operator actively constructed and enforced by the *Index Thomisticus*? By reading, as this chapter does, the criteria that were specified in the hiring, training and assessment of the *Index Thomisticus* keypunch operators as a way of understanding what was held to be an ideal keypunch operator, the techno-social order that was sought in this early encounter between automation and the humanities will be brought into view.

DOI: 10.4324/9781003138235-5

Seeking also to recentre the perspectives of keypunch operators, this chapter asks: what do we know of how the role of keypunch operator could be experienced by those who held it? And what possibilities beyond the *Index Thomisticus* might the experience of having worked as a keypunch operator have opened, or indeed closed, for individuals? In this, attention is again given to underlining the complexity of the space that this book explores. Keypunch operators arguably experienced epistemic injustice (Fricker 2007) in the context of the *Index Thomisticus* and digital humanities. However, their training nevertheless helped many individuals to secure good jobs in industry, jobs they would not otherwise have had access to. And while the main focus of this chapter remains on the local and the situated, attention is also drawn to the wider resonances of these processes, beyond Gallarate, and beyond the humanities, through an emblematic case study of the construction and portrayal of the role of the keypunch operator in the then-burgeoning and internationally-focused information processing and Machine Translation industry, given particular impetus by the Cold War.

Recruitment

That the role of keypunch operator was, indeed, explicitly advertised to young women is attested by the recruitment notices that were carried in Italian newspapers about the training school's courses and bursaries. In 1961, for example, at least four notices were carried in *L'Italia* and *La Prealpina* about a competition for study grants opened by Busa (*L'Italia* 1961a, 1961b; *La Prealpina* 1961a, 1961b). Eligible to apply were females over 14 years of age who had a typing diploma and had attained or were in the process of completing their lower middle school diploma (*L'Italia* 1961a). In other words, applicants with the legal minimum level of formal education were explicitly sought as keypunch operators, suggesting the role was actively framed as low-skilled from the earliest years of the training school.

The necessity of keeping costs down may partly explain why the role was framed in this way. The perception of keypunch operators' labour as manual or clerical and thus inherently less valuable and difficult than that of scholars is arguably also symbolised by this low hiring-bar. A procedural rationale may be relevant too: individuals with lower levels of formal education tended to be preferred for keypunch operator posts (Hicks 2017, 68–9; cf. Nace 1965, 568–9). This may have been linked to the belief that higher levels of accuracy could be obtained if individuals did not understand the material they were transcribing (see below). But by 1945, in the UK, "A government-wide inquiry found ... that better-educated 'grammar school girls' made much better punchers, able to produce consistently more characters per hour with higher accuracy" (Hicks 2017, 68). This is not to say that other models did not exist, or that they were unknown to Busa. If that particular report was not available to him, at least one other profile of keypunch operators did enter his purview. For example, a 1963 letter from Prof. Dr. Ferdinand Cap, regarding the Translation and Documentation Department of the University of Innsbruck, discussed the high-quality materials being created there. He wrote: "the typists who make the fair copies must combine mastery of mathematical and chemical expressions with good linguistic knowledge, and their work in turn must undergo a final check" (Cap 1963).

Discovery

Of the training school, Busa wrote that "for all those admitted, the requirement was that it was their first job" (Busa 1980, 85). Most of those interviewed confirmed this to have been the case. It is difficult to imagine young people harboring aspirations of becoming keypunch operators and it makes sense that interviewees recall applying to the school at the behest of others. A recent study, drawing on a dataset from 1996–8 has established a link between "finding a job without actively searching ('nonsearching')" (Kmec, McDonald and Trimble 2010, 213) and the acquisition of employment in a sex-segregated workplace (Kmec, McDonald and Trimble 2010). Given the "small world" nature of the field of digital humanities, and the prominent role intrapersonal connections are argued to have played in the structuring of the field (e.g. Gao 2021), a data-driven, historically-focused study of this phenomenon may add a useful empirical basis to analyses of the role and prominence of segregated labour in the emergence and development of computing in the humanities.

Many interviewees recalled learning about the *Index Thomisticus* project via Mother Cleofe, principal of the Canossian Institute, run by the Canossian Daughters of Charity, which many of them attended. Passarotti summarised that "It was the main private school in Gallarate (for girls only) ... While the Canossian Institute included primary, secondary school and one specific kind of high school ('Scuole Magistrali' in Italian: it was the school for teachers)" (Passarotti 2019b). Established in 1887 and located at Via Poma 1, 21013,[1] it was less than 2 kilometres from the Aloisianum.

In interviews, Mother Cloefe is recalled as a formidable and wise presence, who had understood at an early stage that keypunch training could open valuable employment opportunities for some of her students: "Mother Cleofe had said it beforehand ... take this course because you won't, you won't have any problems getting a job" ... "You'll find one right away, in fact" (Cervini et al. 2014). Of the cohort of keypunch operators interviewed, The Operator was hired earliest, around 1954, before the founding of CAAL proper. She too recalled the influence of Mother Cleofe:

> ... in 1953. Because I had finished, I had finished high school, the training school for teachers ... at the institute, but I had also completed a course in stenography to, to get a job. I went ... to say goodbye to the school's Principal [Mother Cleofe], and she mentioned it for the first time. "Look", she said, "there's this Father Busa who would like six girls to attend...". Back then there were six, she said, six young women, six, who

attended a course on, on the IBM machines. It was the first time that I …
and I said yes, let's give it a try (laughs).

(The Operator et al. 2014)

For present-day readers, the significance of being able to potentially secure not
just a job, but a good job, can perhaps be best appreciated when it is considered
against the reviews set out in Chapter 3 of the working conditions that many
experienced during the Italian economic miracle. That their Principal was correct in her estimation of the opportunities that keypunch training could open is
borne out in a number of interviews, as some interviewees discussed the valuable
employment they could access on account of having competed their training
with CAAL (see below). This reminds us of the resourcefulness of many of keypunch operators, and some older women around then, as they went on to create
a value from their training that was significant and that had not, perhaps, been
envisaged by Busa and others around him.

That it was, moreover, a consecrated member of the Catholic Church, in the
person of Mother Cleofe, who was supposedly encouraging the young women
towards the training school on the grounds of further employment is notable too.
The question of women's employment outside the home had been a highly vexed
issue in early post-war Italy. Carroll cited some of the speech that Pope Pius XII
gave immediately before the first national conference of the Union of Italian
Women (UDI) in 1945. Emphasising the doctrinaire that a woman's purpose in
life was procreation, he warned: "Women who do go out to work become dazed
by the chaotic world in which they live, blinded by the tinsel of false glamour
and greedy for sinister pleasures" (Caldwell 1991, 22). By the mid-1960s, however, "the vexed debates about women's work outside the home had also given
way to a grudging acceptance" (Caldwell 1991, 22).

That Mother Cleofe was, as recalled in interviews, apparently encouraging able
young women towards the labour market from the mid-1950s suggests that the
views of the Catholic Church and wider Italian society that would have sought to
confine women to the domestic sphere[2] may have been dominant but they were
neither singularly held nor, it seems, universally adhered to. That Busa was not
hiring married women—whose work for the *Index Thomisticus* may have been
perceived as a dereliction of their domestic duties—and that they were being
admitted to a training school, rather than formal employment, may have been a
productive distinction in such matters. Another way of interpreting this is through
the prism of Mother Cleofe's, and indeed Busa's religious vocations. The Canossian
Daughters of Charity include education among their acts of charity,[3] suggesting
that Mother Cleofe's guidance to the young women may have arisen in this context.
Interviewees did, however, recall having been encouraged towards the training
school because it would help them to get a job, perhaps suggesting that Mother
Cleofe's guidance did not emanate from her vocation alone. It does seem to be the
case that, notwithstanding what may have been their differing motivations, individuals like Mother Cleofe, and of course Busa, could take a rather practical view
and were willing to encourage or engage young women as apprentices.

Other interviewees learned of the school through family and friends with a direct connection to Busa. Crosta entered the school around 1961: "right after finishing high school after two years of doing nothing. (laughs) Nothing. ... my uncle, an engineer, back then the mayor of Gallarate, told me, 'go to Father Busa'. And I started from there" (Crosta et al. 2014).

Mainardi recalled that she commenced training around 1964. She was also routed to the *Index Thomisticus* through the Canossians, seemingly following a slightly circuitous route: "Right after the third year of high school – I had a friend who was already working there and through her – she also went to the Canossian school. And I had – well that's where I went to high school" (Mainardi et al. 2014).

In this way, the oral history interviews capture the previously undocumented routes through which Busa sought to attract pupils to the training school. A snowball effect appears to have been created. Leveraging his contacts from across Gallarate's social spectrum, Busa raised interest in the school with Mother Cleofe and the Canossian Daughters of Charity; with political figures like the Mayor of Gallarate and local industrialists[4] along with individuals mentioned in interviews such as Favaro Nazzareno.[5] It is male industrialists and political figures who are mentioned in the acknowledgements and paratexts of the *Index Thomisticus*, but the bridging and networking work of Mother Cleofe must have been consequential too.

That Mother Cleofe is remembered in the oral history interviews, rather than in more formal publications or archival sources pertaining to the *Index Thomisticus* is not particularly unusual. With regard to the study of literary history, for example, Kaltenbrunner has summarised how:

> Canonical views of literary history typically exclude whole groups of potentially relevant actors, such as women as writers, translators, and mediators in the literary scene ... Although various currents of feminist and critical theory have drawn attention to such bias ..., they have not managed to actually replace longstanding canonical traditions.
>
> (Kaltenbrunner 2015, 208)

Those canonical traditions are not yet replaced in digital humanities either. Yet, through oral history it has been possible to recall to the historical record the role of Mother Cleofe, and to show that women played a variety of overlooked roles, from keypuncher to networker and even advocate, in the *Index Thomisticus* project and its wider orbit. Most optimistically, perhaps, through these recollections we are reminded that neither gender nor technology were or are immutable, confined to one register or necessarily determinative of persistent devalued conditions. Even within the limiting conditions of the *Index Thomisticus* it is clear that technology, and female networks, could be made to operate for the benefit of women so as to ultimately open, beyond the *Index Thomisticus*, possibilities for interviewees to gain jobs that would not otherwise have been available to them.

Testing and selection

It seems almost paradoxical, and to speak to the social-basis of skill evaluation, that despite the fact that keypunching was "dead-end" (Hicks 2017, 21), coeval commentary nevertheless emphasised the consequences of it going wrong:

> In a machine installation, card punching is often the most expensive operation. Low production or many errors in card punching can sky-rocket machining costs. It is therefore most important to select good card punch operators and keep turnover down.
>
> (McNamara and Hughes 1955, 417)

Above, the consequences for the *Index Thomisticus* of its work going wrong have been considered with reference to the scholarly accuracy of the project. Yet, budget considerations must have been as relevant to the *Index Thomisticus* as any other project. For even if keypunching work was framed as merely clerical, and could be recompensed at low rates, in the *Index Thomisticus*, as elsewhere, the foundational nature of keypunch operators' tasks meant that they were often required in numbers far greater than workers upstream and downstream of them. This is suggested, for example, in a funding bid drawn up by Busa, proposing the engage-ment and remuneration of a cast of administrative, technical and scholarly workers, including 30 female keypunch operators to be paid 30,000 *lire* each per month; two female typists in the administrative division to be paid 100,000 *lire* per month;[6] a male head of department to be paid 100,000 *lire* per month; a male academic assistant, 150,000 *lire* per month; two male researchers for lemmatisation 100,000 *lire* each per month, and two male programmers 120,000 *lire* each per month (Busa n.d.). Thus, while five keypunch operators could be hired for the cost of each academic assistant, keypunch operators were, in the aggregate, among the costliest of project staff, given that they were numerically the largest cohort of the *Index Thomisticus* workers.[7] The need for judicious selection of operators cited above must have been as relevant to the *Index Thomisticus* as to any other keypunching operation.

Before the introduction of aptitude tests for selecting keypunch operators, IBM summarised their ideal attributes of education and personality, framing the role as requiring moderate levels of education and stereotypically docile workers:

1   Education—preferably high school graduate. Two years of high school, or the equivalent in commercial training, may be taken as a minimum.
2   Neatness.
3   Agreeable personality.
4   Alertness.

(IBM Corporation 1936, 1)

By the 1950s and 1960s, aptitude tests were being used to select female keypunch operators to work across a range of industries including banks, insurance firms, the pharmaceutical industry and government departments (McNamara and Hughes 1955, 418–23). Evoking the extent to which their roles continued to be devalued, and framed as unskilled, doubts are expressed in the literature on aptitude testing about its applicability to the keypunch operator:

> Although mental ability tests have correlated with clerical success, they did not appear to hold much promise for card punch operators, possibly because of the routine repetitive nature of the job. However, since there is the possibility of finding an optimum range of mental ability for this job, additional research may be warranted.
>
> (McNamara and Hughes 1955, 422–3)

And while it may be expected that the shift to aptitude testing would herald a less subjective and personality-driven mode of assessment than that of the 1930s, the formal instruments that followed continued to interpret certain characteristics as reliable predictors of ability, thus referencing a highly subjective ontology of human potential. Indeed, the testing of aptitude, rather than levels of educational or vocational attainment, implies that some people are innately suited to performing certain kinds of tasks (Abbate 2012, 51). Ultimately, aptitude testing of card punching (and programming) would prove a better indicator of existing competencies than a reliable predictor of who would be successful in a given post and organisation (see, for example, McNamara 1967).

Busa's writings show that he too was concerned with picking suitable candidates for the post of keypunch operator. In 1968, for example, he hoped that:

> Centres of Psychology and Communication will find:
>
> – suitable texts to test people's proof-reading ability,
> – programs to train such people,
> – the rules of human behaviour regarding mistakes in the preparation of computer input.
>
> (Busa 2019j[1968], 124)

Implying that the *Index Thomisticus* training school had devised a regime that identified suitable candidates with a high degree of precision, he later wrote that admission to the training school was most selective: he recalled that just 20% of those who completed an initial month of testing were recruited (Busa 1980, 85). In contrast with IBM's early description of keypunch operator requirements cited above, this may be read as a progressive step in that it seems to acknowledge that keypunching did require skill beyond having an agreeable personality. Of course, a certain performance of prestige and popularity is detectable in this claim. For the school to have been able to operate such an exclusive admission process it follows that it must have been highly subscribed. Moreover, in the implied rigor of this admission process we are arguably also to read an expression of Busa's hierarchical power and attention to detail, given that he saw it fit to reject 80% of applicants to the school.

Yet, as so often with the *Index Thomisticus*, when the surface of its formal publications is imaged with the infrared reflectography of oral history and archival research, the historical picture that is revealed seems rather more complex than previously portrayed and recognised. While the picture of the school's approach to testing is difficult to reconstruct from extant records with certainty, selective admission does not seem to have been in force throughout the lifetime of the school, and the power dynamic that is implicit in Busa's recollections of the school's selective admission from among an abundance of candidates also appears rather more unsteady when scrutinised more closely.

That selective admission to the *Index Thomisticus* training school was not permanently in place is suggested by the previously discussed document of Regulations (see Chapter 3), which specifies that admission of male operators would be at the level of 20% at best, and be determined through "competitive examination" (CAAL n.d.). No corresponding statement regarding female keypunch operators is made. This seems strange and the motivations for this are unclear. Perhaps it is to be understood in connection with IBM's early articulation of the qualities desired of a punched card operator above, which are so vague and stereotyped as to hardly require selective admission?

Yet, oral history interviews suggest that an abundance of admission mechanisms were pursued during the years under examination. Some candidates appear to have been admitted to the training school directly and without selection; others took some kind of aptitude test first. Yet more may or may not have taken an aptitude test but did receive some initial training, followed by a test to determine their punching accuracy, which decided their continuation. Indeed, as recalled in interviews, techniques and locations of testing changed, as did the identity, if apparently not gender of those who administered the tests, in that it is women who are recalled in this role.

One possible explanation for the different approaches to evaluation that were mobilised by the *Index Thomisticus* pertains to the level of typing skill that candidates had attained prior to their application to the school. If candidates were already highly competent typists, then aptitude testing was presumably redundant. Also relevant may be the number of candidates who were interested in taking up a place in the school at any given time. A notice of recruitment published on 26 July 1961, which aimed to recruit male machine operators also mentioned opportunities for female keypunch operators and informed readers that they could send their applications to CAAL's administrative office in via Cerva, 35, Milan (*La Prealpina* 1961b). Far from the abundance implied by Busa above, that interest in this may not have been high is hinted at by another article that appeared on 4 August, which again reminded readers that CAAL's secretariat was continuing to accept applications from young women who wished to train as keypunch operators (*L'Italia* 1961b).

That the keypunching executed by the operators of the *Index Thomisticus* was different to that done in settings where IBM's aptitude tests were routinely used was indicated by Busa. He stated that keypunchers who had been trained in literary punching by CAAL could take up posts in industry and easily adapt to the forms of punching required there. Yet transfers in the opposite direction had not, he claimed, been successful: "those girls first trained in business key punching are unable to grasp literary punching" (Busa 1964, 67). From this follows the question of whether the *Index Thomisticus* sought to develop specialised instruments for evaluating literary keypunching? And whether they were shared with the humanities computing centres that were being set up during the 1950s and 1960s, who would likewise have needed to hire keypunch operators? This merits further research. If this were the case, then the existence of such instruments might be read as a recognition that candidates of particular aptitude and ability were required for this specialist work.

Some references do indeed suggest that specialist instruments for keypunch operator aptitude testing or evaluation may have been developed by CAAL. A 1964 Catholic News Service press release refers to such instruments as being among the outputs of the centre (O'Neill 1964, 3).[8] Busa also gave at least one presentation that may have been relevant to this. A letter from the Assistant Chief of the Applications Engineering Section, Data Processing Systems Division of the U.S. Department of Commerce, Mary Elizabeth Stevens, mentions how Busa had given a report on "training personnel to keypunch textual material in different languages for the concordances" at a meeting of a conference programme committee in Washington around 1958 (Stevens 1959). But the nature of the distance between the details that are included in press releases like those cited, and the detail of what was actually happening in the *Index Thomisticus* day to day is unclear. And it might indeed have been expected that the oral history interviews could address some of this uncertainty.

Oral history interviews do recall that IBM Milan was involved in the selection of keypunch operators for the *Index Thomisticus* in late 1953: "I did it at IBM, where there was that manager secretary or similar. She had us take the test on the machines ..." (The Operator et al. 2014). A curious detail in this account is the mention of having taken the test on a numeric rather than alphanumeric keyboard. Busa wrote that he worked episodically in IBM Milan from 1949–54, before he set up CAAL and the training school (see Busa 1980, 85). Presumably, then, alphanumeric keyboards were available in IBM Milan. Could The Operator's detail of having been tested on a numeric keyboard indicate that she had taken a general IBM evaluative test for keypunch operators rather than one that was designed for the multilingual text comprised of alphanumeric symbols and special characters that had to be punched for the *Index Thomisticus* project? It may be relevant that The Operator had previously been trained in stenography, suggesting the purpose of her test may have been to evaluate her accuracy and speed rather than aptitude. Quite logically, the external literature suggests that aptitude tests should be used with entry level candidates while tests directly on the machines were more suitable for evaluating experienced operators (McNamara and Hughes 1955, 423).

Aptitude tests, or psychotechnical examinations, as they are sometimes referred to in documentation pertaining to the *Index Thomisticus* project, are known to have been in use by c.1961. de Tollenaere wrote how:

> Pupils admitted to this school must have finished at least elementary education, must be able to type and have passed a psychotechnical examination of the IBM in Milan. After an initial course of three weeks, learning to handle the machines, punching begins.
>
> (de Tollenaere 1963a, 8)

Likewise, some recruitment notices state that each applicant would need to complete a psychotechnical examination, and, if they were successful in this, they would be permitted to attend, over a period of two weeks, the theoretical courses and other training provisioned by CAAL (*L'Italia* 1961a).

The standard IBM aptitude test in use at this time was the "Card Punch Aptitude Test" (CPAT), also called the "Card Punch Operative Aptitude Test" (CPOAT) or M04–6351 "Card Punch Aptitude Exam" in IBM and wider literature. CPAT was a pen-and-paper test that lasted 12 minutes and was designed for evaluating female applicants to entry-level keypunching posts. Part 1, lasting seven minutes comprised a letter-digit substitution test; Part 2, lasting five minutes, comprised a name-checking test. The latter consisted of 150 pairs of names and individuals who sat the test were asked to mark those that were identical (McNamara and Hughes 1955, 423).

The psychotechnical test taken by one *Index Thomisticus* keypunch operator in 1963 referenced the abundance of applicants that Busa would also recall: And [Busa] had us take a test, I remember we took a test, an aptitude test. They had these worksheets and there were very many of us: we were forty, forty young girls and they chose ten" (Cervini et al. 2014). The test had a paper-based aspect, which involved interpreting "peculiar diagrams … all colorful, superimposed diagrams" (Cervini et al. 2014) by writing down what she thought they represented. She recalled that speed of reaction and memory skills were also tested via a machine with a button for candidates to press when a specified colour was displayed. Parallels between this test and the IBM CPAT overviewed above are not immediately obvious.

Bossi, who took the same test in 1962, recalled that testing was then done "GB [Gianna Bossi]: where the *Banca Popolare di Novara* has its offices today" (Cervini et al. 2014). She did not specify which branch of the bank she was referring to, and her formulation indicates that the offices may not have been held by the Bank when she took the test. Other interviewees recalled that they too took aptitude tests in the premises of a bank. Banks were among the earliest adopters of IBM equipment in Italy. The same bank as mentioned by Bossi, with the qualifier that it was near Milan, is recorded by IBM as having received an IBM 7070 in 1961 (see IBM Corporation 2003a). At that time, when hiring staff, companies that rented IBM equipment could use the standardised aptitude tests that were supplied by IBM (McNamara 1967, 52), or devise their own tests. So, it is possible that candidates for the training school sat in on IBM aptitude tests that were being administered by the bank but, again, commonalities between the texts described by the interviewees and the CPAT of IBM are not obvious. And there remains, of course, the possibility that the young women were not taking aptitude tests for keypunching at all, but rather that they were taking the psychophysiological assessments that we have seen mentioned in apprenticeship legislation (see Chapter 3).

Whether applicants took an aptitude test or not, a stage of training, and sometimes further testing, was required. Not acknowledged in Busa's formal publications, the interviews show that a female keypunch operator played a substantive role in the actual training and subsequent evaluation of candidates. It was necessary to provision this initial training, it seems, because candidates with the desired stenography or typing diplomas were not applying to the keypunching school in sufficient numbers. The Operator also claimed that it was she and not IBM Milan staff who had the skills necessary for delivering this training; IBM Milan did not have anyone "qualified for precisely that job" (The Operator et al. 2014). Recalling again the otherwise overlooked role of female networks, and female social capital in recruitment for the *Index Thomisticus*, The Operator also mentions her links with the Canossians: "... I was with the nuns and at that time the nuns had students. And they had these courses in stenography, so I would ask the nuns, 'send me the best ones' [laughs]" (The Operator et al. 2014). Individuals like The Operator knew from experience what reports like that of the UK government had found: education and training were indeed necessary for this work.

Echoing the then-contemporaneous discourses that centred keypunch operator precision in the training and execution of their work (e.g. McNamara and Hughes 1955, 420), The Operator likewise centred precision as the decisive criterion in determining who would be admitted. She recalled testing candidates for 15 days, admitting those who reached the required standard and rejecting the rest:

> TO: we needed them to learn to type, without looking at the keyboard.
> ... it was necessary because you look over here, you look over there, you look over here, you look over there ...
> MP: ... You get lost, like medieval copyists.
> TO: Yes.
>
> (The Operator et al. 2014)

By the early 1960s, then, admission to the training school does indeed appear to have become selective. The direct contributions of individual keypunch operators to a praxis-oriented process of selecting and training candidates, and indeed, of Mother Cloefe and the Canossians in the sense that they seem to have identified and encouraged their best pupils to apply to the school has been overlooked in reporting on the *Index Thomisticus*. But their contributions were far from inconsequential, especially when considered next to discussions mentioned above that emphasise the importance of selecting effective keypunch operators.

Abbate has examined the aptitude tests for programming that were used extensively by the computing industry in the 1950s and 1960s:

> They typically consisted of sets of multiple choice or fill-in-the-blank questions involving basic algebra and various types of logic problems. ... No knowledge of computers, advanced mathematics or engineering was required to do well on these tests.
>
> (Abbate 2012, 51)

Those tests were, Abbate argues, potentially empowering for women:

> Aptitude testing could work to women's advantage by providing a seemingly objective measure of their technical ability, thus countering gender stereotypes and the effects of previous constraints on their education. A woman who had never had the chance to earn a college degree–or who had been steered into a nontechnical major–could walk into a job interview, take a test, and instantly acquire credibility as a future programmer.
>
> (Abbate 2012, 52)

Throughout this section, the difficult of establishing the kinds of tests, whether aptitude or otherwise, that the keypunch operators took, and the difficulty of establishing the distribution of those testing methods across the cohort of keypunch operators as a whole has been emphasised. The following analysis is offered, then, in a highly speculative mode that acknowledges this wider uncertainty.

Busa's hiring practices were, from some perspectives, valuable and empowering ones. They opened possibilities for young people to learn new and valuable skills that enhanced their employability. Yet, the aptitude or admission testing used in the incunabular period of digital humanities, as seen through the prism of the *Index Thomisticus*, does not seem to have opened possibilities for empowerment that are comparable with those observed by Abbate in the context of aptitude tests for programmers across the wider computing industry. The *Index Thomisticus* admission tests allowed individuals without existing training to secure a place in the training school, and to train on unit recording equipment. Yet, due to the rigid labour divisions of the project, roles other than keypunch operator were not open to young women. And once an individual had secured the role of keypunch operator, from there the emphasis was unwaveringly on constructing and operationalising the roles of keypunch operators as sub-professional, sub-altern even. The low level of formal education to which such roles were tacked, the limited training offered, the low levels of remuneration including the absence of social security contributions and Busa's discussions of keypunch operators' roles ultimately being taken over by machines (see Chapter 5) all emphasise that the keypuncher post was not aligned with opportunity but rather with statis. Concomitantly, the opportunities that might have been opened for keypunch operators to use the *Index Thomisticus* as a stepping-stone to employment in the emerging field of humanities computing, or as a stepping stone to the wider data processing industry were foreshortened by the highly conservative and unequal techno-social and socio-pedagogical order of the *Index Thomisticus*.

Today, in the digital humanities and educational institutions more widely opportunities for workers to move between administrative and managerial, academic and technical lanes arguably remain limited. This is reflected in the # alt-ac body of literature (e.g. Rogers 2015), written by those inside and outside the academy, in non-tenured roles that can offer opportunities to draw flexibly and creatively on academic, technical and other learning and expertise in ways the traditional academy still does not support well. Even within the digital humanities, the career-path stability and sustainability difficulties faced by individuals engaged in technical work that is nevertheless crucial to the discipline like, for example, Research Software Engineers, remains unresolved at a sectoral level, despite important ongoing work by organisations like the Society of Research Software Engineering in the UK and the pioneering work of King's Digital Lab at Kings College London (see e.g. Smithies and Ciula 2020).

Yet, far from perceiving this as an inevitable instance of "how things were", some keypunch operators did recall having been aware that the possibilities opened to them through the *Index Thomisticus* were circumscribed. This is implied in a vignette told about a female programmer who visited Gallarate, "And this was the German woman that had to program the calculating machines. She came from, from New York. That's why she could program (laughter)" (The Operator et al. 2014). In other words, this interviewee was aware that the woman who was employed in New York had more opportunities to develop her computing skills than Italian women like her had at that time, and wished to foreground this in her oral history interview.

If aptitude tests could function as sites of gender subversion and incipient change in the wider computing industry, they do not appear to have had a similar role in the early stages of digital humanities, at least in the context of one of the field's most formative and influential projects. This suggests that it was not enough for women and other minoritised groups of the incunabular period of digital humanities to seek to subvert, or indeed benefit from, the generative potential opened by instruments like aptitude tests that were being taken up in the wider computing industry. The keypunch operators' horizons of opportunity could not be remade through their actions alone, but were also shaped dynamics beyond their control, including the nature of the institutional and organisational contexts in which research into computing and the humanities was first pursued. In the case of the *Index Thomisticus*, the rigid and conservative nature of its setup seems to have operated against the generative potential that was, in however modest a way, being unlocked in some pockets of the wider computing industry around this time.

Subsequent research on the role of evaluative mechanisms and processes of selection across a broader cross-section of historical digital humanities projects may be informative for refining this initial and speculative theorisation of selection instruments as axes of authorised power in the earliest stages of the field, and lead to better understandings of the history and sociology of knowledge as it has been localised in the digital humanities and its workforce. Likewise, this book suggests the relevance of oral history to this task, in the way that individual testimony can tether, with lived experience, the rhetorical portrayals found in project reporting like that of Busa, which may reflect the aspirational elements of principal investigators and their projects better than the lived experiences of their day-to-day workers.

Training

IBM documentation states that training was essential for keypunch operators and determinative of the quality of the work they could deliver in post (e.g. IBM Corporation 1936, 1). Despite the numbers of (predominately) women who trained as keypunch operators, few accounts of the process, structure and content of that training from the perspective of those who actually took it are extant. Even in oral history interviews, as far as I've been able to establish, detailed, first-person accounts of training are uncommon. In an interview conducted with an individual named Bubbles Whiting, for example, she skips quickly over her training on Hollerith machines in the UK: "I left school in 1947. I was trained in London [?] to do this and very fortunate indeed I was to have all this training because I had a very good job at the tender age of 14 ..." (The Centre for Computing History 2016).

Instead, extant accounts of keypunch operator training tend to be authored by those who planned or delivered this training. Nace, for example, reported on the use of captioned video lessons to train young, deaf women in keypunching (Nace 1965), as did Rybak (Rybak 1969). It is telling that this "instructor narrative", as we might call it, can feel obliged to justify and explain itself. Nace, for example, opened his paper by making clear that he had written it following an invitation to do so (see Nace 1954, 563). Rybak takes care to emphasise the exemplary nature of the training delivered in his institution such that the "placement record of our deaf girls was remarkable" (Rybak 1969, 34).

With regard to the *Index Thomisticus*, sustained first person accounts of the training that keypunchers received are likewise absent, even from the oral history interviews drawn on in this book. Could this be because those who took keypunch training internalised the messages that were communicated to them about the purported simplicity and mechanical nature of their work? Or that their training might merit being recalled in detail only when there was something notable or exceptional about it? That an awareness of this possibility should have been better reflected in the design of the respective interview questionnaire is something that has become apparent in retrospect. The hypothesis that when interviewing individuals whose agency or actions have been devalued, particular attention should be given to designing pathways that might better elicit the recollection and narration of the particulars of their experiences is thus an outcome of this book.

In addition to the limitations of interview design just observed, it is surely also relevant that interviewees appear to have received minimal levels of training only. Beyond that given in the first weeks of operators' two-year apprenticeships, "training" seems to have been conceptualised as the embodied and gender-specific execution of the punching and verification of the *Index Thomisticus* and the other projects that CAAL undertook. Regarding the punching of Russian-language texts, for example, it was recalled that Busa simply instructed, seemingly out of the blue, a cohort of operators to punch the respective texts: "All right, so, he called over a group of young women and said we had to do Russian. He called a young man who knew Russian and he taught us the base [to read Cyrillic], we didn't learn Russian" (Cervini et al. 2014). Yet, even with regard to the limited training that seems to have been delivered, it is difficult to understand its nature, structure, content, its particular challenges and so on. To try to fill some of these gaps, some further contextualisation of the training that keypunch operators might be expected to have received will now be assembled from overviews of the educative missions of IBM and Jesuit order, given those institutions' intimate links with the *Index Thomisticus* project.

IBM is well known for providing numerous training programmes and educational activities for staff and customers. In 1932, it established an Education Department in Endicott, New York to manage this arm of their activities. Pictures from 1946/7 show certificates of completion and attendance being given out on IBM punched cards (Aswad and Meredith 2005, 89). Women too were trained by IBM at an early stage, among other courses run from the schoolhouse in Endicott was "Systems Service for Women", first established in 1935. Women who occupied this role were described as, among other things

> aiding [IBM's] customers in the application of [IBM] machines to their accounting problems and in training their personnel in the operation of our machines, which training is carried on in Customers Operators schools conducted by these young women.
>
> (Pritchard 1940)

As we have seen, in the *Index Thomisticus* project it was also young women who provided training to keypunch operators and who also liaised with external clients about potential contracts.

At least one female keypunch operator mentioned having taken a short spell of training in IBM Milan.[9] Guidance on keypunch training given in IBM materials published in the United States may be of uncertain applicability to the Italian context,[10] yet interesting commonalities with, and divergences from, the *Index Thomisticus* set up can be noticed in these accounts. In one IBM document, the need for the trainer to impress upon operators "the simplicity of the punching operation" is emphasised (IBM Corporation 1936, 5). The instructor was advised to reassure the student: "if you are already familiar with typewriting the operation of this machine will prove to be amazingly simple and enjoyable" (IBM Corporation 1936, 10). Given the ostensible simplicity of their task, and the standard application-contexts of keypunching (where numerical rather than alphanumeric data would have been input), it is perhaps unsurprising for it to be implied that training courses could produce competent workers in two or three weeks, as the *Index Thomisticus* seems also to have expected. Other discussions are more circumspect, however, when estimating how long it took to train keypunch operators to a high level:

> A rough rule of thumb is six months' experience for key punch and equipment operators ... an individual with average intelligence and with an average degree of aptitude for this type of work should be able to master the fundamentals sufficiently within six months to meet the minimum qualifications for an experienced operator. Much more time is usually required to become proficient.
>
> (Van Ness 1963, 152)

IBM documentation suggests that training modules should be delivered in the following order: "(1) Mechanical operation of punches (2) Keyboard exercises and (3) Punching from actual business documents" (IBM Corporation 1936, 1). Moreover, operators should receive instruction in the use of the duplicating machine, verifier and automatic machines (for example, the gang punch). Emphasis is also put on the necessity for operators to work without looking at the keys (see IBM Corporation 1936, 5) and on the need for monitoring and evaluating the accuracy of their work. Methods for checking whether "she is performing the exercise properly" (IBM Corporation 1936, 5) are elaborated.

While punching from real-world documents certainly did form part of *Index Thomisticus'* keypunch operator training, whether they could take classes in more fundamental matters, like the "Mechanical operation of punches" is unclear. It is difficult to believe that operators could have gained the skills they needed without some instruction in the fundamental operation of accounting machines. Yet, the pattern in all other aspects of their training seems to have been to provide them with the minimum needed to do their work, so this cannot be assumed. The Operator recollected that she had, in fact, been interested in learning about the machines

TO ... in order to modify the tasks. To not always do those same tasks, always punching, because punching like that will actually weaken your eyesight.

MP: Oh, this is interesting. What did you want to do?

TO: I wanted to learn all about electronic calculators because later on I also did a basic course on electronic calculators.

(The Operator et al. 2014)

The training that she sought seems to have become accessible to her at a later time only, and not, it seems, within the *Index Thomisticus* project.

If the training in keypunching that was delivered by the *Index Thomisticus* seems to have corresponded significantly with that recommended by IBM, it seems to have departed from the educative aims of the Jesuit order. Of the Jesuit approach to education generally, Jones has written:

Collectively and historically, the Jesuit mission has often included the founding of schools ... the curriculum of their colleges—which were comparable to modern secondary schools—was built like all Renaissance education on the humanities as found in classical texts and languages.

(Jones 2016, 118)

In contrast with this view of Jesuit curricula, the training that CAAL provided was, in the very narrowest of senses, vocational and applied rather than humanistic. Many of those interviewed recalled that they had not been informed about the context of their work or of the nature and purpose of the *Index Thomisticus*. Asked whether they were aware of their role in the overall project, for example, Brogioli and Vanelli responded:

BV : No, the project was, it was taboo for us; we didn't know what the project was.

MP: You had no idea of the purpose behind what you were doing?

GB: No.

BV: No. Nobody explained it to us, the job was what they told you to do so ...

GB: Yes, they taught us how to use the machine, what we had to do but, but ...

BV: But not the purpose.

GB: Neither the motivation behind it nor the purpose.

(Brogioli et al. 2014)

The themes that we might expect to feature in a Humanistic curriculum, like a critical engagement with the history and social and cultural contexts of automation or "the machine", including its place in learning and scholarship seem to have been entirely absent from the curriculum of Busa's training school. Leaving the historical context that might explain that absence aside for now, it is fascinating to note digital humanities would be criticised as late as the 2010s, for its lack of intellectual orientation towards cultural criticism:

> We digital humanists develop tools, data, metadata, and archives critically; and we have also developed critical positions on the nature of such resources (e.g., disputing whether computational methods are best used for truth-finding …) But rarely do we extend the issues involved into the register of society, economics, politics, or culture in the vintage manner …
>
> (Liu 2012)

It is an open question as to whether this points to a further, previously over-looked aspect of Busa's legacy, entailing an orientation towards the instru-mental and an overlooking of the social and cultural aspects of the digital humanities, not only in an epistemological sense, but also in terms of the research trajectory of the field. The now distinctive and vibrant critical turn in the digital humanities, connected, for example, with fields like black digital humanities, feminist digital humanities and global digital humanities, has come about in post-2010 period only.

Returning to the training school, it seems curious, at least from this remove, that it should not have foreseen training individuals in a way would have allowed them to go on to work in the emerging field of humanities computing and literary computing. That this pathway already existed is sug-gested by Busa's publications. In 1964 he wrote about how there had emerged "about fifty institutes that use computers to research into words: of these more than fifteen are engaged in preparing computerised concordances for the study of words, the rest deal with applied linguistics" (Busa 2019f[1964], 90). Indeed, the international resonances of the texts that the keypunch operators were punching were signified not only by the multilingualism of those texts but also in the way that the digital humanities was, even at this early stage, in the process of seeding itself across what would become a global arena of activity (see e.g. Risam 2016).

While it can hardly be irrelevant that women were not admitted to Jesuit colleges until the twentieth century, the Jesuit order did contribute to the education of women before this point, suggesting that, from an ideological perspective at least, the limited nature of the training Busa provided may not have been demanded by his Jesuit context (see e.g. Gorman 2005). Yet the *Index Thomisticus'* training provision can be interpreted as functioning to obstruct young women's attainment of Humanistic knowledge, not only in the sense of the exemplary Jesuit commitment to fostering critical thinking (e.g. Von Arx 2012) but also in the sense framed by Jones above in terms of its orientation to classical texts and languages. Those interviewed all concurred that they received no instruction in Latin, Greek, Russian, Hebrew, German, Aramaic, Nabatean or any of the other languages they punched. When The Operator was asked "Did you know Latin?" she responded, "Yes, I had fin-ished high school" (The Operator et al. 2014). Otherwise, just a few individuals who were interviewed (Mainardi et al. 2014; Crosta et al. 2014) recalled having learned Latin in school. Most interviewees, however, had not completed high school.

Of course, the belief that knowledge of the ancient and modern languages that operators were transcribing could interfere with the accuracy rates of their work may have been relevant. Yet, by seeking to admit young women who had not learned Latin to the punched card school, and by not delivering any Latin tuition on the job, even though they spent a significant amount of their time punching Latin, Busa was excluding, in a highly consequential way, those young women from the world that he was exhorting others to build.

The significance that Busa attached to and proposed for the Latin language is set out in a charmingly eccentric essay that he wrote in Latin and presented to the third *Congrès Int. pour le Latin Vivant* in Strasbourg in 1963. Subsequently published in the proceedings of this conference in 1964, the published version records that he addressed attendees as "pacifist soldiers of Latin, which you rightly assert to be the best vehicle of communication" (Busa 2019f[1964], 90). Busa proceeded to enumerate examples of why he believed Latin to be this singular vehicle: it allowed researchers with the requisite lexicographical resources to "greatly extend ... human communication ... to communicate with the fathers of the sciences that we have today and who were pre-eminent in past ages" (Busa 2019f[1964], 90). Thus, he argued, the Latin language presented the field of Linguistics, which was being stymied by the "incredible difficulties of computer translation", with a great opportunity (that would, of course, be supercharged by lexicographical resources like the *Index Thomisticus*). Implicitly evoking the concerns that were then mounting about the viability and cost-effectiveness of machine translation, concerns that would see the setup of the ALPAC committee in April 1964, and their subsequent issue of a report that proved disastrous for the funding-base of machine translation in the medium term (see Alpac 1966), Busa observed: "although more money than one could ever imagine had been assigned to research into computer translation by military and technical institutions, almost nothing has been achieved, so that now there is much scepticism about this matter" (Busa 2019f[1964], 90). It presumably would not have helped his argument to have mention his own connections with computer translation research or that CAAL had been keypunching Russian texts for use in the Georgetown Machine Translation System that had been installed on an IBM machine in a location in Italy that was home to institutions of what is now called the European Union (see below).

So, Busa's proposal was that the scientific community could switch to writing and communicating in Latin, thus, he seemed to suggest, doing away with any need for machine translation. He exhorted his audience "At least let Latin and computer translation fight it out as rivals and competitors, and let them be weighed in the balance: would not Latin win, if only we wanted?". Elsewhere in the essay, he suggests that Latin would, moreover, be a "suitable computer language for science", thus proposing that scientific communication and scientific programming languages could all be written in Latin.[11] Busa closed by promising his audience: "If, instead of dreaming, we are prepared to act, work, produce, achieve, construct and co-operate, by God's good grace, Latin will again be the international language of science" (Busa 2019f [1964], 91).

Even if this essay seems to have been communicated in a playful register, there is no suggestion that Busa was being insincere in his depiction of the weight he personally attached to the Latin language or insincere about the significant role he believed it could have in the future of human and machine communication. And while he did observe that the discipline of linguistics was concerned to understand and promote communication or "provid[e] tools for people to communicate with each other throughout the world" (Busa 2019f[1964], 90), his essay addressed scientific communication and scientific computing only. Thus, in his essay, Latin is positioned as being synonymous with the scientific past and a harbinger of a new international, scientific future.

Busa emphasised in this essay that the fundamentals of Latin could be imparted to scholars within "one year at the most" (Busa 2019f[1964], 91). Yet keypunch operators were not, whether in the hypothetical world of Busa's ideation, or in the actual, day to day world of CAAL to be afforded instruction in Latin. Though they might be required to play a fundamental role in the encoding of the Latin words and code on which future science and scientific computing would run, they were to be intellectually and communicatively excluded from this world. And this exclusion was arguably important to enforce, for if the Latin language could be learnt by keypunch operators "on the job", in a time-frame that amounted to less than half of the time that was required for their apprenticeships, the boundary markers that the *Index Thomisticus* project was constructing between scholars and technicians might be revealed as rather less stable than otherwise communicated.

To the question "what difference did computers make?" to early-adopter scientists, Agar responded that "one difference that computers made to science was deepening the division of labour – and expanding one side of the division, professional computing services" (Agar 2006, 900). Agar also suggested, as was the case with the *Index Thomisticus*, that "computerization, using electronic stored-program computers, has only been attempted in settings where there already existed material and theoretical computational practices and technologies" (Agar 2006, 873). This suggests that Agar's "deepening division of labour" was already in process in setups like Busa's, which had initially elaborated electro-mechanical and human-augmented computation and, in due course, would enfold electronic, stored programme computers into its methodology. Indeed, the particular case study of the *Index Thomisticus* offers an interesting case study of this "deepening division of labour" in the emerging field of digital humanities, where it arguably manifested in a multi-level, "push and pull process" between scholars and technical staff.

A "push" may have been exerted by the keypunch operators through their level of interest in applying to the training school, reminding Busa of his somewhat uneasy reliance on recruiting appropriate technical staff. That the *Index Thomisticus'* was reliant on having its material keypunched by a group of young women who were, despite the rhetoric of the project, developing specialised skills that were not possessed by others in the project surely cannot have gone unnoticed. Thus, a "pull" process could be exerted, to bring power back to the scholars, by departing from a traditional Jesuit curriculum and withholding from female technical staff crucial aspects of the knowledge base and production of the project, which furthermore acted as pathways to digital humanities as it was emerging on the international stage. From this reading, it can be suggested that scholars in the humanities may have sought to devalue the work of keypunch operators and others in response to the "deepening division of labour" that computation was heralding for the humanities, as it offered a way to occlude any apparent loss of power from the scholar to the swelling ranks of technical staff.

Whether Busa was emphasising, publicly or privately, that the keypunch operators were able to get good jobs in industry after leaving the *Index Thomisticus*, that they were a source of cheap labour in the present, and that their roles would be automated in the future, one thing was clear. Busa apparently did not see a place for keypunch operators in present or future acts of knowledge creation in humanities computing, computational linguistics or other related areas of scholarly endeavour. Gender differentials certainly shaped perceptions of the level of skill that a given role entailed in the *Index Thomisticus*, and in computing setups more broadly. Yet the devaluing of keypunch operator labour can also be seen as being part of a wider and older process, which recalled the social and intellectual divisions between scholars and their amanuenses, to which the *Index Thomisticus* was linked through the long thread of concordance making.

Certification and graduation

Not all exclusions or even archival absences are permanent, however. From the Certificate that was given to Bossi, which she brought to her oral history interview in 2014 and which has since been accessioned to Busa's archive, some details of the training that was provisioned to operators from November 1961 to September 1962 can be recovered. Dated 8 September 1962,[12] the formatting of the "Certificate of Professional training" (CAAL 1961) indicates that it had been prepared in a template form that was amenable to adaption and personalisation. Bossi's Certificate specifies that she attended "Professional Training Course No. 102 for female card punchers". The course was authorised by the Ministry of Labour and Social Security and her Certificate was issued in accordance with "the law of 29 April 1949, n. 264 and subsequent modifications and additions". It carries the signatures both of Busa and the "Director of the Office of Labour and full employment of Varese". The gender default of the Certificate recipient was Mr ("Sig."). Space was left for additions were the Certificate to be awarded to a Ms ("Sig.

na"), the intervention required to signal the female presence. Perhaps this reminded the reader that the "Sig.na" represented a divergence from the default male (see Criado Perez 2020, 1–25), though this has hardly a linguistically uncommon title.

The Certificate states that, in this case, basic courses in numerical and alphabetical punching had been successfully completed. No indication is given that the literary and multilingual punching that operators executed was quite specialised. Arid figures about hours and machine types are instead listed, enumerating a largely data-driven quantification of keypunch work. Specified is the "operation of the machines": Bossi spent about 347 hours working with the 026 machine (a printing card punch); about 196 hours on the 056 (a verifier); and about 104 hours on the 858 (a cardatype machine). About 100 hours were spent on "order operations and controls". The latter reference may refer to those manual and cognitive tasks that were essential to operating keypunch machines but did not involve punching as such (see IBM Corporation 1955, 5). No explanation is otherwise given of such rubrics.

Under the section of the Certificate that reported on "ability and behaviour", it initially seems curious to find "programming" specified. The programming of electromechanical accounting machines was done in a way that is quite different to how digital computers are programmed today. Not having stored memory, accounting machines were controlled by plug boards, which could have dimensions of "three feet by two feet and contain perhaps a thousand holes" (Winter 1999, 10 citing Cutbert Hurd). Each time a different task had to be performed with the machines it was necessary to rewire its plugboard or swop a new one in or out (Hicks 2017, 66). Removable plug boards do feature in photos of CAAL (e.g. Busa Archive #0163).

The IBM 026's "program unit", which Bossi is also recorded as having used, did allow a limited set of functions to be programmed.[13] They included: an indication that a field should be manually punched; the shifting of the keyboard to alphabetic mode for a given column; automatic duplication; automatic skipping; and the hard coding of the length of a punched card field or operation (IBM Corporation 1961, 19–20). That programming is listed with indicators of ability and behaviour on keypunch operator Certificates may be understood with reference to scholarship on the history of programming, and the masculinisation of the electronic computing industry that gathered momentum from last midcentury. As discussed in Chapter 1, having initially existed as a feminised endeavour, as programming professionalised and was done on digital computers, it transformed into, and was indeed valourised as a highly masculinised area in the UK and USA (see e.g. Abbate 2012; Ensmenger 2012; Hicks 2017). Thus, it seems possible that when the Certificate was drawn up, programming had not yet acquired this association[14] and, as far as it was implemented on electromechanical machines, it remained a feminised aspect of computing projects and workforces, associated with low-skilled female workers.

Other criteria of "ability and behaviour" assessed on the Certificate given to Bossi echo some of the desirable qualities for keypunch operators that were set out by IBM in the 1930s. They include checking by sight; discipline and urbanity; professional involvement; and willingness to acknowledge errors in one's work. Criteria left blank on the Certificate pertain to planning; machine assistance; oral and written traits; directive capacity and sporting activities. These latter criteria relate to physical exertion; leadership and management skills; and the oral and written skills that assist people in making their voice heard. As Beard has argued, the silencing of women's voices has been synonymous with the attempted control of women, and their exclusion from power, right across the western canon (Beard 2018). Thus, it does not seem outlandish to suggest that those skills may have instead been assessed or attested when the Certificate was to be awarded to a male machine operator.

With the exception of "checking by sight" it is difficult to see how the other criteria specified, like "urbanity", could have been objectively assessed. These criteria are not so much skills as markers of gender-sanctioned dispositions and attitudes. They are criteria that centre stereotypes of women as compliant, reliable, undemanding and docile (Milkman 1987; Abbate 2012, 3–7; Wyer et al. 2013). The Certificate may be read as codifying this stereotype, setting it as one that keypunch operators should model to successfully complete their training. By explicitly including, without further structural qualification or mitigation, an individual's willingness to acknowledge mistakes in their work as a measure of their evaluation, the Certificate seems to tether individual keypunch operators to other sexist tropes too. Arguably, the Certificate, to the extent that it accurately reflects the circumstances of the keypunch operators' training, functions to draw attention away from the efficacy of the training regime itself, and other structural factors, pre-empting critical reflections on or articulations about its efficacy by placing responsibility for ownership of mistakes on the operator alone. Perhaps this is why, at least as far as it is attested by the archival record, few female *Index Thomisticus* keypunch operators seem to have independently raised complaints and it was, instead, the young male technical staff who, via a priest, felt secure enough to communicate their discontent? (see Chapter 4).

Afterwards

By 1968, IBM equipment had been installed in Italy in 98 commercial banks, 42 savings banks and was being used by utility companies, service and data processing centres, the pharmaceutical industry and nuclear research centres too (IBM Corporation 2003a). The *Index Thomisticus* keypunch operators would secure jobs right across those sectors. Many of those interviewed mentioned their subsequent employment at EURATOM, which was located in Ispra, some 30 miles away from Gallarate.

The European Atomic Energy Community (EURATOM) was created in Rome on 25 March 1957 by Belgium, France, Italy, Luxembourg, the Netherlands and West Germany (Guzzetti 1995, 7) and its research remit included all facets of nuclear research. Its manifestation in Ispra was a true stronghold of science and technology, not unlike the more famous CERN centre in Geneva, endowed with offices, laboratories, and major installations, including the research reactor Ispra I, built by the Italians, the management of which was transferred to EURATOM on 1 March 1963.

(Guzzetti 1995, 17)

EURATOM was

also the headquarters of the European Scientific Data Processing Centre (CETIS), which used powerful computers to provide various services to the Commission and other Community institutions, and also to undertake research into [machine translation], documentation systems and mathematics.

(Guzzetti 1995, 17)

Given its research remit, EURATOM sought to "provide the scientists at Ispra with a rapid and economic Russian-English translation service" (Perschke 1968, 98). Machine Translation (MT) was, from the mid 1950s to the mid 1960s, a topic of national and trans-national interest, generously funded through "government, military and intelligence sources" (Hutchins 2000, 4). Undertaken against the backdrop of the Cold War, the focus of MT research in the East and West was predominately, though not exclusively, on Russian and English (Hutchins 1978, 119–21). An IBM 7090 had been installed in Ispra in 1961, at the cost of about 3 million dollars (Busa 2019e [1962], 80), so the necessary hardware was in situ. But "the American projects were already so far advanced as to make it appear impracticable to start [MT] development de novo" (Perschke 1968, 98). Instead, a MT system that had been designed in the USA, by a research group in Georgetown University, would be adapted for the IBM 7090 and installed at Ispra. That the scientists at Ispra had, like Busa, turned to America to secure computing machines, routines and expertise is indicative of the post-war decline in computing and technology in Italy and on the continent (De Marco et al. 1999, 28), certainly when held against the economic, technological and scientific ascendency of the USA, which was among those countries that profited from the diaspora from Europe of researchers and intellectuals during the fascist-era (e.g. Sieg-mund-Schultze 2009; Turchetti 2003). The scientists at Ispra and EURATOM were among those

young Italian scientists [who] began working on this somewhat new, but promising scientific area either by trying to acquire the knowledge and technology mainly developed in the United States or, more ambitiously, by trying to fill this already existing wide gap.

(De Marco et al. 1999, 28)

Recalling the role Busa played in facilitating the EURATOM and Georgetown trans-Atlantic collaboration he later recalled:

I connected the Anglo-Russian project of Leon Dostert and Peter Toma (of Georgetown University, Washington, DC) with the Computing Center of the EURATOM of Ispra, which is on Lake Maggiore in Lombardy. My contributions were on an exchange basis.

(Busa 2004, xix)

The interests of the Jesuit order notwithstanding, the links that Busa helped to forge between EURATOM and Georgetown had multifaceted significance for him and CAAL too. Jones argued that CAAL received payment from EURATOM for the Russian texts that keypunch operators mentioned having worked on whilst still apprentices to the *Index Thomisticus*:

... Cold War defense helped to fund both atomic energy research and research into [MT] (in the same facility at Ispra in Lombardy), and through a process of exchanges, more directly perhaps than many have realised, that research helped to fund the first centre for humanities computing 30 kilometers away in Gallarate.

(Jones 2016, 113)

Intellectual and strategic foresight opportunities also accrued to Busa. Vanhoutte has identified that:

when the use of automated digital techniques were considered to process data in the humanities, two lines of research were activated: [MT] and Lexical Text Analysis (LTA). [Pioneers of] ... the MT line of research and were not humanists by training, whereas Busa and [others] were LTA scholars and philologists.

(Vanhoutte 2010)

By forging connections with Georgetown-based individuals like Léon Dostert and Peter Toma in the early 1960s, Busa was not only connecting with pioneers of a cognate research field in which he had an existing interest (see Jones 2016, 110). Martin-Nielsen has positioned the cold war as a linguistic war, "Men's minds would only be won over, politicians and military leader's agreed, if America developed the capacity to communicate with and understand both allies and foes" (Martin-Nielsen 2010, 132). To be able to meet this linguistic challenge without the requisite number of Russian translators, the USA - allocated huge funding sums to MT research. Early MT actors, like the influential Dostert, had access to richly abundant funding streams, and they were intermeshing their research with the geopolitics of information, and thus the cold war, in a way that was radically more pronounced than LTA scholars.

The MT group based in Georgetown's Institute of Languages and Linguistics was one of the largest and most important groups in the USA at work on MT at that time (Bar-Hillel 1960). Led by Léon Dostert, they collaborated with IBM too, and Peter Toma, who would also go on build a strong reputation in MT, joined the group in 1958 (Vasconcellos 2000, 93). By 1963, the system that Georgetown's research ultimately gave rise to, the Georgetown system of MT had been installed at EURATOM (Hutchins 2003, 133), with Busa's help.

By the middle of the decade, references in Busa's publications to MT work, and of the fundamental applicability of his research to it, would become fewer. This occurred in anticipation of and after the disastrous ALPAC report of 1966, which saw funding to MT dramatically decline. And Busa would later become defensive about how the history of MT research could challenge his territorial claims of novelty. As late as 2004, he felt it necessary to defend his unsteady claims of chronological and conceptual pre-eminence:

> I have already said that hermeneutic informatics was the first to come into existence. Shortly afterwards, in the early 1950s, if I am correct, the move toward automatic translation started. The magazine MT – *Mechanical Translation* was started at MIT, launched, I think, by Professor Billy Locke and others. The Pentagon financed various centers. I was involved in this.
>
> (Busa 2004, xix)

Busa's forays into the MT world led him to a vantage point from which he could survey his research anew, allowing him to identify new interconnections for and with his research.[15] Indeed, his connections with MT left signals that shape the topography of digital humanities to this day. Digital humanities centres have a prominence and significance as brokers of national and international computational and data-driven exchange and collaboration that is distinctive in the wider humanities (e.g. Fraistat 2012). That Busa's connections with MT research played a role in his accentuation of the centre will now be argued.

An important pivot in the longer process of connecting EURATOM and Georgetown was a meeting that was held between Dostert and Busa in Frankfurt on 6–7 April 1961. "Out of that meeting Busa drafted a two-page memo of agreement, outlining a formal collaboration between CAAL and the [Georgetown] linguistics group, which led to the installation [of the Georgetown MT system] at CETIS at EURATOM, Ispra" (Jones 2016, 111–12). The memo records Busa depicting CAAL as having been, anterior to the meeting, somewhat parochial and resolves that: "CAAL … will be no more an individual, isolated project; in fact, it starts now, Tübingen conference, contracts with EURATOM etc to be inserted in the world growing up of the information processing techniques …" (Busa 1961a).

It is, in fact, Dostert who is recorded suggesting "the idea of an international service of free electronic processing of concordances" (Busa 1961a) at this meeting, an idea that Busa would develop further in a 1962 paper. There he wrote that with funding from EURATOM, CAAL would engage in knowledge dissemination and the international networking of centres, delivering also the "dream of international centres: services by individuals or by the institutes to freely provide the first electronic versions of linguistic materials on cards or on tapes" (Busa 2019d[1961], 73). As Jones has observed, "this plan ... drove much of the activity of CAAL in the crucial mid-century period" (Jones 2019, xv). Though today this development is portrayed as idiomatic of Busa's internationalist outlook, and as highly influential on the humanities computing ecosystem that followed, the germ of the idea appears to owe more to Busa's connections with Dostert and the MT community in the course of forging the EURATOM–Georgetown collaboration than has previously been acknowledged.

That feminised keypunch labour would create the cards and tapes to be made available by the international centres is, of course, implicit rather than explicit in Busa's paper. Yet punching is directly referred to in the Memo of the meeting with Dostert, where it is positioned as a fundamental bridging activity, and even bargaining chip of the proposed collaboration. The memo records how Dostert set out the scientific and institutional benefits that could be secured for CAAL—and for Busa professionally, in terms of his profile and esteem—through the proposed collaboration with Georgetown. And he arguably positions the work of the keypunch operators as crucial for unlocking these benefits. This is suggested by the following statement, which precedes the enumeration of those benefits:

> [Mr Dostert] feels it will be useful to the CAAL to accept the punching of the patents for the USA Dept. of Commerce: for scientific results, for prestige, for making easier contributions from international Foundations: provided it will be not only a pure service but a service for scientific research.
>
> (Busa 1961a)

That Busa could bring to the table a workforce trained in keypunching must have been valued by Dostert and Georgetown. In 1960, the Georgetown project had opened a keypunch operation in Frankfurt, Germany,[16] to punch dictionaries and other texts used in their MT research. The centre was opened in Frankfurt rather than New York in expectation of "an easy supply of personnel with knowledge of the Russian language, or at least competence in the Cyrillic alphabet and that overall costs for such an operation would be significantly less than in the United States" (Heller 1997). Costs would be kept low by hiring housewives who were interested in returning to the labour market. The operation went on to house "9 keypunch operators, 13 verify operators, 20 keypunch machines, and 10 verify machines, plus supervisory and support personnel" (Heller 1997). Texts for EURATOM were also punched there (Macdonald 1963, 212). The centre closed in late fall 1962 (Heller 1997), "because the volume of keypunching required no longer justified the maintenance of a separate facility" (Macdonald 1963, 212).

And this closure seems to have opened the way for CAAL to punch texts for the EURATOM-Georgetown collaboration, and for other research and strategic partners of those entities. As Busa put it:

> I supplied them, from my laboratory at Gallarate, with Russian abstracts of biochemistry and biophysics in Cyrillic script on punched cards, a million words. These were translated with the Georgetown programs.
>
> (Busa 2004, xix)

For Georgetown, the link with Busa must have meant that the remediated text required for some of their research and research collaborations could be supplied by punched card operators trained by the *Index Thomisticus*, whose labour cost significantly less that it would have done in the USA, thus ameliorating the closure of Georgetown's keypunching centre in Frankfurt.

While not seeking to detract from the expertise and personal characteristics that Busa drew on in forging connections between EURATOM and the Georgetown group, the work of the keypunch operators was arguably also decisive in the realisation and execution of the collaboration between Georgetown, EURATOM and CAAL. That he is recalled as having personally called at the house of one operator may reflect Busa's eagerness to engage the services of the keypunch operators for EURATOM:

> GL Father Busa came to my house to invite me to the EURATOM in Ispra. To do translation in Russian.
> MP: Oh?
> GL: Translation. We would punch in Russian with those characters.
> MLS: In Cyrillic.
> GL: In Cyrillic, right, the term escaped me. Yes, Cyrillic.
>
> (Lombardi et al. 2014)

The importance of the keypunch operators to this transatlantic collaboration was not articulated in oral history interviews as per my analysis above; nor was it articulated as such in archival or secondary literature, whether referring to this particular collaboration or to the contributions that keypunch operators made to MT more widely, by elaborating its data-foundations. Instead, and by now this will hardly be surprising to the reader, the work that keypunchers contributed both to MT and humanities computing projects, or in Vanhoutte's formulation, to MT and LTA research in Italy, USA and beyond was routinely obfuscated or diminished and even ridiculed.

The press reporting of the January 1954 demo held by the Georgetown group and IBM to demonstrate their[17] collaborative research on MT can be viewed as a microcosm through which to better view this in process.[18] The research that was demoed had been led by Cuthbert Hurd, Director of the division of Applied Sciences at IBM, and Dostert who had devised the rules of syntax that were operationalised in the research (Booth 1955, 8). IBM had provided financial support, computing time and the programming expertise of Peter Sheridan (Vasconcellos 2000, 93; Hutchins 2004, 2005). Much of the linguistic coding was done by the Czech linguist Garvin (see also Danes 2009).

The demo showcased an IBM 701 or "electronic 'brain'" (as the IBM press release, and many of the newspaper reports[19] derived from the press release dubbed it (see IBM Corporation 1954)) that ran programs to translate Russian to English. The total Russian vocabulary used in the demo was 250 words (Hutchins 2005, 3). The experiment "produced English translations of a small set of highly constrained Russian sentences using a computer program that performed dictionary lookup, analysed morphology, and applied some simple grammatical rules" (Vasconcellos 2000, 87–8). It has been described as the "first substantial attempt at non-numerical programming" (Hutchins 2005, 10). Reports of the demo also foreground how the MT and LTA worlds at this time, as viewed through the research of the *Index Thomisticus* and the IBM-Georgetown demo, shared more than a stemmatic kinship, each representing a particular lineage of a pervasive, wider structural sexism.

As with the *Index Thomisticus* project, the most fundamental stage of an MT workflow was getting written or printed text into a computationally tractable format. Press reports of the IBM-Georgetown MT demo, and the "girl" who keypunched Russian sentences for it, echo the portrayal and conditions of the keypunch operators who worked on the *Index Thomisticus.* [20] Similar to the *Index Thomisticus,* a female who did not know Russian was chosen to punch the Russian text (Hutchins 2005). The *New York Times* front page described how the "girl operator" input Russian-language phrases using an English-language keyboard: "The operator did not know Russian. Again, she typed out the meaningless (to her) Russian words: 'Vyelyichyina [...].' And the machine translated it: ..." (Plumb 1954). The emphasis above on the operator's ignorance of Russian might be interpreted as an appeal to integrity in the sense that it sought to pre-empt any suggestion that the demo was rigged. Indeed, *New York Herald Tribune* reporting on the demo noted how "I.B.M. engineers gave assurances that there was no pint-sized bilingual Russian inside the instrument pulling the right levers" (Ubell 1954, 1)

But it is also the case that the IBM press release seems to riff on the keypunch operators' dearth of Russian linguistic knowledge in a multi-layered way, emphasising the operator's, rather than the machine's otherness and out-of-placeness. In a juxtaposition of the capabilities of the operator versus the machine, it is the contribution of the woman that is portrayed as mechanical, almost senseless. This is underlined by the onomatopoeic import of the verbs ("punched", "rattled" and "tapped") that are used to describe her work or connected with it. The anthropomorphised machine, the "brain" (a commonly used term for computing machines, even if often used with some irony), does not punch or tap or rattle. It is portrayed as something measured and controlled—in ostensible contrast to the operator, the machine supposedly understands and translates, and does so smoothly and quickly (see IBM Corporation 1954).

As Abbate has written: "[m]asculinity and femininity were part of the cultural vocabulary that was used to define what a computer was and who was best qualified to use one" (Abbate 2012, 4).The sustained juxtaposition of femininity with the advanced computing of MT, and the merging of femininity with the devalued work of keypunching speaks clearly to this, seeming to suggest that femininity is, in fact, incompatible with computing.

Other inflections of the structural sexism that devalued women's contributions and sought to foreclose the domains to which they might contribute feature in the demo coverage too. The *New York Herald Tribune* discussed the kinds of sentences that MT would ultimately be able to handle: "She taxied her plane on the apron and then went home to do housework" (Ubell 1954, 1). The immediate aim of the example was to show that MT methods were expected to deliver effective approaches to homographs and polysemantic words.[21] But the example is itself polysemantic, also communicating the idea that women had neither rightful place nor future in MT research or the computing industry.[22] The necessity of input data having to be encoded on punched cards (via feminised labour) is noted in the article as a great inconvenience. But the reader is reassured that "Dr. Dostert said that it will not be too long – possibly three to five years – when automatic text-reading machines will feed in Russian sentences automatically into the machines without punched-card intervention" (Ubell 1954, 1). In the next chapter, we will find Busa similarly wishing for the automation of keypunch labour, and thus emphasising the precarity of feminized labour in computing projects. The article concludes with the observation: "To do all this [automatic translation] the machine performs about 60,000 operations a sentence. During the demonstration yesterday, it had two 'nervous breakdowns'. Random errors crept in which automatically shut the 701 down. 'She' didn't cry" (Ubell 1954, 1). The misbehaving machine, then, was coded feminine when a deviation from its ideal and intended state was being signalled.

In this way, in Italy and the USA, in early MT and humanities computing projects, some of which attracted international media coverage, women's outsider status was constructed and disseminated. In newspaper reports, and scholarly articles, portrayals of women's supposedly mechanical, unskilled, unthinking and, as such, temporary labour could be collocated with mentions of computing and computers. This portrayal can also be detected in the treatment of *Index Thomisticus* female staff, and the structural sexism that it was founded on, whatever about the calls of its staff for fairer treatment of workers.

But the IBM-Georgetown demo in New York also had a more tangibly causative impact on the *Index Thomisticus'* keypunch operators in the way it opened up employment opportunities for them in EURATOM. The success of the demo led to "new funding and major national and international support for machine-translation research ..." (Jones 2016, 110). This included the large grant that Georgetown received from the CIA, under cover of the NSF the following year (Vasconcellos 2000, 88 fn. 5) which supported research focused mostly on "the translation of Russian texts in the field of organic chemistry" (Dostert 1957, 6). The system that this research gave rise to, the Georgetown System of Machine Translation, as we have seen, would be installed on an IBM machine at EURATOM (Hutchins 2003, 133). Following an initial probationary period, "a research contract was concluded with Georgetown University in 1963 putting the Russian-English MT system at the disposal of CETIS after making a number of modifications to suit the particular requirements of the Ispra establishment" (Perschke 1968, 98). The direct employment opportunities opened for CAAL's keypunch apprentices in Ispra were over and above what seems to have been Busa's earlier sub-contracting of their work.[23]

That the involvement of *Index Thomisticus* keypunch operators was planned or already in motion from July 1961 is suggested by archival photographs. Pictured in EURATOM, standing around the IBM 7090 Data Processing System[24] are Busa; Mr Lecerf and Mr Braffort (from EURATOM), Peter Toma and others from Georgetown. Also pictured, and as usual, unnamed in the corresponding hand list prepared by Busa, are at least 11 of the young women who worked for CAAL as keypunch operators.[25]

Various recollections of EURATOM occur in *Index Thomisticus'* keypunch operator oral histories. As might be expected, the perception of keypunch operator roles as mechanical does seem to have prevailed. One interviewee recalled that in EURATOM they were not informed about the purpose of, or rationale for their work: "BV: But it was just a temporary thing, in fact, we can barely recall it because they didn't explain to us what exactly we were doing" (Brogioli et al. 2014).

But other recollections of EURATOM, and indeed of the other locations were operators worked, also occur in interviews:

> GL [Graziella Lombardi]: [In] '63 I went to Ispra and stayed in Ispra until '74, when I had my second daughter.
> MP: And in Ispra, however, you didn't work for Father Busa, you were working at the EURATOM?
> GL: No, for IBM.
> MP: For IBM?
> GL: IBM hired us.
> MP: As keypunch operators?
> GL: As keypunch operators.
> GL: Yes, I ended up staying home earlier, I had my second daughter and then I didn't go back. I had a wonderful experience, those years I worked in Ispra were truly ...
>
> (Lombardi et al. 2014)

Lombardi's recollections are notable not only for how she states that she was hired by IBM rather than EURATOM while in Ispra (perhaps in the context of the Georgetown collaboration?) but also for the happiness with which she recalls her experiences there. A debated trope of women's oral history interviews,[26] Lombardi centres her family at the nucleus of her experiences and chronology, perhaps indicating that her grounds for assessing the enjoyment that she derived from her work were not restricted to markers of professional reputation or esteem, but were connected with life-work balance. And Lombardi is far from the only interviewee to recall her post-*Index Thomisticus* entry into the labour market in a positive way.

Possessed of highly desirable skills, interviewees received multiple job offers:

> MM [Mirella Mainardi]: We were highly sought after. Coming from Father Busa's school, we were the most sought after. Can you imagine that an employee from *Credito Varesino* came to my house, rang the doorbell and said, "Come work for us"?
> MM: It's no coincidence, no coincidence, we all met again at the bank.
> NR [Nadia Re]: At the bank they took all of us as a group.
>
> (Mainardi et al. 2014)

Their training completed; the young women exited the narrow passageway of the *Index Thomisticus* onto a wide landscape that was criss-crossed by an abundance of employment paths:

> MC: Because we didn't have – seeing today, how young people can't get a job – it wasn't hard for us at all. On the contrary, I applied and in ten days I got three offers. In *Credito Varesino, Banca Alto Milanese* and this other pharmaceutical company in Linate. I then chose *Credito Varesino*.
>
> (Cervini et al. 2014)

Maria Luisa Segatto also emphasised the transferability and generative nature of her training, attributing to it, rather than her personal merits, the paths she subsequently traversed:

> MP: Right, as far as I understand, this experience, with punched card machines, was fundamental in helping you find a job?
> MLS [Maria Luisa Segatto]: Of course, I got a job in the bank's Mechanography Center where I worked until retirement. ... I didn't have an adequate degree to work at the bank but I was able to get a job in the Mechanography Center. I was there for ten years and then moved on to other tasks. However, if I hadn't arrived through that training, I wouldn't have gotten it.
>
> (Lombardi et al. 2014)

As such, it is striking that although the Italian job market that the interviewees encountered after leaving the *Index Thomisticus* was a socially conservative one, many of those interviewed recall their experiences post-*Index Thomisticus* in a positive way.[27] One way of understanding this is with regard to the contours that can be illuminated, and the sense of multi-narrativity that can brought to otherwise macro analyses of social and cultural trends via an oral history-led historicisation of individual and small-group lived experience, as attested by this book. Another way of understanding this is through the potential of "Oral history [to] illuminate the collective scripts of a social group, revealing, for instance, how and why peoples' memories of their workplaces or communities are created" (Sangster 1994, 8).

In interviewees' "collective script" of their post-*Index Thomisticus* employment we can arguably witness them quietly, elegantly and collectively pushing against the mores that questioned their suitability to enter and thrive in the (technological) workforce. Indeed, "women's narratives" have been shown to include "understatements, avoidance of the first-person point of view, rare mention of personal accomplishments and disguised statements of personal power" (Etter-Lewis cited in Sangster 1994, 7). These narrative devices can be detected in interviewees' recollections as they contrast their experiences of the *Index Thomisticus* with the period that followed. As discussed, most recall having been ushered towards the *Index Thomisticus* by the adults around them, of then having worked in constrained circumstances, with little knowledge of the purpose or context of their work and of having worked for a Boss who was mostly absent or perceived by them, at that time, as domineering.

However, in their recollections of the post-*Index Thomisticus* period they mention not only the multiple job offers they received but how they felt able to pick and choose from among those offers, gently emphasising their growing independence, confidence and self-determination. This point seems to be made in connection with EURATOM in various ways, for example, when interviewees recall the abundance of offers their received and what might be interpreted as their playful attitude to those offers:

> BV: Afterwards, I remember I turned down a definitive job offer at Ispra because I was young, because it was far, because they offered me a job at the *Busta*. But two of us were not sure if we wanted the job there so we raffled it off and the other woman got it. And then there was another offer in Varese for *Cariplo*.
>
> (Brogioli et al. 2014)

In contrast with the *Index Thomisticus*, one interviewee recalled that her new employer imparted to her a proper sense of the purpose of her work, and she took time to recall this in her interview:

> BV: When I arrived, they had just recently opened this Data Elaboration Center, I don't know, it was called the Mechanography Center, mechanography. For example, back then the first task was to do the reading, the meter reading, they used to do the monthly meter reading ... from the meter reader's book. So, they would give us the cards with the previous month's reading, we would insert the current one, and we would check

the difference to make sure it coincided with the meter readers. And after that, the bill was issued.

(Brogioli et al. 2014)

Reading this as a "disguised statement of personal power", this interviewee can be seen to signal her growing understanding of information as a currency of esteem and progression in the professional workplace and of how her new employer did not use information as a currency of worker alienation. Indeed, the "collective script" of these accounts might be understood to be one of growing confidence and awareness of the importance of keypunching skills, which ultimately helped some interviewees to access jobs that they enjoyed, took pride in and from which they earned a good wage.

This is not to say that interviewees excluded Busa from their recollections of the post-*Index Thomisticus* period. Interviewees do recall that Busa gave them help and guidance in finding subsequent employment. For example, one interviewee mentions that on one occasion when she sought employment, Busa suggested a particular service centre in Viale Monza, Milan, and contacted the appropriate person there on her behalf: "he said, 'If you want to get a job, let's try it, I'll ask this Lady'. It was in Viale Monza, it was similar to working with him, that's why I had a job there" (Cervini et al. 2014). That a priest should have been involved in communications with potential employers was not usual in Italy at this time, and employers often sought satisfactory references from an individual's parish priest before hiring them (Dunnage 2002, 158). The wider context of this was political, and entailed the Italian government, employers and the Church in attempting to ensure that Communists could be excluded from employment. Dunnage has written of how "The Catholic Church … played a significant role in limiting the influence of the Left in Italian society in return for the state's support of its moral positions" (Dunnage 2002, 158).

Whatever about references, interviewees also respectfully communicated that the leveraging of Busa's networks was not a prerequisite of finding subsequent employment. They secured jobs as a result of applications they initiated and submitted to companies like Enel, a gas and electricity company, for example. And this was true across the cohort: "MC: And later many women went to, they weren't in this group, but many went to Gallarate, to Busto's Banca Alto Milanese. … Always as keypunch operators. All of them got jobs, each one better than the other" (Cervini et al. 2014). Yet, according to interviewees' recollections, those jobs were all secured outside of the field of digital humanities itself. Their work may have been crucial to the emerging field but this still did not translate into a possibility to work within this field. In this way, interviewees recollections of the post-*Index Thomisticus* employment landscape can seem to dialogue with the contention that:

Asking why and how women explain, rationalise and make sense of their past offers insight into the social and material framework within which they operated, the perceived choices and cultural patterns they faced, and the complex relationship between individual consciousness and culture.

(Sangster 1994, 6)

MT and humanities computing projects, then, often benefited from a reciprocal interaction with the structural sexism of the social, technical, cultural and disciplinary contexts of their pursuit and making. Some reinforced harmful and ill-informed stereotypes and labour practices by designing their workforces along sex-typed lines; in doing so, they intertwined exclusionary and regressive practices and processes in emerging new fields, fields that would go on to play a decisive role in our information age, while being nevertheless perceived as an objective and even socially progressive arena of activity. Recent work is showing the implications of these "blind spots" in the design and deployment of digital tools, processes and infrastructures, which have been implicated in the digital replication and reamplification of inequalities of gender, race, class and other modes of difference (e.g. Losh and Wernimont 2018; Mullaney et al. 2021).

Noble, for example, has shown how "women, particularly Black women are misrepresented on the Internet in search results and how this is tied to a longer legacy of White racial patriarchy" (Noble 2018, 107). O'Neil and others have shown that Artificial Intelligence and Machine Learning are disproportionately affecting some individuals and communities, amplifying and exacerbating existing social inequalities (see O'Neil 2016). And that the attendant consequences of this are not confined to those who are directly impacted has also been demonstrated. Hicks has explicitly linked the decline of the British computer industry to gender discrimination (Hicks 2017). Likewise, research into fields like algorithmic accountability is working with the intention of making computing more ethical, to make it more than a mechanism for reifying, however unintentionally on the part of individual developers, the world views and life experiences of a small and elite group of technologically competent individuals, to the exclusion or harm of all others (e.g. Wieringa 2020).

To return to the specific context of the *Index Thomisticus*, a forerunner of such processes, it should come as no surprise that the most experienced of the individuals whom we interviewed chose to walk away. In the case of The Operator, in particular, it is clear that she had amassed a wealth of technical and project-management knowledge, that she had an intellectual curiosity about the technical aspects and methodology of the project and that she knew Latin. She had also played a central role in training new keypunch operators. Indeed, her experience on the project must have made her one of the most qualified and experienced humanities computing project workers of her day. Nevertheless, she received little support or opportunity to develop her skills and expertise. During her interview she stated that the years she spent working for Busa were of little use to her in her subsequent teaching career:

MP: [to TO] What did you do after you finished working on the project? After 1963? Was this project experience useful for getting a job, working ...
TO: ... No.
MP: No related jobs?
TO: No because ... I was teaching.
MP: Oh, teaching? What did you teach?
TO: Primary school.

(The Operator et al. 2014)

It was a loss, on a human, technical and intellectual level that individuals like The Operator decided to walk away. Still, the agency of this act should not be under-estimated. As feminist and archival scholars have argued, acts of exclusion are not entirely in the jurisdiction of the powerful, but dynamics and performances of exclusion can be embraced by non-hegemonic groups as part of a wider struggle to expose and even re-centre power. As Lawrence has it, "women's silence ... may be read as a strategy of resistance and choice – a ritual of truth" (Lawrence 1994, 156). Accordingly, the "silence" that The Operator embraced in walking away from the field may be understood as a decisive and powerful response, one that foregrounds the responsibility that attends the inherent complexity of the task of attempting to reassemble and retell previously hidden stories.

Notes

1 This information was found on the following webpage: http://www.canossian.org/en/2014/10/22/terrority-of-milan-gallarate/, which is no longer available but a version of it remains in the Web Archive: http://web.archive.org/web/20160907233953/http://www.canossian.org/en/2014/10/22/terrority-of-milan-gallarate/ (accessed 20 December 2019). Attempts to contact the Canossian order for further information about the school and its links with Busa went unanswered in the timeframe of this study.

2 According to the views of the Catholic Church, it could be deemed a misrepresentation to say that their views sought to confine women to the home. The Catholic Church's emphasis on the centrality of the family to national life, on the equality of women and men in the eyes of God, and on the social good of the duties that are to be performed by women, in the context of their essential identity of mother and caregivers, is an important aspect of Catholic Social teaching to this day (see e.g. https://www.vatican.va/themes/famiglia_test/santopadre_en.htm). Caldwell's work, among others has, however, demonstrated the contradictions and complexities of the Church's fashioning and elaboration of this view of women (see Caldwell 1991, 16–27).

3 See: https://canossianssacramento.wordpress.com/about/canossians-in-mission-2/.

4 Of the industrialists in the town, Jones has written that "Gallarate's economy had been based on the textile industry since the nineteenth century, which was still in the mid-twentieth century in the hands of local families. It was to the patronage of these families that Busa turned for his own initial travel expenses, ... and ... for financial support and advice for the research centre he wanted to build" (Jones 2016, 108).

5 Nazzareno was a machine operator in Busa's school who subsequently became a computer scientist (Passarotti 2019b).

6 That female typists working in the administrative section of CAAL should be paid a very different amount to those working in the machine department is a

fascinating detail of this budget. (Busa 1969d may shed some light as to why this was the case).

7 Based on the budget included in this proposal, with total projected costs of 14,319,000 for phase A of the proposed work, keypunch operators were, in the aggregate, the second most costly group to hire. Only the project's scholarly editors, who were projected to cost 16,320,000 in the aggregate, were more expensive (see e.g. Busa n.d.)

8 Issued by the Press Department of the National Catholic Welfare Conference, this briefing seeks to centre Roman Catholic actors in the timeline of the *Index Thomisticus* in a way that they are not necessarily centred in other reports on the project, which, in turn, reflect other agenda. This reminds us not only of how the *Index Thomisticus* project could be enmeshed in a number of dialogues and agenda beyond the context of computing and the humanities strictly defined but also of the rhetorically and strategically complex stage on which Busa's work took place.

9 According to media reports, IBM Milan staff were involved in the training of male machine operators in the earlier stages of the project, see *La Prealpina* 1958.

10 Searches for Italian translations of IBM instructional materials in Busa's archive, and via a request to IBM corporate archives, Poughkeepsie, did not yield useful results. Nor did the keypunch operators indicate that they had access to such resources or that they had been secured or created by the *Index Thomisticus*.

11 Latin software and serializations of programming languages were developed for the domain of computing in the humanities, the best known perhaps being that of "*Kleio*", developed by Manfred Thaller, see Thaller and Nyhan 2016.

12 This certificate has been digitised and made available on the 'Reconstructing the First Humanities Computing Centre' website (http://www.recaal.org/pages/busa. html). The text accompanying the digitised image includes the note "This handwritten certificate, dated September 8, 1962, is accompanied in the Busa Archive by a (final?) printed version for the same operator, with variant assessment numbers, hours worked, and a later date stamp of 10 October (the year smudged), indicating additional training".

13 The IBM 026 program unit consisted of a program card (on which was punched the procedure that was to be automated) wrapped around a program drum. A star wheel sensing device then ran around the card and interpreted its instructions; program control levers raised and lowered the star wheels (see IBM Corporation 1961, 18–19).

14 For a discussion of the verb to "program", especially post ENIAC, but also covering earlier uses of the word see Grier 1996.

15 As noted elsewhere (Nyhan and Passarotti 2019, 59) this can be detected in Busa's output by comparing, for example, (Busa 2019b; c[1958]) with earlier publications, the former attesting Busa's growing understanding of the wider research context of his work.

16 It was led by Roger A. Heller, with whom Busa was also in contact since at least May 1961 (Busa 1961b; Heller 1961). Peter Toma, with whom Busa was in regular contact for a time, contributed to the centre in various ways including training its staff (Heller 1997).

17 Dostert's Assistant recalled how IBM "made certain the event was widely covered by the press. By the time I arrived, Georgetown was the focus of international attention. My very first assignment was to send offprints of a report on the experiment ... to a list of linguist luminaries and power-brokers of the time" (Vasconcellos 2000, 88).

18 For an overview of how the collaboration came about see (Hutchins 2004).

19 See especially Hutchins 2005 for a discussion of the press reporting of the demo.

20 Busa was directly aware of this particular demo, see (Busa 2019c[1958], 63–4).

21 Hutchins notes that this claim was carried in the *New York Herald Tribune* only and that it was perhaps an invention of the journalist who penned it. The caution with which Hutchins treats the example seems to stem from his awareness of the difficulties of automatically translating such phrases rather than the gender stereotypes that it evokes (Hutchins 2004).
22 A belief that would be robustly challenged with regard to the wider workplace in Friedan's seminal work just nine years later (Friedan 1963).
23 Interviewees did not indicate that they were aware of their work having been sub-contracted.
24 The acquisition of this equipment is mentioned also in IBM chronologies of their activities in Italy. See: https://www.ibm.com/ibm/history/exhibits/italy/italy_ch2.html.
25 See Jones 2016, 112–13, for an analysis of this "exchange basis".
26 On the complexity of the intersections of gender and memory, including how intersectionality may be factored into such analyses see (Leydesdorff, Passerini and Thompson 2017).
27 This has also been observed in the post-second world war Canadian context by (Pierson 1986).

5 On the making of the myth of the lone scholar

Digital humanities as aetiology

Introduction

Absence is not without consequence. Neither is it an inert state. The very noticing or coming into view of absence can alert us to that which was consequential but remained unseen or unacknowledged. One oral history interview recalled the time spent by the *Index Thomisticus* project in Boulder, Colorado (c.1969–71), shortly after it had taken its leave of Gallarate. With data entry largely completed, the time in Boulder was recalled as having been spent on verification and correction mostly:

> GC: ... When we went to America it was revision more than anything else. ... we would print the texts, many of them, on a sheet.
> ...
> MP: You would correct all of it manually?
> GC: Yes, by then were rereading. You could say we were correcting drafts.
> (Crosta et al. 2014)

In Boulder, the *Index Thomisticus* staff was much reduced.[1] Crosta was the sole link to what had previously been its troop of technical staff. During her interview, she expressed dissatisfaction with what she perceived to have been the project's lack of progress in Boulder "But for work, I think it was a dead period. ... Dead. It's such a shame [Busa] insisted on going to America ..." (Crosta et al. 2014).

Verification had been a core task of the *Index Thomisticus* and of its feminised labour. Can the project's lack of progress in Boulder be entirely unrelated to the fact that the team of keypunch operators who had helped to drive it forward in Gallarate, over many years, had been dispensed with? Now that the keypuncher operators' absence from most *Index Thomisticus* publications also reflected, for the first time, their literal absence from its quotidian functioning, a window on to the significance of their contributions may have been opened to those connected with the project. Still, the importance of keypunching labour to the *Index Thomisticus* project continued to be obfuscated or overlooked in publications about it.

DOI: 10.4324/9781003138235-6

The previous chapters have argued, through examples drawn from the history of concordancing, the use of office machines and computing, feminised labour in the post-war Italian economic miracle and depictions of gender and technology utilised in cold war contexts, that Busa was not unusual or exceptional in his gendering and devaluing of keypunch operator labour. Indeed, it is perhaps because such framings were so prevalent that this labour could be hidden in plain sight, until this study.

The focus of this chapter returns more closely to gendered epistemology and the emergence and development of digital humanities. With regard to the literature of the field, this chapter asks how was the work of keypunching devalued in print? And how could it be devalued in print even when, it is argued, many of the authors and readers of those articles would have known from their personal experience that the work of data capture, usually by feminised labour, was *sine qua non* of humanities computing research projects? Rather than an inevitable or inconsequential feature of Busa's reporting, or that of the subsequent humanities computing and digital humanities communities' reporting on Busa and the *Index Thomisticus*, this can be understood as a core aspect of the field's "literary inscriptions" (Latour and Woolgar 1979, 50–1), a concept that has been elegantly explained as "representations of scientists' claims about the outcomes of their practice, sent to other places to convince and enrol allies" (Clarke and Fujimura 1992, 4).

Accordingly, this chapter pays attention to the ways that keypunching was represented in formal publications on the *Index Thomisticus*, to how those representations were picked up on, how they were replicated in a large measure of the humanities computing and digital humanities literature, and the gendering of the disciplinary formation and depiction of the field within the academy that this suggests. Finally, it reflects on how and why those inscriptions could be put productively to use in the inscriptions of the emerging field of humanities computing, or digital humanities itself. It is quite fascinating to note that Busa's representations of keypunching versus scholarly labour are communicated not only through direct discussions of the esteem he accorded to this work, but also through silence and omission, which will be seen to structure discussions of scholarly and keypunching work alike.

Representation

Busa's inscriptions portray keypunching versus scholarly work as deserving of inversely proportional levels of esteem. This is communicated in various ways, direct and indirect, not least through the juxtapositions of this work that accumulate in Busa's oeuvre. As we shall see, these juxtapositions seem to have regularly been taken at face value by subsequent scholars and their purchase was not confined to academic economies of esteem. Busa's generous estimations of the scholar's work foregrounded and, to some extent, documented and memorialised their role in the *Index Thomisticus*. His lowly and negative estimations of keypunching work its significance to the *Index Thomisticus* sowed the seeds of its decades-long exile from the collective memory of the (digital) humanities and the history of computing.

When discussing and describing the work of the scholars, Busa was at pains to emphasise what he portrayed to be the sophistication and difficulty of their task. Their work putting "data into elementary information units" entailed "an exquisitely philosophical work of classification" (Busa 2019h[1966], 107). It required them to "avoid being submerged in a series of problems that plumb the very depths of metaphysics" (Busa 2019h[1966], 107). Though the scholars' names are not routinely given they are accorded a distinct collective presence in respective texts. Some vague sense of them as individuals is preserved through the use of the active voice to describe their work and unambiguous references to "the scholar" or "a scholar". For example: "The scholar marks the text to indicate how it should be recorded on the cards, ..." (Busa 2019b[1958], 43).

References to keypunching work often do not directly acknowledge the fact of operators' existence. In seeking to challenge archives that have excluded or marginalised the contributions of lesser-known individuals like keypunch operators, one must look askew at compendia that are "inimical to women's interests [and] agency" (Chaudhuri, Katz and Perry 2010, xv). While necessarily operating without certitude, one of the ways that this book has sought to do this has involved utilising the contextual, historical and technical knowledge about the nature and detail of individuals' work that has been set out in earlier chapters to detect and excavate what seem likely to be disembodied or implicit references to keypunching labour and those individuals who executed it. For example, in a discussion of the work of validation, work that certainly was the preserve of the keypunch operators, Busa talks not of metaphysical forbearance but evokes stereotypes of women's work as involving less expertise and exertion than that of men, suggesting that in the following it is the work of the keypunch operators that is being referred to. We read that "The necessity of avoiding and finding errors is a very pragmatic and perhaps plebeian task – I would even say a very humble task" (Busa 2019j[1968], 120). Indeed, it may be argued that the accumulation of such imprecise and yet ostensibly critical references contributed as much to the devaluing of keypunching work as the more directly dismissive references surveyed below. Directly dismissive references can be responded to; imprecise and suggestive references are more difficult to detect and engage with and yet they seem to pervade the literature on the *Index Thomisticus* in a powerful if otherwise unsurely-detectable way.

Busa did allude to the difficulties that attended the scholar's work:

> the essential problem of the pre-editing phase has been to develop a set of rules to be used in detecting quotations and their limits; the difficulty lies in the marvellous varieties of inconsistency which we have encountered in the use of italics and quotes.
>
> (Busa 1964, 68)

Yet he did not discuss the errors that such difficulties may have led to. In fact, published discussions of errors in the scholars' work or references to times when Busa disagreed with their classifications are not currently known. As argued in Chapter 5, that such disagreements did not happen, and that mistakes were not made by scholars is, however, completely implausible. Busa wrote of how the pre-editing of the texts involved marking up what they "contained implicitly" (Busa 2019j[1968], 120–1). The scholar's work must have been at least occasionally interpretative and hermeneutic and, as such, open to debate.

Busa's silence on errors in the scholarly work contrasts loudly with his 1968 complaint about errors in the keypunching work. This seems to reinforce the gendered epistemologies the *Index Thomisticus* was arguably constructing, which positioned men as planners, designers and thinkers and women as handmaidens of machines, beholden to the instructions of the men. This portrayal forms, in fact, the basis of the only sustained discussion of *Index Thomisticus* keypunching work currently known. Categorising, with his characteristic dry wit, one batch of work as manifesting "an Olympic level of inaccuracy" (Busa 2019j[1968], 123), Busa discussed the mistakes made in other batches too:

> 8.3 Work code n. 35. 41,888 text cards were punched in 470 man-hours. 2,185 mistakes, i.e. 5%, were found and corrected during punching. The first IBM 056 check revealed a further 682 mistakes, i.e. 1.6% ... another ... 245 mistakes, i.e. 0.5%. These cards were then printed and checked against the original document. Would you believe me if I told you that another 37 mistakes were discovered only at that moment? We totalled up 3,149 mistakes, i.e. 7.18%.
>
> (Busa 2019j[1968], 122)

That those error rates are higher than what might otherwise be expected is the case:

> Through the use of punch machines with spring-loaded knife mechanisms, plus automatic feed and ejection, punchers could attain incredibly fast speeds of 300–400 forty-five-column cards per hour – or more than six cards per minute. Many workers could punch six holes per second, at an error rate of under 3 percent.
>
> (Hicks 2017, 67)

Busa's 1968 text continues by relating that a so-called "empirical classification" of errors and their causes was devised by the *Index Thomisticus*. This comprised 3 atomised classes of error: those arising from "the document, those due to the operator, and those due to the atmosphere and ambience of our centre" (Busa 2019j[1968], 123). The pertinent material, processual and structural factors that are flagged in IBM literature as relevant to understanding why operators made mistakes are little attended to by the "empirical classification".[2] Moreover, the difficulties of the keypunching work that were raised or alluded to in oral history interviews, like its tedious, de-contextualised, poorly remunerated and low-prospect nature were not, it seems, on the compass of the *Index Thomisticus* as reified in this classification.

The reasons that are put forward to explain keypunching errors pertain to operators' personal failings. If Busa depicted the epistemic virtues of the scholar as including the self-discipline that delivered them from metaphysical diversions, the epistemic vices[3] of the keypunch operator included their inability to extricate themselves and their emotions from domestic diversions. Yet, the *Index Thomisticus*' "empirical" approach offered no evidence-based substantiation of the causality he asserted:

9.1 This fault, when it was repeated, seemed partially to be the result of a lack of motivation or encouragement in human relations within the Centre. It also resulted from the biotype and character of the operator. The accidental interruptions seemed to be the result of temporary emotional situations. Believe me, it is not wise to give a text that is difficult to punch to an operator whose children are doing exams or having an operation. When a bachelor punched Michelle instead of Washington, I realized that there was a 97.4% chance that he had a row with his fiancée the previous evening … Accidental distractions are also caused by noise and adverse weather conditions, etc.[4]

(Busa 2019j[1968], 123)

That the operator in the above sentence is indicated to be male is a peculiarity of this text, for the operators are otherwise indicated to be female throughout this text and according to the evidence extant the women only held the post of keypunch operator. That the operator is here indicated to be male may be due to a linguistic error in the text, which was published by Busa in French. It could also be that the default male here stands for the female operator to affect a certain sense of probity given the training school's morality requirement (see Chapter 3) and considering that, in the sentence in question, Busa is mentioning a romantic relationship between unmarried people.

Given the emphasis put on women and the domestic context at this time (see Chapter 3), Busa's attributing of the female operators' mistakes to the domestic realm, and the association being created in this passage between the domestic realm of relationships and children, arguably served to emphasise just how unlike he and his fellow Jesuit scholars they were. Indeed, how unlike the male, "child-free 'ideal worker'" (Abbate 2012, 142) of any stripe they were, stereotypes that have also been shown to have held powerful sway in the history of computing, technology, the cold war and beyond. Feminised keypunch labour was thus represented through lenses of error, domesticity, poor emotional regulation and difference, the authority of this representation perhaps implicitly heightened in the way it was recorded by an individual who was very much the ideal worker.

Drawing again on widely circulating gender stereotypes, the keypunch operators were associated with frustration too, as Busa inscribed the emotional cost of their errors for him. Not explicitly identifying the keypunch operators as the source of the problem, yet issuing the following as the concluding points of a discussion that centred errors made in the transcription of texts, and the necessity that work with computers be built on the highest levels of accuracy (Busa 2019h[1966], 108–9), he sought to reassure the reader who may be encountering difficulties in their computing project:

> … your work will eventually turn out well after you have been sitting half a dozen times on the stairs of your laboratory, with your cheek laid pensively on the palm of your hand, feeling an urge to commit either dismal suicide or mass murder!
> … I … suggest that you prepare a phrase-book of innocent but effective exclamations, graded like the Mercalli scale for measuring earthquakes, to refer to at critical moments in your work!
>
> (Busa 2019h[1966], 109)

A silly attempt at humour, Busa's comments would be deemed clumsy today but their core message is rhetorically powerful. By addressing the mistakes of keypunch labour, and emphasising the burden it placed on him, Busa reinforced his position as the learned and heroic scholar on whom the task of sorting out the mistakes of defective labour and subordinate workers fell. This narrative, expressed more carefully, was repeated elsewhere too. In an article in the *U.S. Catholic,* it was reported that the intra-personal problems that Busa encountered in the course of his work could be more difficult than the technical problems he encountered. Those human-centred problems are reported as having required Busa to be patient, to draw on what might now be called his emotional intelligence, and to assign to each collaborator the job "they can handle" (O'Grady 1966, 37).

The emphasis thus put on the low attainment of the keypunch operators may also have been useful in rationalising their confinement to the lowest-ranking roles. It perhaps offered a justification for the asymmetrical and unmeritocratic power relations that characterised the project. Indeed, when the scattered references, explicit and implicit, in Busa's texts are viewed in the aggregate a subtle but troubling subtext seems to emerge. We are, perhaps, to understand that despite the purportedly selective system that was used to admit suitable candidates to the training school, despite the training they were provisioned and even with the use of a tracking system to monitor their output (see below), their work continued to be found wanting by a very large margin indeed. According to this reasoning, the project might not be viewed as unmeritocratic at all.

Thus, the voices of the keypunch operators themselves went unrecorded and the representations of them and their work that entered the public domain were Busa's, filtered through a masculinist and hegemonic labour context, and communicated with the authority of a scientific or academic publication. One of the most interesting aspects of those representations is how they "shed light on … conflicting perspectives on gender rights and obligations" (Chaudhuri, Katz and Perry 2010, xviii) as they converged on the project of the *Index Thomisticus* and the take-up of computing in the humanities. A rich seam for the exploration of this is in Busa's discussion of the emotions that are indicated to have breached the dam that separated the terrains of the keypunch operators and scholars alike.

For Busa, the male scholar, the emotion he evokes in the excerpt above can be read as being not only justified but useful, in that it is discussed in the context of the successful outcome of the project. The productive emotion of the male scholar thus stands in marked contrast with the "temporary emotional disturbances" of the operators, which supposedly resulted in errors in their work. Keypunch operators' embodied emotions can thus be understood as being as out of place as they were, given their invisible and yet supposedly definitive tethering to the domestic realm. In this way, in reporting on the *Index Thomisticus*, whether directly by Busa or in that published by media outlets, the collocation of gender and technology with displays of emotion, skill and even "work" in the sense of action in a workplace, could produce radically different readings of the skill, dedication, future prospects and professionalism of an individual, and indeed of technology itself.

The gender data gap manifest in the historical record of the emergence and development of the digital humanities as refracted through the *Index Thomisticus* project is pronounced. Despite the comparative abundance of data that exists on the identities of the male actors who contributed to the *Index Thomisticus* (including sponsors, supporters, collaborators and, albeit to a lesser extent for the period under scrutiny, scholars, technicians and programmers), data on its female keypunch operators and other females connected to the project is sparse. Digital humanities is far from alone in this. And this need not be construed as intentional or driven by malfeasance, "It is simply the product of a way of thinking that has been around for millennia and is therefore a kind of not thinking …: men go without saying, and women don't get said at all" (Criado Perez 2020, xii).

And yet, while expressly not seeking to imply that the *Index Thomisticus'* data gap was brought about by maliciousness, the origins and inevitability of that data gap are in question. According to Busa's own publications he was possessed, in 1967, of detailed documentation on the contributions of each individual in his centre to the data foundations of the *Index Thomisticus*. Broadly in line with the principles of scientific management espoused by Frederick Winslow Taylor, IBM recommended its customers use a data-led monitoring system to detect "abnormal performance or unusual variations from standards" (IBM Corporation 1946, 12) in keypunch operators' work. Taylorism achieved acclaim for:

Using time-motion studies, log books and other observational methods, ... [and] develop[ing] a framework for optimizing the manufacturing
process by creating standardized operating procedures and rigorous
measurement of employee output. Thus was born the factory assembly
line, where each worker was recast as, in effect, part of the machine.

(Wright 2014, 35)

Busa's writings suggest that he sought to bring the principles of scientific management to CAAL, but arguably in a half-formed way. He reported adopting
one part only of Taylor's equation: that of continuously tracking and monitoring the work of operators (yet interviewees made no mention of this system).[5]
Largely reflecting IBM's suggested approach for quantifying operator output
(IBM Corporation 1946), Busa described CAAL's tracking system:

Each person working in our Centre prepares a punch card for half a day's
work, or less. This contains their own identity, the quantity and references of
the material used, the mistakes they made while working, and those each one
found while checking their own work or that of another. Thus, it is always
possible for us to trace each mistake and to find out who made it. We have
split our operations into three groups: production, checking, and correcting.

(Busa 2019j[1968], 122)

As keypunch operators prepared punched cards, and did the work of verification, the system as described may have been used to track keypunch
operators only. That such a tracking system was in place indicates that the
Index Thomisticus must have had, at some point, a record of the identity of
each individual keypunch operator and a quantification of their data contribution to the project. Yet, individuals' names were not recorded in outputs
about the *Index Thomisticus*. Indeed, "... a name is more than a name. It
denotes power and status, belonging or not belonging" (Perry 2010, 9–10).

Notwithstanding the excerpt above, the *Index Thomisticus* tracking system
does seem to have departed from that recommended by IBM and Taylorism in
other respects. Taylorism required detailed attention to "standardised operating
procedures" in addition to employee tracking. In the context of keypunch
operators work, those standardised procedures can be understood to include
the already alluded to IBM-recommended instruments and processes for opti-
mising the speed and accuracy of punching. By merely providing keypunch
operators with, for example, "German documents, [which were] however, a bad
and dark photocopy of a typed text" (Busa 2019j[1968], 123), further annotated
by scholars, Busa was disregarding the standardisation and systematisation that
Taylorism presented as the necessary corollary to the quantification of workers'
output. Thus, the keypunch operator's errors were centred but little serious
attention, in the sense of the review of process and approach that Taylorism
would have called for, seems to have been paid to how the mistakes that the
keypunch operators were making actually came about.

The above discussion of CAAL's tracking system emphasises error, and the project's ability to link specific errors with the individuals who made them. Here again we can detect a departure from the IBM literature, which seems to caution against an overemphasis on error, instead advocating for its contextualisation in longer trajectories of output:

> For new operators, the number of cards punched per hour or the number of errors being made are not so important as how much *improvement* [sic] is being made from week to week. … Only after the operator has reached a level rate of production should her proficiency be given an absolute evaluation.
>
> (IBM Corporation 1949, 7–8)

And IBM further cautions that "The supervisor must bear in mind at all times the psychological reaction that reports or records may have upon personnel, and … [they] must be used with caution" (IBM Corporation 1946, 14). To the extent that willingness to acknowledge errors in one's work was listed as a criterion to be met by those who graduated from the training school, the dimensions of the *Index Thomisticus'* psychological cautiousness with error identification and tracking is unknown. Yet the *Index Thomisticus'* association of error with the technical elaboration of the work, and the individuals who executed it, is apparent.

Punched cards, then, were not only the means through which the text of the *Index Thomisticus* was captured, transformed, quantified, published and otherwise disseminated. Punched cards were also used as a "tool of management control in the workplace" (Agar 2006, 869). Just as CAAL sought to tame the *Index Thomisticus'* legion of complex words on the standardised rectangle of the punched card so it sought to tame and dataify keypunch labour, and those who executed it, on those same cards. Little wonder that already by the 1930s, the psychologist Elton Mayo had "blamed the Taylorized workplace for depriving workers of their sense of self" (Carnes 2007, 113).

And as the tracking system sought to dataify keypunch labour, suggesting that keypunch operators were machine-like, or could perhaps become part of the machine, Busa emphasised that scholarly work was entirely separate from and superior to machines. The computer, he wrote, was merely a "*hochgeschwindkeittrottel*" (high velocity cretin) (Busa 2019e[1962], 82) and a "combinatorial machine" (for instance, Busa 2019h[1966], 107). While acknowledging that the work of the scholars aided the machine, and it aided them, he emphasised that they neither would, nor could be, replaced by computing devices. On the disambiguation of homographs, for example, it is observed "Such work requires the competent responsibility of the scholar and it cannot be accomplished by machine. However, once such a classification has been made, mechanical recognition of different forms of the same word could follow" (Busa 2019b[1958], 45). Not so for the work of the keypunch operator, however: "The possibility of punching text cards automatically, starting with the examination of the text by means of a photocell or by other means exists but as yet there are no practical methods for carrying it out. Naturally it will be gratifying when such techniques are operational." (Busa 2019b[1958], 55). In the elucidation of such a perspective, Busa was echoing contemporary discussions–directly connected to the emerging computing industry's task of creating a business case that could sell costly and unproven digital computers—about the benefits that might be derived from integrating digital computers into administrative computing contexts, where it was expected that staff categorised as clerical, including those in punched-card departments, could be then be dispensed with (Haigh 2001, 75–80). As Haigh observed, it would become clear that "existing clerical work was much less routine than had been assumed" (Haigh 2001, 80).

In due course, technologies like Optical Character Recognition (OCR), Handwritten Text Recognition (HTR) and Automatic Speech Recognition (ASR) would indeed allow text and audio to be automatically transcribed, though with quite different accuracy levels depending on factors like the typeface and quality of the source text (Smith and Cordell 2018). Yet this has also proven true of the work of the scholars. Natural Language Processing tools and platforms now automatically perform tasks like part of speech tagging, lemmatisation and tree-banking, even for languages like Latin, though again with different accuracy levels for different languages (Ruder n.d.).

In the course of reporting on "human errors in the preparation of input for computers" Busa did not, as he had done elsewhere obscure keypunch operator's agency with claims that he had actually punched the *Index Thomisticus*. Thus, the text under discussion is contains rare, direction mentions of the keypunch operators at work:

> you know that many Latin words end in m, and only a few in n. I had two female operators who, with miraculous consistency, punched n instead of final m. I discovered that they came from the Veneto, where in dialect there is a high percentage of final – *ns*, but never final – *ms*.
>
> (Busa 2019j[1968], 124)

That the most sustained, published discussion of the keypunch work occurs in the course of a discussion of the errors made in the work is not unusual, however. Whether in the context of concordance-making, when working with early-modern text technologies or in early-modern laboratories, technicians and amanuenses came into view mostly via discussions of aberrations. Blair, has discussed how early modern scholars sometimes ventriloquised mistakes through their otherwise silent amanuenses (Blair 2014). As Shapin put it: "Importantly, technicians' capacity to subvert—that is, to make mistakes and trouble—came to constitute an understood moral resource for explaining and excusing experimental failure" (Shapin 1989, 558). Perhaps this is why Busa tracked and documented the errors that were made during keypunching instead of taking time to address the situated, systemic and epistemic particulars of CAAL that arguably also played a role in the making of errors. The former approach may have benefited the rhetoric of the *Index Thomisticus* more than the latter.

That the keypunch operators' mistakes might best be understood as props in a wider narrative about the differences between scholars and keypunch operators (and thus technical staff) that was enacted through the *Index Thomisticus* is suggested by how Busa's private or project-internal portrayals of the scholars differed starkly from his published portrayals of them.

Highly personal documents in Busa's archive tell a different story about the scholars and their work, and Busa's attitude to this. They show that Busa did, in fact, track the arrival and departure times of the scholars who worked on the project and that he recorded observations (including his dissatisfaction) about their discipline and the quality of their work. Physiological and psychological reports on individual scholars were also drawn up by medical doctors and psychologists in Gallarate. Those reports explicitly comment on individual scholars' fitness to undertake the work required of them (Redacted 1963a, 1963b). This includes discussion of physical issues that could affect an individual's ability to read carefully, and at length, and discussion of potential personality-based and psychological issues that might impair their ability to complete the work required of them. Public discussions of the *Index Thomisticus* project and its workings seem to indicate that the "scholars" of the project did not complete aptitude tests, yet these documents indicate that some scholars in fact completed intensely personal medical and psychological evaluations, which deemed some unfit to pursue the work at hand.

It is all the more fascinating, then, that the public versus private portrayal of keypunch operators is a reverse image of the public versus private portrayal of scholars. Though few documents pertaining to the operators are included in Busa's archive, some archival documents suggest Busa's more nuanced and more privately held assessment of keypunch labour and its importance to a humanities Computing setup. If we understand the word "basic" to mean "essential" in the context of a 1962 letter to Z. Ben-Hayyim, in the Academy of the Hebrew Language, we learn that Busa did indeed recognise the centrality of their work:

... my advise is as follows.

1 Provided that no linguistic centre is able to make full use of a big computer,
2 And that it will always be easy to find a free use of a big computer for hours, if the programs are ready,
3 And that the programs we are preparing at our Centre will be freely available to everybody—and with special affection to the old friends of mine
4 And that the evolution of the computers is fast and directed towards miniaturisation and becoming cheeper [sic]

5   I think that the truly basic installation is a section for punching and verifying the text cards

6   ....

7   The staff for a keypunch section could be:

8   One person for each 026 or 056,

9   One person for the cardatype,

10 Two persons for checking by reading what has been punched by three keypunches

11 One person for supervision

12 11. The most important thing is to get a good personnel. To test and to train it could be a good thing to start with only one couple of 026–056 [sic].(Busa 1962)

Yet, in the *Index Thomisticus'* inscriptions, keypunch labour was portrayed as ancillary to the real work. Busa's publications thus seem to establish keypunch operators and scholars' incommensurate capacity and capability for independent and reliable work. Appeals to difference are constructed, explored and ostensibly justified, between "ideal" scholars and domestically-bound keypunch operators, between emotionally-afflicted operators and the justifiable emotions of Busa, between the scholars who would not be overtaken by the machine and the women who it would replace. In this appeal to difference, one cannot but be reminded of the words of Lerner:

> … historically, what makes dominance acceptable, is putting a negative mark on difference. This group or that group is different from us; they are our "Other". And because they are our "other" we can rule them. It is upon such ideological distinctions that class dominance was made acceptable even to the people who did not directly benefit from it.
>
> (Lerner 1998, 135)

Yet the scholars of the humanities computing and digital humanities community did stand to benefit from the "class dominance" that the *Index Thomisticus* arguably contributed to building between the work of the scholars and the key-punch operators, or between scholars and the technical staff who were sub-ordinate to them. Or, more kindly put, even among professional researchers, claims and narratives of all kinds can be accepted at face value until grounds to challenge them arise. This book, and its effort to reveal a hidden history of feminised labour in the digital humanities seeks to offer that challenge, pointing also to how knowledge of the emergence and formation of the discipline has been constructed and reproduced by the wider field.

Acknowledgement

The triumphalist portrayals of Busa's work that are explored in the following sections did not, of course, win universal accord in humanities computing and digital humanities. Van Zundert, for example, has reflected on how the *Index Thomisticus*:

> was presented in a form already well known to scholarly editing: a fifty-six-volume print publication concordance. The computational aspect was used simply to automate and scale a tedious and error-prone editorial task. The utility and sense of that of course goes without question. What interests me here, however, is that the automation was geared toward reiterating on a larger scale a scholarly task that was in essence well known and rehearsed; computational power was harnessed to produce an instrument well within the confines of the existing paradigm of print text and its scholarly applications.
>
> (Van Zundert 2016, 901)

Articles that strike a similar tone of ambivalence regarding the sophistication of Busa's work or his founding father status include, for example, McDonough 1967; Lessard and Levison 1997; Winder 2002. [6]

A large quantity of the secondary literature on Busa and the *Index Thomisticus* project published by the fields of humanities computing and digital humanities echoes the evaluative differentiations and omissions that are found in Busa's own publications, as discussed above and in previous chapters. This is true with regard to the self-image that Busa fashioned through his publications and also with regard to his portrayals of his workforce.

For example, the obituary published for Busa by the Association for Computers and the humanities emphasised his connection with IBM above all else: "Roberto Busa is considered by many to be the founder of the scholarly application of computing in the humanities and is most well-known for his collaborations with Thomas Watson, the founder of IBM" (Bellamy 2011). Busa did not directly collaborate with Watson in any commonly understood sense of the term. Moreover, and without wishing to be pedantic, Watson retired in 1956 (and died that same year), some 24 years before the *Index Thomisticus* would be fully published. The rhetorical point of this claim is arguably to associate Busa, and thus the field of digital humanities with "Great man" narratives, like that of Watson, lending it esteem and validation by association, associations we have seen Busa himself build in discussions of the *Index Thomisticus*.

Correspondingly, few mentions of the team who worked directly with Busa on the execution of the *Index Thomisticus* occur in the secondary literature. Of keypunch operators in particular, still fewer references exist. One clear exception to this statement is the work published by de Tollenaere, where he directly addresses the composition of Busa's team and even names one member of the keypunch team (de Tollenaere 1963b, 43). Wisbey is another exception. In a longer discussion of Busa's methodology, he wrote how: "... the scholar pre-edit[ed] the text before punching ... The scholar also inserted special reference marks. ... Once this preparatory work had been done a card punch operator transcribed the text ..." (Wisbey 1962, 165). Citing Busa as his source, Wisbey thus perpetuated the scholar-invisible technician binary.

Burton's description of Busa's set up is one of the most detailed secondary accounts of its time. Drawing, too, on Busa's publications she writes:

> By 1964 the number of people working at the center [CAAL] had increased to sixty: six for managing and secretarial work, fourteen for thought-processing (Latin pre-editing group, Latin lemmatising group, Hebrew group, and a soon-to-be-arranged Greek group), four computer programmers, 32–37 for machine operations (key-punching texts, verifying, listing, sight-checking, punch-card processing, computer processing) ...
>
> (Burton 1981a, 3)

Burton names various individuals who collaborated with Busa, for example, Antonio Zampolli (Burton 1981a). She also refers to the staff of the centre:

> At this center the staff completed the preparation of the corpus of fifteen million words in nine languages (Latin, Greek, Italian, German, English, Hebrew, Aramaic, Nabataean, and Russian) and four alphabets (Roman, Greek, Hebrew, and Cyrillic) from texts dating from Aristotle to nuclear physics abstracts ... By then Busa calculated that the thirty years of work he and others had spent on it amounted to roughly one million man hours.
>
> (Burton 1981a, 3)

Despite this attention to the centre's labour distribution and staff, in the publication under discussion, and elsewhere, Burton proceeds to elide the contributions of the keypunch operators: "After keypunching the 90,000 lemmata from Forcellini's *Lexicon totius Latinitatis* ... he [Busa] listed the 130,000 graphically different words found in the Thomistic corpus ..." (Burton et al. 1984a, 111). So too: "During the next five years Busa processed about two million words of text using only this punched card equipment ..." (Burton 1981a, 2).

Burton's eliding of the contributions of the operators (and other technical staff) follows Busa's lead. This was not uncommon and is, of course, repeated in successive articles on Busa's work. Those elisions often replicate the devices of obfuscation used in Busa's own writing: work is mis-attributed, agency is subsumed by the passive voice, and the role of the machine is privileged over the role of the (usually female) human. An example of the first is found, for example, in the work of Rupert:

> Over the last two decades Roberto Busa, with generous assistance from IBM, has transcribed onto magnetic tapes the entire corpus of Aquinas, several works by other medieval theologians, as well as the Vulgate, many Qumran texts, and the selected works of modern authors such as Kant.
>
> (Rupert 1985, 188)

An example of the second is found, for example, in the work of Brunner, creating the impression that Busa worked alone:

> The Busa/Watson meeting resulted in IBM's willingness to support the creation of a machine-readable version of the text of Saint Thomas Aquinas. Data entry would not be completed until 1967, and another thirteen years would be consumed by text verification and data processing tasks leading, ultimately, to the production of a sixty-volume, 70,000-page concordance to the works of Saint Thomas.
>
> (Brunner 1989, 49)

An example of the third is Hockey's comments on the many years that Busa spent working on the *Index Thomisticus*: "It may seem a long time before publication, but it would not have been possible to attempt such a mammoth undertaking without substantial mechanical help" (Hockey 1980, 15). And of course, neither Busa, Hockey nor the field of humanities Computing were alone in their overlooking of the mammoth feminised human labour that was also required. As Hicks has observed of the contributions of women to second world war code-breaking, but is indicative of feminised computing over the longer-term:

> Conceived of as a passive support to the 'real' work of codebreaking, rather than an integral part of the codebreaking itself, women operators paradoxically found themselves and their work undervalued in histories that were being rewritten to privilege the role of the computers they ran.
>
> (Hicks 2017, 42)

And while the influence, as measured quantitatively with bibliometrics, of the texts cited above may vary, these elisions are also detectable in one of the most highly cited texts on the history of digital humanities, arguably compounding the invisibilising of keypunch operators to new and wider audiences, however unintentional:

> Father Busa imagined that a machine might be able to help him, and, having heard of computers, went to visit Thomas J. Watson at IBM in the United States in search of support ... Some assistance was forthcoming and Busa began his work. The entire texts were gradually transferred to punched cards and a concordance program written for the project.
>
> (Hockey 2004, 4)

Of references in the secondary literature to Busa's staff, mentions occur of the quite amorphous category of "assistant", for example: "We cannot forget, however, that Professor Busa did not find the course charted which he began so many years ago, but that he himself had to explore it, little by little, with the help of his assistants" (Duro 1968, 49–50). Raben too mentions "assistants", but indicates that they were clerics, thus excluding, once more, lay keypunch operators: "Although adept at coupling technical support from IBM with manpower provided by the Church, he still spent decades creating his masterpiece" (Raben 1991, 343). As this book has explored, punched cards and punched paper tape could store instructions, however "more often, the human operator of the punched-card machinery would follow instructions, so that the organisation of computation combined human, machine and method" (Agar 2006, 874). The omissions noted above not only obscure feminised keypunch labour and those who executed it but they ultimately present an unbalanced, and overly machine-centric view of a workflow and an emerging field that was founded on humans, machines and method alike.

By 1981, the role of humans in the *Index Thomisticus'* workflow—whether it was the fundamental technical and methodological input of collaborators like Tasman, or the daily input of interns and employees like keypunch operators—had become almost undetectable in many secondary discussions of Busa's work. The final instalment of the *Index Thomisticus* was published in 1980 and so the publications that appear after this date were no longer commenting on work in progress but reviewing the output. They can be read as definitive assessments of the *Index Thomisticus*. In the following discussion of Burton, Busa alone is portrayed as deserving of credit for the outcomes of the *Index Thomisticus* project:

> He showed that the machine could be successfully adapted to accept language in one form (a set of poems), then read, analyze, sort, and process that language until it emerged in another, intelligible, form, that of a concordance. He thus demonstrated that what had seemed a purely mental operation contained a mechanical, or as he termed it, "material" component. ... He has revolutionised the fields of concordance-making and of computer applications.
>
> (Burton 1981a, 4)

It is against this process of overlooking, followed by forgetting, that the article published by Winter in 1999 is especially important. It emphasised, for a readership no longer familiar with many of the technologies that Busa had used, that manual work had actually played a crucial part in the *Index Thomisticus* project: "Father Busa, with IBM's enabling help, was at the pivot point (or was the pivot point) between handmade scholarly tools and machine-made scholarly tools" (Winter 1999, 16).

Nevertheless, beyond Winter's conceptual foregrounding of the project's reliance on human labour, he did not give much attention to either those individuals who provided labour or the labour they provided. Though Winter was certainly innovative in drawing the workforce of the *Index Thomisticus* into view, they are otherwise eclipsed in his article by Busa, whose achievements include no less than having seen "a need for the impossible" (Winter

1999, 7). In the timeline that Winter sketches of key dates in computing, for example, he acknowledges the significance of transferring the text of the *Index Thomisticus* onto punched cards. But he nevertheless omits the key-punch operators from that action: "1967 Thomas Aquinas text card-punching completed. R.Busa/IBM" (Winter 1999, 4).

Later in that same text, when summarising Busa's "1957 algorithm" he alludes to the work of the scholars ("the scholar") and the keypunch opera-tors ("a clerk"). Redolent of Busa's own texts, Winter lauds the work of the scholar: "the scholar's task is two-fold, and Herculean. He must first examine the form cards ... This is morphology on the practical level. It is intense work" (Winter 1999, 15). Citing Tasman, and directly influenced by Busa's writings too, he rehearses the standard perfunctory overview of keypunch labour: "A clerk ... copies the text. ... A second clerk retypes the phrase ...." (Winter 1999, 14).

If an early tendency of the publications under discussion was to portray Busa as a *de facto* lone scholar, in due course his status as founding father of the field of humanities computing, and later, digital humanities came to be emphasised.[7] In this vein, Unsworth, for example, wrote: "Most fields cannot point to a single progenitor, much less a divine one, but humanities comput-ing has Father Busa, who began working (with IBM) in the late 1940s on a concordance of the complete works of Thomas Aquinas" (Unsworth 2004). Ramsay similarly noted:

> But the field is unusual in that it can point both to a founder and to a moment of creation. The founder is Roberto Busa, an Italian Jesuit priest who in the late 1940s undertook the production of an automatically generated concordance to the works of St. Thomas Aquinas using a computer.
>
> (Ramsay 2008)

Busa has been portrayed in this way by individual scholars and by the field's major scholarly associations, as mentioned above (see also, for example, Hockey 2004; Weingart and Jorgensen 2013; Smith 1985; Genêt and Zampolli 1992; Miall 1992).

An intriguing example of the way that Busa's team members were also eclipsed by his rising renown, suggesting that Busa's reputation as progenitor was aided by the overlooking of his team's contributions, occurs in an article written by Raben for a Festschrift that was dedicated to Busa in 1987. In the article in question, Raben recalls the 1964 Literary Data Processing Con-ference, held at Yorktown Heights, USA, where Busa and Raben both gave papers. The published proceedings of this conference show that Busa did include discussion, more detailed than was his tendency, of the tasks of the 60 staff who worked with him on the *Index Thomisticus* from the early to mid 1960s. Moreover, in that 1964 paper, Busa identified significant aspects of the *Index Thomisticus* project that he himself did not have the expertise to implement ("I am not myself a programmer" (Busa 1964, 74)), again quite clearly signalling that he collaborated with others in the execution of the *Index Thomisticus*. Yet, despite having attended this conference, and having presumably attended Busa's talk, which was also included in the published proceedings, Raben too would later imply that Busa worked alone:

> Through his perseverance and intellectual application, Roberto Busa has demonstrated the efficacy of utilizing the newest technology to comprehend the thought of a master synthesizer of 700 years ago. ... To Roberto Busa, eager pioneer in the blending of philosophy, linguistics, and technology, must go major credit for demonstrating the value of this new synthesis.
>
> (Raben 1987, 227)

Thus, much of the secondary literature of humanities computing and digital humanities followed the trend that had been established by Busa in overlooking and minimising the feminised labour and labour outputs on which the success of the *Index Thomisticus* was built.

But why did many in the humanities computing and digital humanities communities fall into line with this portrayal? It is not plausible to suggest that authors of the earliest papers were simply unaware of the reliance of the *Index Thomisticus* on human labour. Scholars of humanities computing and digital humanities know from their daily praxis that text capture was (and is) an unavoidable aspect of text-based digital humanities projects and that this work is done–even today for categories of documents that are not amenable to automatic capture–or augmented by humans. In noticing the secondary literature's lack of critical engagement with either Busa's or their field's sidelining of the contributions of the keypunch operators (and other technical workers), we gain an insight into how seamlessly Busa's narrative was enfolded with hierarchies of knowledge and horizons of opportunity at the unfolding intersection of computing and the humanities. Indeed, as I will now argue, the field of digital humanities, no less than Busa, stood to benefit from his anointing as founding father.

The myth of the founding father

The fields of humanities computing, and later digital humanities often minimised the contributions of the technical staff on Busa's team and foregrounded Busa as a notional *pater familias*. This was done even though other founding fathers were known and certain difficulties, and curious associations, flowed from the positioning of Busa as founding father. What was it, then, about the narrative that Busa embodied that proved so appealing to the field of humanities computing and digital humanities? What can the emphasis that has been put by the digital humanities community on some parts of the Busa foundation story, and not others, tell us about how the community imagined itself? And what does the embracing of this narrative tell us about the kinds of knowledge and associations that humanities computing and digital humanities aspired to create? Before suggesting some possible answers to this question, a few of the difficulties that arise from the linking of the emergence of the fields of humanities computing and digital humanities to the work that Busa embarked on in the late 1940s will be set out.

The emergence of humanities computing has often been traced to the meeting that took place between Thomas J. Watson, Sr., the CEO of IBM and Busa in 1949. Busa's account of this meeting has taken on the status of a creation myth for the field (see Jones 2016). For many years, the account of this meeting that circulated was based entirely on Busa's own published account of it:

> I knew, the day I was to meet Thomas J. Watson, Sr., that he had on his desk a report which said that IBM machines could never do what I wanted. I had seen in the waiting room a small poster imprinted with the words: "The difficult we do right away; the impossible takes a little longer," (IBM always loved slogans). I took it with me into Mr. Watson's office. Sitting in front of him and sensing the tremendous power of his mind, I was inspired to say: "It is not right to say 'no' before you have tried." I took out the poster and showed him his own slogan. He agreed that IBM would cooperate with my project until it was completed "provided that you do not change IBM into International Busa Machines.
>
> (Busa 1980, 84)

Already in 1981, de Tollenaere's work had raised questions about the detail of Busa's portrayal of this meeting. Far from having allayed Watson's concerns, de Tollenaere had claimed that "IBM in New York was sceptical about [Busa's] proposal and therefore it was that IBM Italia had provided Busa with technical assistance, card material, and machines free of charge" (cited in Burton 1981a, 1).[8] Jones' work has further problematised Busa's telling of the encounter. Watson and Busa's November 1949 meeting was not recorded in Watson's formal datebook (Jones 2016, 28), which may suggest many things of which we cannot be sure, for example, that the meeting was not deemed important enough to have been recorded. Moreover, Busa's command of English was not yet strong at the time of his meeting with Watson (Jones 2016, 3). In fact, Tasman later recalled that it was necessary to avail of the services of an interpreter so that he and Busa could converse in English in those earliest days (Tasman 1968). So, one wonders whether Busa would really have been able to interact with Watson with the ease that is indicated in his account of the meeting above?

Moreover, Jones has shown that IBM's support of Busa was less certain than Busa's later portrayal of it and how Tasman's recollection was that he "believe[d] [IBM] expected me to shake hands with the Jesuit and things would disappear" (cited in Jones 2016, 37). Suggesting the plausibility of

Tasman's recollection, Busa did formidable work to vouchsafe what he must have recognised to be the uncertain support of IBM, including having, for example, a statement of his good character sent to Watson by Cardinal Spellman of New York and by engaging in an extensive letter writing campaign enlisting scholars and scholarly associations write to IBM stating their support for the project (Jones 2016, 86–7).

Why, then, did the field of humanities computing and digital humanities show such a lack of critical engagement with Busa's one-sided portrayal of this meeting? Could it be because Busa's account of his meeting with Watson was not only charming but sociologically powerful too: it gave an emerging and distributed community of practice a point of common descent to cohere around and from which to trace descent. Yet it arguably also raised difficult questions for the field, questions that it may not have been ready or willing to explore.

Glossed over in Busa's recollection of his meeting with Watson is the post-second world war context of that meeting, a context that raises many questions about the historico-ethical and capitalist inheritance of computing in the humanities. This ranges from the broad challenges that the carnage, suffering and destruction wrought by the technological warfare of the second world war posed to the techno-utopian rhetoric that was espoused by Busa and others, along with the more specific challenges that might be raised were the object biographies of the particular accounting machines that were used by some early humanities computing projects better known. Indeed, Jones has written how, in 1946, when

> European demand for [accounting machines] became evident, and IBM found it difficult to deliver new machines due to postwar shortages and import restrictions, it began selling "as-is" equipment, decommissioned punched-card machines from the U.S. military.
>
> (Jones 2016, 36)

The questions that follow, about the intersections between emerging humanities Computing and the industrial-military complex, have only recently started to be explored by scholars like Jones (2016, 33, 60, 69, 131) and McPherson (2012).

Further difficulties arise when the implications, or logical conclusions, of the pinpointing of the field's emergence to the late 1940s, as is implied in the quotes from Unsworth and Ramsay above, are followed through. The first of Busa's texts to discuss mechanically-assisted concordancing was published in 1951. In 1949, Busa was not yet working on the *Index Thomisticus* proper. Rather, he was concording cantos of Dante and hymns of Aquinas for what would be described as a kind of proof of concept for the *Index Thomisticus* (Winter 1999, 10). As we have seen, Busa was doing this not with stored program or digital computers,[9] but with electromechanical accounting machines and human labour. Thus, by tracing the field's emergence to Busa's work in the late 1940s, its origins are arguably not being tranced to an intellectual or technical paradigm shift. Rather, its origins are instead being traced to efforts by Busa, Tasman and IBM employees, including keypunch operators, to replicate, semi-automatically and with office machinery, the well-established processes of the analogue concordance tradition. Put this way, the appeal of the Busa origin legend to the field of humanities computing is not that apparent.

And if we assume that the field is not literally tracing its lineage to 1949 but rather to the *Index Thomisticus* in the sense of the output of the work that began around 1951, the matter remains complicated. The *Index Thomisticus* was published in hard copy from 1974–80. Busa's published concordance attained a scale, and level of detail, that had not previously been seen in humanities computing scholarship (Rockwell and Passarotti 2019). Nevertheless, by the time it was finally published, the creation and manipulation of concordances and concordance software had become an area of central activity in humanities computing (see Oakman 1980, 69). Even a cursory glance at the *Directory of Scholars Active* (Raben 1977), for which data was collected semi-annually from 1966–72, shows that the production and output of concordances had dominated the work of the field for a number of years by 1974 (see also Hockey 1980). Software that could be used to automate aspects of the production of concordances was an established focus by this point too. Early examples, which were run on the mainframes of their respective institutions, included Toronto's PRORA (1966) and Oxford's COCOA (1967) (Lancashire 1986, 54).[10] By the early 1970s:

> programmers began making their concordance-generating programmes "portable" ... Oxford's COCOA, followed by OCP, the most powerful portable batch concordance generator now available for mainframes, and Waterloo's WATCON (by Philip H. Smith, Jr.) were joined by John Bradley's COGS (1977), Alan Reed's CLOC (1979) and William Tuthill's HUM (1981).
>
> (Lancashire 1986, 55)

In other words, the concordance landscape as it looked in 1980, when the *Index Thomisticus* was published, had shifted quite dramatically from the time when Busa began his work some thirty years earlier. Though certainly the result of a great deal of work, and an important piece of scholarship, when the *Index Thomisticus* finally appeared it was initially in the form of a very traditional reference work.

As such, whether Busa's "foundation act" is traced to the late 1940s, or the actual publication of the *Index Thomisticus* (1974–80), it is difficult to find evidence of hallmarks like innovation and seminal intellectual contributions that are often associated with the great men and women of *wissenschaft*. This is not to say that there is not much to be admired in Busa's work. It is, however, to ask how far the actual detail, as opposed to the perception, of Busa's work shaped the perception of his expertise and scholarly contributions and the status that was accorded to him subsequently? Perhaps the impulse that mythologised Busa's contributions is not so far removed from the impulse that devalued that of the keypunch operators.

Amplification

If the difficulties noted above have been little discussed in digital humanities' publications, what has been emphasised from among Busa's achievements? In the earliest literature, the emphasis was often placed on locating the disciplinary context of Busa's work: it was "[a]mong the most significant published work ... in lexicographical analysis by computer" (Wisbey 1962, 164). Zampolli categorised the work as "lexicological and lexicographical" (Zampolli 1973, 343). Raben also emphasised the lexicographical aspects of Busa's work (interestingly, Raben's wording and the information that he gives about Busa suggests that Busa had not yet acquired the renown of present times in the early 1990s):

> The importance of the computer as a lexicographical tool was apparently first demonstrated in a computer-assisted study of Thomas Aquinas conducted by Roberto Busa, a Jesuit teaching linguistics at the Aloisianum in Gallarate, Italy.
>
> (Raben 1991, 343)

Following from the emphasis on words that the categorisation of his research as lexicographical and lexicological implies, various publications mention that Busa's processing of words rather than numbers was a distinctive achievement. This is implicit in Burton's discussion of how he "showed that the machine could be successfully adapted to accept language in one form (a set of poems), then read, analyze, sort, and process that language ..." (Burton 1981a, 4). This was also emphasised by Jones:

> for perhaps the first time in IBMs research the "words" in the code (the term "word" was used for any discrete string of digits making up a unit of data) represented actual natural-language words – linguistic data.
>
> (Jones 2016, 44)

And by Rockwell:

> Busa's project may have been more than just the first humanities computing project. It seems to be one of the first projects to use computers in handling textual information and a project that showed the possibilities for searching any sort of literature.
>
> (Rockwell 2013)

The issue of scale that Rockwell noted has rightly been emphasised by others too, for example, "It's undoubtedly the case that many at the time were thinking of ways to use computers to conduct research in the humanities, but the scale and sweep of Busa's project stands alone" (Ramsay 2011b).

Blending the perspectives above, Busa's work is also described as having inaugurated the relationship between the various scholarly fields that deal with words, often at scale, and computing. Many of those digitally-augmented fields are now often viewed as occupying an important place in the "big tent" of digital humanities. Pritchard wrote of the impact of Busa's work on "classics and the computer" (Pritchard 2008). In the context of religious research, it was argued that

> the pioneering work of Roberto Busa sj., ... broke through the 'theological' diffidence towards computer-aided studies. In fact, many disciplines and departments in this field have now started studies, research projects and sometimes specific institutions for such work.
>
> (Melloni 1990, 393)

Others hold that Busa inaugurated fields that became distinct from humanities computing: "[Busa] is Universally recognised as one of the pioneers of computational linguistics" (Passarotti 2013, 22). The trans-disciplinary significance of his work is also emphasised, whether in terms of how it transcended "the disciplinary boundaries of corpus linguistics, and of medieval philosophy" (Passarotti 2013, 22) or through discussions of the *Index Thomisticus'* importance "for theology, the history of ideas, historical linguistics, lexicography, and textual studies" (Burton 1981a, 4).

The texts discussed above do not, then, tend to locate Busa's contributions to particular research questions, methodological approaches or to particular schools of thought. Rather, these texts tend to frame the significance of Busa's research in an extremely broad way. Thus, his work and legacy has proved endlessly malleable and minable for the field that has strived to portray itself as his descendent and successor. And it is in this regard more than any other that the utility of portraying Busa as the field's founding father can be seen, notwithstanding the difficulties that this also raises. As each new technology for processing or analysing text has unfolded, it seems, the digital humanities has been able to make a claim that Busa's work somehow gave rise to it. With this manoeuvre the field can, through its links to Busa, portray its historical trajectory as one of steep upward advancement and innovation, and its identity as one that has moved incrementally from outsider to insider.

This approach has been followed even when the developments that are being claimed are anachronistic or implausible. For example, Hockey has written how "the first electronic text project in the humanities began in 1949 when Roberto Busa started work on his *Index Thomisticus*" (Hockey 2000, 5). As argued elsewhere, in 1949, when Busa began work, and for many years after, he planned that the outcome of his work would be a printed concordance. There is no indication in his writings, or his work, that he planned an electronic text project in 1949. Or that he planned, until a later stage of his work, one that was in any way comparable to those electronic text projects have since become synonymous with digital humanities. Indeed, it seems unlikely that Busa could have conceived of an electronic text project in 1949, before the invention of the hardware, networks, protocols and infrastructure etc necessary to display and distribute these projects (see Nyhan and Passarotti 2019, xix–xxi).

Other, later evaluations of Busa's work have also sought to present the subsequent path that the history of computing in the humanities and beyond has followed as a logical and inevitable outcome of the work that Busa began in 1949. For example:

> Busa ... saw the potential of computer assistance for tracking patterns across a massive corpus and subsequently embraced the affordances of the new media for textual study. Busa's computer-assisted experiments in corpus linguistics should thus be regarded as a turning point in the use of computers for the study and production of texts, one that would continue with the introduction of hypertext in the 1980s, the widespread take-up of the Internet in the 1990s, and the current experiments in social and cloud computing today.
>
> (Hockey 2004)

Another example of the seemingly boundless developments that Busa's work gave rise to can be found in Irvine, for example. In the quote below it is not enough to claim that Busa's work gave rise to the field of AI, it apparently also led to platform capitalism:

> Watson's meetings with Busa may well have launched the priest on a course to seek investors in his own research laboratory and data-driven empire, one that effectively translated "IBM into International Busa Machines" ..., but the greater empire would be built on the investment in Busa: this is the transmutation of Watson the angel investor into Watson the linguistically intelligent supercomputer, and thus the computational transvaluation of linguistic data into capital.
>
> (Irvine 2015, 4)

And the link to Watson, this time Watson the machine, is echoed and remade by Jones: "In historical context, it's worth noting that Watson's kind of cognitive computing is ultimately descended from the kind of work Busa and Tasman helped to inaugurate, the processing of language instead of numbers" (Jones 2016, 70). While Busa and Tasman did indeed take important steps in the processing of language rather than numbers they were far from the only individuals who were working in this area at this time (see e.g. Nirenburg, Somers and Wilks 2003). Moreover, more work is required so that the work of

Busa, and that being undertaken by the machine learning community, for example, can examined against each other and contextualised with regard to later developments in computing. As it stands, the direction of travel proposed in discussions of the path from Busa's processing of words to developments in machine learning, AI, cognitive computing and so on is at worst tenuous and at best requiring of further research. Yet, this pirouette is often repeated in the secondary literature on Busa. This apogee of this tendency was reached in some of the obituaries that were written about Busa by his fellow clerics. Silencing the contributions of generations of computer scientists, engineers, physicists, mathematicians, information scientists, librarians, humanities computing scholars and others, it was claimed in the Catholic press that it is due to Busa that the internet, hypertext linking, and the ability to create electronic documents and emails all exist. This article also contains the curious comment that if the reader can "read this article", this must also be due to Busa (see L'Osservatore Romano 2011).

And though the discussions above centre discussions of Busa's contributions to technologies and techniques, his legacy is evoked in other contexts too. For example, in a time of increased questioning of the value of the humanities, estimations like those of Passarotti connect Busa's work with the value of fundamental, humanities blue-sky research:

> … without knowing it, people benefit daily from the results obtained from the project which led to the *Index Thomisticus*. Today's ubiquitous relationship with digital texts allows us to forget how many seemingly trivial procedures are in fact the applied result of years of basic research, from the encoding of alphanumeric characters to the operations of search engines. In this sense, the *Index Thomisticus*, created with the aim of "analysing the texts of St. Thomas with a computer", was an extraordinary project of fundamental research whose design, development and testing would ultimately enter all our homes.
>
> (Passarotti 2013, 22)

This review of the ways that Busa's work and legacy have been portrayed by the digital humanities community suggests that the secondary literature has placed great emphasis on making claims about what was new and allegedly future-making in Busa's work. The motivation for this is here understood as being connected with the necessity of justifying digital humanities as an academic field of enquiry within academia (see Nyhan 2016). Thus, this chapter argues that in the lack of critical engagement with Busa's own claims that much of the secondary literature demonstrates; in the broad-brush evocations of his achievements; in the attempt to propose a causal link between Busa's legacy (and thus the field of digital humanities) and a triumphalist legacy of technological progress, we can read a desire on the part of digital humanities to engage in the business of constructing a genealogy of utility, an "aetiological construct" (Ó Corráin 1998, 182).

This aetiology has allowed the field to trace its descent from a Busa who has been portrayed as being almost outside of his time in the way that his work was so utterly forward-looking and cutting-edge. The techno-utopian lineage in which the field has sought to place itself not only extends back to Busa, but forward into new futures too. In this way, the implications of Busa's work are still claimed to be unfurling, as columns of successful technologies, from hypertext to AI, spring from Busa's shoulders and march forward in succession. And in this teleology, we are, perhaps most importantly of all, to read an implicit claim of validation for the fields of humanities computing and digital humanities. Thus, from discussions of Busa's achievements and legacy we can ponder the ways that disciplines and professional communities use history to respond to the needs of the present and to try to will the grander futures they desire into existence.

That Busa depended on a mostly overlooked workforce to manually implement the foundations, and some pivotal stages of the elaboration of the *Index Thomisticus* is a rather less glamorous story than that of, for example, Winter's account of the Busa who saw a "need for the impossible" (cited above). Thus, I argue, we have seen a systematic neglect of those elements of Busa's workflow design, use of technology, and workforce organisation that raise questions that could unsettle the aetiology of digital humanities and, perhaps, the identity of the digital humanities scholar as it was fashioned after Busa. Indeed, emphasis on the human labour that was contributed to the *Index Thomisticus* project emphasises the great deal of manual work that digital humanities projects almost invariably continue to require. This could divert attention away from the promise of the digital humanities, and its growing associations with fields like data science and machine learning, that attract much funding and prestige and likewise emphasise their automated credentials (even if they likewise depend on significant levels of human labour in the context of, for example, dataset curation and training).

And while not wishing to diminish the benefits of building such an aetiology, or wishing to demand that digital humanities' aetiology should be immune to the idiosyncrasies, inconsistencies and flights of imagination that are an integral part of all storytelling, this book shows that there is much to be lost when fields, disciplines and communities focus on triumphalist narratives alone, and overlook the more difficult, or less glamorous parts of their histories.

With regard to Busa in particular, this also suggests that the apparently "new" in Busa's contributions should not continue to be accorded a significance that occludes all else. There is much to be gained from situating Busa's work and working practices within longer histories of textual scholarship and textual labour. The emergence and development of humanities computing and digital humanities, may well, from such a vantage point come to be understood as being as much about the intermingling of the old as the devising of the new. This can open new opportunities for the field of digital humanities to reflect on previously unarticulated assumptions about the purpose and role of disciplinary histories, and to reflect on whether it is time to admit new interpretations of the field's history, founders and project staff, scholarly and technical alike, to its aetiology.

Notes

1 Archival documents indicate that there was some chopping and changing of the team who would move to Boulder with Busa (see e.g. Busa 1969c, 1969d). The team that ultimately went, as recalled by Crosta (Crosta et al. 2014), seems to tally with the archival picture, which lists one Jesuit; two Dominican Priests, Busa, and his "sister ... as housekeeper, and two girls, age 29, as machine operators and secretaries. All the three are from Italy; one girl is a niece of mine, the other one is the niece of Card. Forni" (Busa 1969d).

2 They include: "Design of source documents and cards [,] Legibility of source documents [,] Number of columns to be punched (or duplicated) and proportion of alphabetic to numerical columns [,] Skill and experience of operator [,] Type of equipment used [,] Type of instruction ... Flow of work [,] Duties other than card punching (auditing, coding or checking) [,] working conditions" (IBM Corporation 1949, 4).

3 For scholarship on epistemic virtues in the humanities in particular see, for example, Paul 2008; von Dongen and Paul 2017.

4 In the original French: "*Quand un célibataire perfore Michelle au lieu de Washington, j'ai appris qu'il y a 97,4% de chances pour qu'il se soit disputé avec sa fiancée la veille au soir ...*".

5 Material remnants of this system are not currently known to be extant in Busa's archive

6 Articles that strike a similar tone of ambivalence regarding the sophistication of Busa's work or his founding father status include, for example, McDonough 1967; Lessard and Levison 1997.

7 Vanhoutte has also written on the processes that led to Busa tending to be seen as father of the field. He has noted that "Susan Hockey's *A Guide to Computer Applications in the Humanities* (Hockey 1980) and Robert Oakman's *Computer Methods for Literary Research* (Oakman 1984) provided the first consistent overviews [of the field] from an academic point of view ... In this respect it's relevant to notice that Hockey identified Busa as the pioneer of humanities computing, whereas Oakman named Ellison" (Vanhoutte 2013, 130–1).

8 Burton portrayed IBM's support of Busa differently 3 years later: in her "Review Essay" of the *Index Thomisticus* she wrote that "In 1949 when IBM, swept away by Busa's enthusiasm, offered to sponsor his index until it was completed ..." (Burton et al. 1984a, 109).

9 Though machines like the IBM Selective Sequence Electronic Calculator (SSEC), a precursor of present-day computers was on display and in operation at the IBM World Headquarters in 1949 when Busa began his work, he does not appear to have had the possibility to use this machine. Jones writes that this was because "it was explicitly defined as for scientific calculations (business users had to pay to cover expenses) and [Busa and Tasman's] work was linguistic and humanistic, but also because their work with punched cards was at too preliminary a stage to require such a large-scale machine" (Jones 2016, 52–3).

10 According to Lancashire, the publication of concordances continued despite the availability of such programmes due to the difficulties encountered by scholars who sought to gain access to computing centres to run them and the material implications of printing them (see Lancashire 1986, 54).

6 Conclusion

What constitutes the foundational work of a discipline, the foundational work of knowledge production? Whose work merits mere attribution, let alone acknowledgement, in histories of knowledge production? On what grounds? And what new understandings of the emergence and development of knowledge-producing communities and professions can be derived from an exploration of these questions?

This book has laid great emphasis on recovering the feminised contributions of overlooked and lesser-known individuals to the history of computing in the humanities, and on seeking to understand why it was their contributions, in particular, that would tend to be either erased, or brought into view during discussions of difference or error. Rereading the history of the *Index Thomisticus* project as a history of gendered epistemology, this book has shown how the quotidian yet important work and identity of female knowledge-makers and technicians was constructed by the *Index Thomisticus* project as existing outside of the work of knowledge production proper. Thus, their work was systematically excluded from, or devalued in accounts of the formation of digital humanities, where masculinist epistemologies—or knowledge that was recognised as such because it was perceived as having been made by, and was furthermore made from, the perspective of men—were instead valourised. In this way, through a case study of the digital humanities, a relatively new discipline, this book has examined how knowledges can be formed and raised questions about how and why this should matter. It has thus sought to explore the role of individual and collective human agency and authority in the emergence and development of a field whose histories are not unusual in having been refracted through techno-utopian and teleological narratives of progress, and the exploits, and indeed, perspectives of "great men". It has also sought to raise questions about the implications of retelling the history of digital humanities in this way, and about the kinds of knowledge producing actors, agents, acts and instruments that might be recognised in studies of the past, present and future of digital humanities and knowledge production settings more generally.

The oral history interviews drawn on in this book, and made available in connection with it, recover previously unknown recollections of individuals' experiences of working in one of the first literary text processing centres, and

DOI: 10.4324/9781003138235-7

on one of the earliest, semi-automated, big data projects in the humanities. Reading these interviews between the lines and against the grain, next to archival material and secondary sources, this book has re-examined the human labour that supported and enabled one of the humanities' earliest forays into automation, particularly looking at the social, hierarchical, historical and organisational contexts that framed the work of the female keypunch operators of the *Index Thomisticus*. In doing so, this book has sought neither to personally disparage Busa nor to deny his achievements. It has argued that the field that would become known as digital humanities itself perpetuated and even amplified the self-mythologising, invisibilising and boundary-setting that this book initially focalised in Busa's writings but traced through a good deal of the subsequent digital humanities scholarship too.

Moreover, this book has placed the labour organisation of the *Index Thomisticus* on a continuum with longer histories of the humanities, especially in terms of amanuenses' generally overlooked and devalued labour and the ideal of the lone scholar that this concomitantly bolstered. And while the hidden labour that has been examined in this book occurred mostly in the context of a historical, text-based and computationally-assisted project, hidden and devalued labour can be detected right across the disciplines of present-day academia. Thus, the history set out in this book speaks to the present and future of the humanities too, through its potential interconnections with later, and separate though still perhaps cognate phenomena, like the precarious labour arrangements of the present university-sector (see e.g. Gallas 2018).

In addition to the broad observations made above, this book also speaks directly to the history of computing in the humanities. From this book follows complex and occasionally contradictory estimations of "the computer", which suggest how difficult it was, and perhaps remains, to accept alien machines and the individuals who use them into the humanities and even digital humanities.

Busa's writings contain various musings on the philosophical and spiritual implications of using computers in humanities research. In one article, for example, he responds to Humanists' condescension towards technical workers, and contends that those same Humanists would not, in fact, be able to answer the questions about language that the "men" who used computers for research had asked them (Busa 2019e[1962], 79). The article goes on to argue that Humanists' inability to answer the questions of technologists pointed to something more profound, suggesting the contributions that computing might make to the humanities:

> The machine warns us that we are not humanistic enough; that although we speak, we are not able to say how we speak. It is the despised machine that repeats to us the invitation "know thyself still more profoundly, scientifically and humanistically: study your speech".
>
> (Busa 2019c[1958], 68)

This is an argument that Busa would return to many times over the following years, and he frequently argued that computing offered something new that could be conceptually and methodologically productive to the humanities (Passarotti and Nyhan 2019).

And yet, this book suggests that through the *Index Thomisticus* project and beyond, a rather more ambivalent attitude towards computing and computers can be traced.[1] Whatever about the intellectual departures that computing might potentially provoke, this book has demonstrated how the female key-punch operators who actually worked on the machines, and captured the data that would subsequent be used by those machines, and the lineages of computers that followed, were relegated to the lowest positions in the *Index Thomisticus'* organisational hierarchy. Neither were they afforded any opportunity to write about the machines or to be acknowledged for their work in writings about the project. The scholars, meanwhile did their thinking away from the machines, just as Busa did. Busa seems to have rarely operated machines and computers himself and to have had little knowledge of programming. Yet (in the case of the hard-copy *Index Thomisticus*) he published the data outputs of the project's human-machine configurations under his name alone, or (in his other publications) analysed the output of those machines, or wrote about the implications of that output. And thus, it was Busa who came to be viewed as the quintessential humanities computing and to some extent digital humanities scholar.

This ambivalence with regard to those who actually practice versus those who theorise about computing in the digital humanities can be detected to this day in ongoing debates like that of "Hack versus Yack". At the time of writing, it is still not unusual for technical digital humanities work to be devalued and seen as unscholarly (Griffin and Hayler 2018). As John Bradley wrote of the Department of Digital Humanities in King's College London, UK, for example:

> ... most institutions view the kind of technical contributions which [the Department of Digital Humanities] makes as a kind of support work—perhaps, in extreme cases, as similar to what is done to the academic's car by his garage mechanics. From this position arises, I believe, the application of the diminutive term "techie" by some to describe those individuals doing this kind of work.
>
> (Bradley 2011, 11)

The not infrequent devaluing of technical digital humanities work, and failure to acknowledge the contributions of technical staff to some digital humanities research outputs has sometimes been portrayed by digital humanities as arising from disciplines, processes and contexts that are external to the field, and that emanate from the Academy itself. This is suggested, for example, in a discussion about peer review that took place via what was formerly a leading digital humanities electronic discussion group. This discussion included talk of the "universal disregard for work in computing among the committees that govern hiring, tenure, and promotion" (Humanist Discussion Group 1987/88b). One contributor pointedly asked: "Do tenure and promotion committees value programming, software reviewing, and other of the activities [sic] so typical of HUMANIST addressees?" (Humanist Discussion Group 1987/88a). Accordingly, to counter the devaluing of technical contributions, and the difficulties of evaluating the multi-authored publications that digital humanities work often necessitates, various initiatives have been set up and guidelines issued (e.g. Off the Tracks 2011; Fair Cite Initiative 2012; MLA 2012).

Thus, in the face of references to the wider academy's tendency to devalue computational work and workers in the digital humanities, it is quite startling to observe that this was also an internal hallmark of the project to which many in the digital humanities trace the origins of the field. Future work might then consider the focus that has tended to be placed in digital humanities publications on collaboration, and its alleged centrality to the field. How might a better understanding of previously undocumented or devalued contributions to the founding of digital humanities allow us to critically evaluate the discourse that has accompanied processes like collaboration and interdisciplinarity in the development and establishment of the digital humanities?

Indeed, once one starts paying attention to fleeting mentions of feminised data-input labour, perhaps devalued, in the literature of humanities computing and digital humanities, those references seem to quickly mount up. To give just a few examples, there is Hockey's mention of "T.C. Mendenhall, writing at the end of the nineteenth century, [who] described his counting machine, whereby two ladies computed the number of words of two letters, three, and so on in Shakespeare" (Hockey 2004, 5). There is Burton's reference to the elaboration of John William Ellison's *Complete Concordance to the Revised Standard Version Bible* (1957), which involved:

> five women working at 'Unitypers' [who] hammered away for five months on metal tape, transcribing the approximately 800 000-word text of the Bible. ... And the ten other women [who for the purposes of verification] punched the Bible text onto cards, ran them through a card-to-tape-converter, and produced four additional rolls of magnetic tape
>
> (Burton 1981, 7)

There is Ott's mention of the nuns who did the lemmatisation for Bonifaitus Fischer's concordance project:

> For this work Fischer had engaged a monastery of Benedictine nuns in Kempen on the Rhine. All of them had an *Abitur* (final secondary-school examinations) with Latin as a second language, and therefore they were very happy with this work which was of course, closely controlled or

surveyed by Bonifaitus Fischer. They did work for some years on the lemmatization.

(Nyhan and Flinn 2016, 60)

Remember that lemmatisation was viewed as the work of the scholar in the *Index Thomisticus* project. And Thaller mentions that Busa also engaged students and religious sisters on a later project:

> We rather soon agreed that I would supervise a few students paid by the Societas Jesu to make the complete works of Ignatius machine-readable; Padre Busa than [sic] took care of having them proof read by the nuns at some monastery in Milano.

(Thaller 2017, 39)

For each of these fleeting mentions, there are, of course, many others that mention an extant dataset that was repurposed for a given humanities computing or digital humanities project (see e.g. Burton 1982; Hockey 2000, 11–23), a dataset that must have been encoded, transcribed or otherwise input through human labour, often feminised. And so there arises once more the question as to how we might in future revise our histories of large-scale projects in the history of computing, to acknowledge and excavate the previously undocumented contributions made by those who have been overlooked or hidden by founding father narratives or discourses about the virtues of collaboration?

Crucial to this book's approach has been a focus on process rather than on outcome; on individuals as much as the machines they operated and on the circumstances that hindered research as much as those that advanced it. In some ways, then, this book is a story of "dead ends" and breakages in the process of doing digital humanities. None of the individuals interviewed for this book continued working in the field of humanities computing. And, in the course of researching this book, as we have seen, it was often stories of error, misadventure or thwarted plans, that brought the work of keypunch operators into view.

By continuing to draw attention to this "failed" aspect of the *Index Thomisticus*, rather than the usual story of its pioneering use of punched card machines, and subsequently computers, it may be possible to continue to reread the history of digital humanities and computing in the humanities productively. The whiggish view of history sets it as a linear series of achievements and successes, thus implying that the shape of the present is the most logical and desirable outcome of the past (see Druckrey 2006 vii–xi). The previously hidden aspects of the history of the *Index Thomisticus* project that are presented in this book alert us to other paths that might instead have been followed, had other power dynamics prevailed. Far from being an otherwise neutral site of technological progress, this book has shown the history of computing in the humanities to have been a site of power that sometimes gave rise to struggle, discontent and exclusion.

As a field, the digital humanities, like society more broadly, is grappling with questions of inclusion and diversity and asking how it can achieve a fairer and more representative *status quo*. It is all the more urgent then, that studies such as the one set out in this book continue to be undertaken. For if we are to set about effecting real and long-lasting change it is essential to understand the longer history of how difference has been constructed and operationalised in the production of knowledge, analogue and digital.

Note

1 See also McCarty, who has discussed, in the context of humanities computing, "the fear that closed down the horizons of imaginative exploration during the years of the Cold War" (McCarty 2014, 283) and its ongoing resonance for the digital humanities.

References

Primary source collections consulted

Busa Archive, Università Cattolica del Sacro Cuore, Milan, Italy

IBM Archives, Somers, New York, USA

IBM Hursley Park Museum, Computer Conservation Society, UK

Oral history interviews

Barras P and Nyhan J (2019) 'A Tall, Stooping Figure in Black Crossing the Courtyard': Philip Barras' Recollections of Roberto Busa S.J. In Passarotti M and Nyhan J (eds) *One Origin of Digital Humanities: Fr Roberto Busa in His Own Words*. 185–196. Springer Nature Switzerland AG: Springer International Publishing.

Brogioli G, Vanelli B, Passarotti M and Nyhan, J (2014) We punched things in Latin, if I can recall, they were St. Thomas' works. Oral history interview, 1 April , Gallarate, Italy. Italian transcript and English translation by Ana Vela and Giulia D'Agostino, published at https://hiddenhistories.omeka.net/exhibits/show/oralhistor yinterviews/interviews.

Cervini M, Bossi G, Passarotti M and Nyhan J (2014) We would copy the Latin, we would computerize it. Oral history interview, 1 April , Gallarate, Italy. Italian transcript and English translation by Ana Vela and Giulia D'Agostino, published at https://hiddenhistories.omeka.net/exhibits/show/oralhistoryinterviews/interviews.

Crosta G, Passarotti M and Nyhan J (2014) I was very fortunate to be able to travel to America. Oral history interview, 1 April , Gallarate, Italy. Italian transcript and English translation by Ana Vela and Giulia D'Agostino, published at https://hid denhistories.omeka.net/exhibits/show/oralhistoryinterviews/interviews.

Lombardi G, Segatto M L, Passarotti M and Nyhan J (2014) If I hadn't arrived through, through that training, I wouldn't have gotten it. Oral history interview, 1 April , Gallarate, Italy. Italian transcript and English translation by Ana Vela and Giulia D'Agostino, published at https://hiddenhistories.omeka.net/exhibits/show/ora lhistoryinterviews/interviews.

Mainardi M, Re N, Passarotti M and Nyhan J (2014) It wasn't well-defined but it was something.... Oral history interview, 1 April , Gallarate, Italy. Italian transcript and English translation by Ana Vela and Giulia D'Agostino, published at https://hid denhistories.omeka.net/exhibits/show/oralhistoryinterviews/interviews.

Righetti D, Nyhan J and Passarotti M (2014) This is my history. Oral history interview, 2 April, Milan, Italy. English transcript published at https://hiddenhistories.om eka.net/exhibits/show/oralhistoryinterviews/interviews.

Slocovich P, Nyhan J and Passarotti, M (2014) I started with hardware, software didn't exist yet, programming did. Oral history interview, 2 April, Milan, Italy. Italian transcript and English translation by Ana Vela and Giulia D'Agostino, published at https://hiddenhistories.omeka.net/exhibits/show/oralhistoryinter views/interviews.

The Operator, Passarotti M and Nyhan J (2014) I was interested in learning a lot about the machines. Oral history interview, 1 April, Gallarate, Italy. Italian transcript and English translation by Ana Vela and Giulia D'Agostino, published at https://hidden histories.omeka.net/exhibits/show/oralhistoryinterviews/interviews.

Tasman P (1968) Paul Tasman Interview by Lawrence Saphire for Oral History of Computer Technology (Interview TC-99, 14 August). Somers, NY: IBM Archives.

Visual sources

Busa Archive #0015 (27/06/52) NEW YORK IBM World Headquarters

Busa Archive #0025 (—/06/56) Gallarate CAAL—Casa Sironi

Busa Archive #0026 (—/06/56) Gallarate CAAL—Casa Sironi v.0025

Busa Archive #0027 (—/06/56) Gallarate CAAL—Casa Sironi

Busa Archive #0028 (—/06/56) Gallarate CAAL—Casa Sironi v.0027

Busa Archive #0077 (17/12/56) Gallarate Aloisianum v.0042

Busa Archive #0084 (17/12/56) Gallarate Aloisianum v.0042

Busa Archive #0085 (17/12/56) Gallarate Aloisianum v.0042

Busa Archive #0127 (03/09/58) Bruxelles Expo '58 v.0129

Busa Archive #0129 (03/09/58) Bruxelles Expo '58

Busa Archive #0134 (03/09/58) Bruxelles Expo '58 v.0129

Busa Archive #0147 (31/03/59) Gallarate Aloisianum e Cuccirelli

Busa Archive #0149 (31/03/59) Gallarate Aloisianum e Cuccirelli v.0147

Busa Archive #0154 (31/03/59) Gallarate Aloisianum e Cuccirelli v.0147

Busa Archive #0163 (31/03/59) Gallarate Aloisianum e Cuccirelli v.0147

Busa Archive #0166 (09/06/59) Gallarate Ditta Cuccirelli

Busa Archive #0167 (09/06/59) Gallarate Ditta Cuccirelli v.0166

Busa Archive #0582 (25/09/65) Gallarate Lab. V. Ferraris

References

Abbate, J (2012) *Recoding Gender: Women's Changing Participation in Computing.* Cambridge; London: MIT Press.

Abrams L (2016) *Oral History Theory.* London: Routledge.

Addison J T and Siebert W S (1994) Vocational Training and the European Community. *Oxford Economic Papers* 46 (4): 696–724. http://www.jstor.org/stable/2663517.

ADHO (n.d.) *Roberto Busa Prize.* https://adho.org/awards/roberto-busa-prize.

Agar J (2006) What Difference Did Computers Make? *Social Studies of Science* 36 (6): 869–907. https://www.jstor.org/stable/25474487.

Aggiornamento (1960) Aggiornamento in data 28 aprile 1960 del Regolamento per l'opera "Index Thomisticus" del 19 marzo 1959. Busa Archive [consulted in digital form at http://www.recaal.org/pages/busa.html; filename BUS_14_1_1_8_0006].

Allinson J (1993) The Breaking of the Third Wave: The Demise of GIS. *Planning Practice and Research* 8 (2): 30–33. https://doi.org/10.1080/02697459308722879.

ALPAC (1966) *Languages and Machines: Computers in Translation and Linguistics.* A Re- port by the Automatic Language Processing Advisory Committee, Division of Behavioral Sciences, National Academy of Sciences, National Research Council, Washington D.C., National Academy of Sciences, National Research Council.

Anderson, Katrina, Lindsey Bannister, Janey Dodd, Deanna Fong, Michelle Levy, and Lindsey Seatter. (2016) Student Labour and Training in Digital Humanities. *Digital Humanities Quarterly* 1.

Andrews, M (1995) A Monoglot Abroad: Working through Problems of Translation. *Oral History* 23 (2): 47–50.

Aquinas T (1882) *Sancti Thomae de Aquino Opera omnia: iussu impensaque, Leonis XIII. P.M. edita.* Ex Typographia Polyglotta S.C. de Propaganda Fide, Romae.

Aspray W (1990) *Computing Before Computers.* Ames, Iowa: Iowa State University Press.

Aswad E and Meredith S (2005) *IBM in Endicott.* Charleston: Arcadia Publishing.

Baird D (2004) *Thing Knowledge: A Philosophy of Scientific Instruments.* Berkeley: University of California Press.

Bar-Hillel Y (1960) The Present Status of Automatic Translation of Languages. *Advances in computers* 1: 91–163. https://doi.org/10.1016/S0065-2458(08)60607-60605.

Barley S R and Bechky B A (1994) In the Backrooms of Science: The Work of Technicians in Science Labs. *Work and Occupations* 21: 85–126. https://doi.org/10.1177/0730888494021001004.

Basalla G (1988) *The Evolution of Technology.* Cambridge; New York: Cambridge University Press.

Bauer S (2015) Your Family's Genealogical Records May Have Been Digitized by a Prisoner. *Mother Jones.* https://www.motherjones.com/politics/2015/08/mormon-church-prison-geneology-family-search/.

Beard M (2018) *Women & Power: A Manifesto.* London: Profile Books.

Becker H S (1998). *Art Worlds.* 2nd edition. Berkeley: University of California Press.

Bellamy C (2011) Roberto Busa Dies Aged 97. *ACH The Association for Computers and the Humanities* https://ach.org/blog/2011/08/11/roberto-busa-dies-aged-97/.

Berg N G (1997) Gender, place and entrepreneurship. *Entrepreneurship & Regional Development* 9 (3): 259–268. https://doi.org/10.1080/08985629700000015.

Betti E (2010a) Il lavoro femminile nell'industria italiana. Gli anni del boom economico. *Storicamente* 6: 1–32 [text cited in the body of the book translated by Giulia D'Agostino]. https://storicamente.org/sites/default/images/articles/media/1448/lavoro_femminile_donne.pdf.

Betti E (2010b) Women's Working Conditions and Job Precariousness in Historical Perspective. The Case of Italian Industry during the Economic Boom (1958–1963). In Agárdi I, Waaldijk B and Salvaterra C (eds) *Making Sense, Crafting History. Practices of Producing Historical Meaning*. Pisa: Pisa University Press, 175–205.

Betti E (2013) *Precarietà e fordismo. Le lavoratrici dell'industria bolognese tra anni Cinquanta e Sessanta. In Zazzara G (ed.) Tra luoghi e mestieri. Spazi e culture del lavoro nell'Italia del Novecento*. Edizioni Ca' Foscari, Venezia. 17–45 [text cited in the body of the book translated by Giulia D'Agostino].

Betti E (2016) Gender and Precarious Labor in a Historical Perspective: Italian Women and Precarious Work between Fordism and Post-Fordism. *International Labor and Working-Class History* 89: 64–83. https://doi.org/10.1017/S0147547915000356.

Betti E (2018) Historicizing Precarious Work: Forty Years of Research in the Social Sciences and Humanities. *International Review of Social History* 63 (2): 273–319. https://doi.org/10.1017/S0020859018000329.

Betti E (2020) *Le ombre del fordismo. Sviluppo industriale, occupazione femminile e precarietà del lavoro nel trentennio glorioso*. Bologna: Bononia University Press [text cited in the body of the book translated by Giulia D'Agostino].

Bianco J S (2012) *The Digital Humanities Which Is Not One. In Gold M K (ed.) Debates in the Digital Humanities*. Minneapolis: University of Minnesota Press, 96–113.

Bing J (2009) Protecting personal data in wartime: The destruction of the alphabetic tabulators in Oslo. *Computer Law & Security Review* 25: 89–96. https://doi.org/10.1016/j.clsr.2008.11.003.

Bishop C (2017) The Serendipity of Connectivity: piecing together women's lives in the digital archive. *Women's History Review* 26 (5): 766–780. https://doi.org/10.1080/09612025.2016.1166883.

Bison I (2013a) Le classi medie: definizione, mobilità e declino nel caso italiano. *Società Mutamento Politica* 4 (7): 155–183. https://doi.org/10.13128/SMP-12973 [text cited in the body of the book translated by Giulia D'Agostino].

Bison I (2013b) Note sullo sviluppo economico-sociale e la classe media italiana: 1945–2009. *Società Mutamento Politica* 4(7), 261–282. http://dx.doi.org/10.13128/SMP-12978 [text cited in the body of the book translated by Giulia D'Agostino].

Black A (2007) Mechanization in Libraries and Information Retrieval: Punched Cards and Microfilm before the Widespread Adoption of Computer Technology in Libraries. *Library History* 23 (4): 291–299. https://doi.org/10.1179/174581607x254785.

Black E (2012) *IBM and the Holocaust: The Strategic Alliance Between Nazi Germany and America's Most Powerful Corporation-Expanded Edition*. Washington, D.C.: Dialog Press,

Blair A (2010) *Too Much to Know: Managing Scholarly Information before the Modern Age*. New Haven; London: Yale University Press.

Blair A (2014) *Hidden Hands: Amanuenses and Authorship in Early Modern Europe*. A.S. W. Rosenbach Lectures in Bibliography. https://repository.upenn.edu/rosenbach/8/.

Blamires A, Pratt K and Marx C W (eds) (1992) *Woman Defamed and Woman Defended: An Anthology of Medieval Texts*. Oxford: Oxford University Press.

Booth AD (1955) *Historical Introduction. In Locke W N and Booth A D (eds) Machine Translation of Languages.* New York: Technology Press of the Massachusetts Institute of Technology and Wiley, 1–14.

Bowden P and Mummery J (2014) *Understanding Feminism.* London; New York: Routledge.

Bowker G C and Star S L (1999) *Sorting Things Out: Classification and Its Consequences.* Cambridge; London: MIT Press.

Bradley J (2011) No Job for Techies: Technical Contributions to Research in the Digital Humanities. In Deegan M and McCarty W (eds) *Collaborative Research in the Digital Humanities.* Farnham; Burlington: Ashgate Publishing, 11–26.

Bray F (2007) Gender and Technology. *Annual Review of Anthropology* 36: 37–53. https://doi.org/10.1146/annurev.anthro.36.081406.094328.

Brunner T F (1989) Databanks in the Humanities: Past, Present and Future. In Proceedings of ACH/ALLC / ACH/ICCH / ALLC/EADH – 1989 "The Dynamic Text". Hosted at University of Toronto, Ontario, Canada. 6–10 June 1989, 49–50.

Bucher T (2018) *If … Then: Algorithmic Power and Politics.* Oxford: Oxford University Press.

Budd K W (2016) The Eye Sees What the Mind Knows: The Conceptual Foundations of Invisible Work. In Crain M G et al. (eds) *Invisible Labor: Hidden Work in the Contemporary World.* Oakland: University of California Press, 3–27.

Burton A (2008) Finding Women in the Archive: Introduction. *Journal of Women's History* 20: 149–150. https://doi.org/10.1353/jowh.2008.0014.

Burton D M (1981a) Automated Concordances and Word Indexes: The Fifties. *Computers and the Humanities* 15: 1–14. https://doi.org/10.1007/BF02404370.

Burton D M (1981b). Automated concordances and word indexes: The process, the programs, and the products. *Computers and the Humanities* 15 (3): 139–154. https://doi.org/10.1007/BF02404180.

Burton D M (1982) Automated Concordances and Word-Indexes: Machine Decisions and Editorial Revisions. *Computers and the Humanities* 16: 195–218. https://doi.org/10.1007/BF02263544.

Burton D M (1984a) Index Thomisticus: Sancti Thomae Aquinatis operum omnium indices et concordantiae. *Computers and the Humanities* 18 (2): 109–120.

Burton D M (1984b) Index Thomisticus: Sancti Thomae Aquinatis Operum Indices et Concordantiae. Roberto Busa Sancti Thomae Aquinatis Opera Omnia. Thomas Aquinas, Roberto Busa. *Speculum* 59 (4): 891–894. https://doi.org/10.2307/2846703.

Burton S K (2003). Issues in Cross-Cultural Interviewing: Japanese Women in England. *Oral History* 31: 38–46.

Busa R (n.d.) Per Completare Lo Index Thomisticus Per L'Esposizione Mondiale Di New York 1964–65. Unaccessioned papers received March 2015. Busa Archive [text cited in the body of the book translated by Giulia D'Agostino].

Busa R (1949) *La Terminologia Tomistica dell'Interiorità. Saggi di metodo per una interpretazione della metafisica della presenza.* Milan: Fratelli Bocca.

Busa R (1950) Announcements. *Speculum* 25 (3): 424–425.

Busa R (1951) *S. Thomae Aquinatis Hymnorum Ritualium Varia Specimina Concordantiarum. Primo Saggio Di Indici Di Parole Automaticamente Composti e Stampati Da Macchine IBM a Schede Perforate.* Milan: Fratelli Bocca.

Busa R (1952) Mechanisierung Der Philologischen Analyse. *Nachrichten fuer Dokumentation* 3, 14–19 [text cited in the body of the book translated by Julianne Nyhan].

Busa R (1957) Die Elektronentechnik in der Mechanisierung der sprachwissenschaftlichen Analyse. *Nachrichten für Dokumentation* 8: 20–26 [text cited in the body of the book translated by Julianne Nyhan].

Busa R (1958a) Letter from Roberto Busa to Mr. Edwin B. Newman, 19 September 1958. (Gal. Rel. Cult. 1940. Rel USA) Busa Archive.

Busa R (1958b) The Index of All Non-Biblical Dead Sea Scrolls Published up to December 1957. *Revue de Qumran* 1 (2): 187–198.

Busa R (1959a) All non-biblical Dead Sea Scrolls published up to December 1957 have been indexed. In *Proceedings of Sacra Pagina, Miscellanea Biblica Congressus Internationalis de Re Biblica (1958)*. Paris: Lecoffre, 7–12.

Busa R (1959b) Letter from Roberto Busa to Rev. P. Angelo Serra S.J., 27 June 1959. (Gall. Rel. Cult. IT. Est. 1942. Rel. It.) Busa Archive.

Busa R (1959c) Letter from Roberto Busa to Prof. Dr. E. Pietsch, 26 March 1959. (Gall. Rel. Cult. IT. Est. 1942. Rel. GE.) Busa Archive.

Busa R (1959d) Letter from Roberto Busa to Mr Allen Kent, 8 April 1959. (Gal. Rel. Cult. 1940. Rel USA) Busa Archive.

Busa R (1959e) Letter from Roberto Busa to Miss Mary Elizabeth Stevens, 27 August 1959. (Gal. Rel. Cult. 1940. Rel USA). Busa Archive.

Busa R (1959f) [P. Busa risponde ai malcontenti …] 7/XI/1959. Busa Archive. Unaccessioned papers received March 2015. [text cited in the body of the book translated by Philip Barras]

Busa R (1960a) Zusammengefasste Darstellung der Erfahrungen des Centro per l'Automazione dell'Analisi Letteraria des Aloisianum. *Kolloquium: Maschinelle Methoden der literaryschen Analyse und der Lexicographie.* Tuebingen, 24–26 November 1960. 6 +26 (litograph) [text cited in the body of the book translated by Julianne Nyhan].

Busa R (1960b) Erläuterungen zu den lexicographischen Arbeiten zu Goethe, Farbenlehre, Bd. 3. *Kolloquium Maschinelle Methoden der literarischen Analyse und der Lexicographie*, 36, 6+26 Tuebingen [litograph] [text cited in the body of the book translated by Julianne Nyhan].

Busa R (1961a) Conversation between Fr. Busa and Mr. Dostert at Frankfurt /M- 6/7– 4-1 8 April 1961. (Gall. Rel. Cult. Est. 1944. Rel. Cult. Germania) Busa Archive.

Busa R (1961b) Letter from Roberto Busa to Mr Heller, 5 May 1961. (Gall. Rel. Cult. Est. 1944. Rel. Cult. Germania). Busa Archive.

Busa R (1962) Letter from Busa to Prof. Z. Ben-Hayyim. Milan, 22 March 1962. (Gall. Rel. Cult. Est. 1943. Rel. Israele.) Busa Archive.

Busa R, Croatto C M, Croatto L, Tagliavini C and Zampolli (1962) Una ricerca statistica sulla composizione fonologica della lingua italiana parlata eseguita con un sistema IBM a schede perforate. In *Proceedings of the XXIth Intern. Speech and Voice Therapy Conference, Padua 1962*, 542–562.

Busa R (1964) An Inventory of Fifteen Million Words. In Bessinger J B, Parrish S M and Arader H F (eds) *Literary Data Processing Conference Proceedings September 9,10,11 1964*. New York; Armonk: IBM Corporation, 64–78.

Busa R (1967) Letter from Roberto Busa to Mr Paul Tasman, 26 June 1967 (1960. Datario). Busa Archive.

Busa R (1968) Letter from Roberto Busa to Mr Paul Tasman 21 March 1968 (1960. Datario). Busa Archive.

Busa R and Zampolli A (1968) Centre pour l'Automation de l'Analyse Linguistique (C.A.A.L.), Gallarate. In Stindlová J and Skoumalová Z (eds) *Les machines dans la linguistique: Colloque International sur la mécanisation et l'automation des recherches linguistiques*. Berlin; Boston: De Gruyter, 25–34.

Busa R (1969b) Letter from Roberto Busa for the Attention of the Director of the Italian Section of the Modern Languages Dpt. 7 June 1969. (1960. Datario). Busa Archive.

Busa R (1969c) Letter from Roberto Busa to Rev. B. McMahon SJ, 28 July 1969. (1960. Datario). Busa Archive.

Busa R (1969d) Letter from Roberto Busa to His Excellency James V. Casey, 9 September 1969 (1960. Datario). Busa Archive.

Busa, R (1969e). Discussions Centrees Sur le LEL. Le LEL de Gallarate. *Revue (R.E.L.O)*. V: 57–63http://web.philo.ulg.ac.be/rissh/wpcontent/uploads/sites/10/pdf/Annee1969/02-03/LELGallarate.pdf.

Busa R (1969f) Le LEL de Gallarate. *Revue (R.E.L.O.)* V, 1–4: 40–54. http://promethee.philo.ulg.ac.be/RISSHpdf/annee1969/02-03/RBusa.pdf.

Busa R (1976) Guest Editorial: Why can a computer do so little? *ALLC Bulletin* 4: 1–3.

Busa R (1980) The Annals of Humanities Computing: The Index Thomisticus. *Computers and the Humanities* 14: 83–90. https://www.jstor.org/stable/30207304.

Busa R (1989) Storia informatica di parole. *Gregorianum* 70: 127–140. https://www.jstor.org/stable/23577767.

Busa, R (1991) *Thomae Aquinatis Opera Omnia – cum hypertextibus – in CD-ROM – auctore Roberto Busa*, pp. 64 + 1. Milano: Editel [CDROM].

Busa R (1992) Half a Century of Literary Computing: Towards a "new" Philology. *Literary and Linguistic Computing* 7 (1): 67–73. https://doi.org/10.12759/hsr.17.1992.2.124-133.

Busa R (1993) CAEL Newsletter. Busa Archive.

Busa R (1994) *Inquisitiones Lexicologicae in Indicem Thomisticum*. 2nd edition. Milan: CAEL.

Busa R (1998) Concluding a Life's Safari from Punched Cards to World Wide Web. In Burnard L, Deegan M and Short H (eds) *The Digital Demotic: A Selection of Papers from Digital Resources in the Humanities 1997*. London: Office for Humanities Communication, 3–12.

Busa R (2004) Foreword: Perspectives on Digital Humanities. In Schreibmann S, Siemens R and Unsworth J (eds) *A Companion to Digital Humanities*. Malden: Blackwell Publisher, xvi–xii.

Busa R (2019a[1951]) A First Example of Word Index Automatically Compiled and Printed by IBM Punched Card Machines. In Nyhan J and Passarotti M (eds) *One Origin of Digital Humanities: Fr Roberto Busa in His Own Words*. Cham: Springer International Publishing, 19–38.

Busa R (2019b[1958]) The Use of Punched Cards in Linguistic Analysis. In Nyhan J and Passarotti M (eds) *One Origin of Digital Humanities: Fr Roberto Busa in His Own Words*. Cham: Springer International Publishing, 39–58.

Busa R (2019c[1958]) The Main Problems of the Automation of Written Language. In Nyhan J and Passarotti M (eds) *One Origin of Digital Humanities: Fr Roberto Busa in His Own Words*. Cham: Springer International Publishing, 59–68.

Busa R (2019d[1961]) The Work of the 'Centro per l'Automazione Dell'Analisi Letteraria' in Gallarate, Italy. In Nyhan J and Passarotti M (eds) *One Origin of Digital Humanities: Fr Roberto Busa in His Own Words*. Cham: Springer International Publishing, 69–74.

Busa R (2019e[1962]) Linguistic Analysis in the Global Evolution of Information. In Nyhan J and Passarotti M (eds) *One Origin of Digital Humanities: Fr Roberto Busa in His Own Words.* Cham: Springer International Publishing, 75–86.

Busa R (2019f[1964]) Latin as a Suitable Computer Language for Science. In Nyhan J and Passarotti M (eds) *One Origin of Digital Humanities: Fr Roberto Busa in His Own Words.* Cham: Springer International Publishing, 87–92.

Busa R (2019h[1966]) Experienced-Based Results with Preparations for the Use of Automatic Calculation in Biology. In Nyhan J and Passarotti M (eds) *One Origin of Digital Humanities: Fr Roberto Busa in His Own Words.* Cham: Springer International Publishing, 105–110.

Busa R (2019j[1968]) Human Errors in the Preparation of Input for Computers. In Nyhan J and Passarotti M (eds) *One Origin of Digital Humanities: Fr Roberto Busa in His Own Words.* Cham: Springer International Publishing, 119–124.

Busa R (2019m[1990]) The Complete Works of St Thomas Aquinas on CD-ROM with Hypertexts. In Nyhan J and Passarotti M (eds) *One Origin of Digital Humanities: Fr Roberto Busa in His Own Words.* Cham: Springer International Publishing, 143–148.

Busa R and Associates (2005) Index Thomisticus. Corpus Thomisticum. https://www.corpusthomisticum.org/it/index.age.

Bush V (1945) As We May Think. *The Atlantic.* http://www.theatlantic.com/maga zine/archive/1969/12/as-we-may-think/3881/.

Butler J (1990a) *Gender Trouble: Feminism and the Subversion of Identity.* New York: Routledge.

Butler J (1990b) Performative Acts and Gender Constitution: An Essay in Phenom-enology and Feminist Theory. In Case S E (ed.) *Performing Feminisms: Feminist Critical Theory and Theatre.* Baltimore: Johns Hopkins University Press, 270–282.

Buurma R S and Heffernan L (2018) Search and Replace: Josephine Miles and the Origins of Distant Reading. *Modernism / Modernity Print* 3. https://modernismm odernity.org/forums/posts/search-and-replace.

Bux W E (1966) *Key-punch Training Course.* Cincinnati: South-Western Publishing.

CAAL (n.d.) Centro per l'Automazione Dell'Analisi Letteraria dell'Aloisianum Gal-larate (Varese). Corsi Liberi di Istruzione Tecnica Per La Specializzazione Pro-fessionale Di Allievi Operatori e di Allieve Perforatrici e Verificatrici di Reparti Contabili Meccanografici. Regolamento. Busa Archive. Unaccessioned papers received March 2015 [text cited in the body of the book translated by Philip Barras].

CAAL (1959) Rapporto Informativo. Oggetto: situazione psicologica generale degli allieve 29 October 1959 [text cited in the body of the book translated by Philip Barras].

CAAL (1961) Attestato di addestramento professionale. 08 September1962. Busa Archive. [Digitised copy consulted at http://archelogos.hypotheses.org/135] [text cited in the body of the book translated by Philip Barras].

Caldwell L (1991) *Italian Family Matters: Women, Politics and Legal Reform.* Houndmills, Basingstoke, Hampshire London: Palgrave Macmillan.

Campbell M (2019) Busa Archive Photos. Private email communication to J. Nyhan. 10 June. Reproduced with kind permission of the author.

Campbell-Kelly M (1990) Punched-Card Machinery. In Aspray W (ed.) *Computing Before Computers.* Ames: Iowa State University Press, 122–155.

Cap F (1963) Letter from Institute for Theoretical Physics. University of Innsbruck. Head: Prof. Dr. Ferdinand Cap to Your Department for Translations, Reference, Abstracts, Documentation. 10 April 1963, (Gall. Rel. Cult. Est. 1944. Rel. Cult. Austria). Busa Archive.

Carnes M C (2007) *The Culture of Work. In Carnes M (ed.) The Columbia History of Post-World War II America.* New York: Columbia University Press, 106–130.

Carrillo E A (1991) The Italian Catholic Church and Communism, 1943–1963. *The Catholic Historical Review* 77: 644–657.

Carroll B A (1990) The Politics of "Originality": Women and the Class System of the Intellect. *Journal of Women's History* 2 (2): 136–163. https://doi.org/10.1353/jowh. 2010.0060.

Carruthers M (2008) *The Book of Memory: A Study of Memory in Medieval Culture.* Cambridge; New York: Cambridge University Press.

Castro Varela M M, Dhawan N and Engel A (2016) *Hegemony and Heteronormativity: Revisiting "the Political" in Queer Politics.* London; New York: Routledge.

Caswell M and Cifor M (2016) From Human Rights to Feminist Ethics: Radical Empathy in the Archives. *Archivaria* 81 (May): 23–43.

Ceruzzi, P E (1991) When Computers Were Human. *IEEE Annals of the History of Computing* 13 (3): 237–244.

Chaudhuri N, Katz S J and Perry M E (2010) Introduction. In Chaudhuri N, Katz S J and Perry M E (eds) *Contesting Archives: Finding Women in the Sources.* Urbana-Champaign: University of Illinois, xiii–xxiv.

Clarke A E and Fujimura J H (1992) What tools? Which Jobs? Why right? In Clake A E and Fujimura J H (eds) *The Right Tools for the Job: At Work in Twentieth-Century Life Sciences.* Princeton: Princeton University Press, 3–44.

Cockburn C and Ormrod S (1993) *Gender and Technology in the Making.* London; Thousand Oaks; New Delhi: SAGE Publications.

Colbans, H. 1958. Machines and Documentation. *Discovery*, July.

Commissione (1959) Commissione parlamentare d'inchiesta sulle condizioni dei lavoratori in Italia, *Relazioni della Commissione parlamentare di inchiesta sulle condizioni dei lavoratori in Italia, VIII, Rapporti particolari di lavoro: contratto a termine, lavoro in appalto, lavoro a domicilio, apprendistato,* Segretariati generali della Camera dei deputati e del Senato della Repubblica, Roma [text cited in the body of the book translated by Giulia D'Agostino].

Computer History Museum (2008) Jean Jennings Bartik – ENIAC Pioneer. YouTube. https://www.youtube.com/watch?v=buAYHonF968.

Computer History Museum (2010) Jean Bartik and the ENIAC Women. YouTube. https://www.youtube.com/watch?v=aPweFhhXFvY.

Considine J (2015) Cutting and Pasting Slips: Early Modern Compilation and Information Management. *Journal of Medieval and Early Modern Studies* 45 (3): 487–504. https://doi.org/10.1215/10829636-3149119.

Conway P (2015) Transformations and the Archival Nature of Surrogates. *Archival Science* 15: 51–69. https://doi.org/10.1007/s10502-014-9219-z.

Cook T and Schwartz J M (2002) Archives, records, and power: From (postmodern) theory to (archival) performance. *Archival Science* 2: 171–185. https://doi.org/10. 1007/BF02435620.

Cory T S (2014) *Aquinas on Human Self-Knowledge.* Cambridge; New York: Cambridge University Press.

Cowan RS (1989) The Consumption Junction: A Proposal for Research Strategies in the Sociology of Technology. In Bijker W E, Hughes T P, Pinch T J and Douglas D G (eds) *The Social Construction of Technological Systems: New Directions in the Sociology and History of Technology.* Cambridge; London: MIT Press, 261–280.

Crain M (2016) Consuming Work. In Poster W, Cherry M and Crain M G (eds) *Invisible Labor: Hidden Work in the Contemporary World*. Oakland: University of California Press, 257–278.

Criado Perez C (2020) *Invisible Women: Exposing Data Bias in a World Designed for Men*. London: Vintage.

Cronin J G R (2021) A reluctant pacifist: Thomas Merton and the Cold War Letters, October 1961 – April 1962. Doctoral thesis, University College Cork.

Cross F L and Livingstone E A (2005) *The Oxford Dictionary of the Christian Church*. Oxford: Oxford University Press.

Crymble A (2021) *Technology and the Historian: Transformations in the Digital Age*. Urbana: University of Illinois Press.

Danes F (2009) Paul Garvin, 1919–1994: An obituary of an excellent (socio)linguist and old good friend. *International Journal of the Sociology of Language* 118: 205–207. https://doi.org/10.1515/ijsl.1996.118.205.

Davies B (2012) *Editions and Translations*. In Davies B (ed.) *The Oxford Handbook of Aquinas*. Oxford; New York: Oxford University Press, 537–540.

Davies M W (1982) *Woman's Place Is at the Typewriter: Office Work and Office Workers, 1870–1930*. Philadelphia: Temple University Press.

Dawson J, McCarty M, Opas-Hänninen L L, Ore E and Unsworth J (2002) The Roberto Busa Award. *Computers and the Humanities* 36: 257.

de Clementi A (2002) *The feminist movement in Italy*. In Braidotti R and Griffin G (eds) *Thinking differently. A reader in European women's studies*. New York: Zed Books, 332–340.

de Freitas R S and Pietrobon R (2010) Why Care about Scientific Controversies? *Journal of Historical Sociology* 23 (4): 501–516. https://doi.org/10.1111/j.1467-6443.2010.01381.x.

De Marco G, Mainetto G, Pisani S and Savino P (1999) The early computers of Italy. *IEEE Annals of the History of Computing* 21: 28–36. https://doi.org/10.1109/85.801530.

de Tollenaere F (1962) Letter from Dr. F. de Tollenaere to Reverendissimo Patre R. Busa S.J., 23 June 1962. (Gall. Rel. Cult. Est. 1943. Rel. Olande). Busa Archive.

de Tollenaere F (1963a) English Typescript Draft for Nieuwe Wegen in de Lexicologie, (Amsterdam, Noord-Hollandsche Uitg. Mij. 1963) Busa Archive.

de Tollenaere, F (1963b) *Nieuwe wegen in de lexicologie*. Mij: Noord-Hollandsche Uitg.

de Tollenaere F (1972) Encoding Techniques in Dutch Historical Lexicography. *Computers and the Humanities* 6: 147–152. https://doi.org/10.1007/BF02402631.

Deegan M and McCarty W (eds) (2012) *Collaborative Research in the Digital Humanities: A Volume in Honour of Harold Short, on the Occasion of His 65th Birthday and His Retirement, September 2010*. Farnham: Ashgate.

Der Spiegel (1957) Elektronen-Gehirne. Zum Ruhme Christi. 3 April [text cited in the body of the book translated by Julianne Nyhan].

Deutsche Forschungsgemeinschaft (2016) DFG-Praxisregeln: Digitalisierung. http://www.dfg.de/formulare/12_151/12_151_de.pdf [text cited in the body of the book translated by Julianne Nyhan].

Di Giovanni S M (2016) *Aggiornamento on the Hill of Janus: The American College in Rome, 1955–1979*. Downers Grove IL: Midwest Theological Forum.

D'Ignazio C and Klein L F (2020) *Data feminism*. Cambridge; London: The MIT Press.

Dinman R (1953) Accounting Machines and the Accounting Curriculum. *The Accounting Review* 28 (4): 577–580.

Dobson J E (2019) *Critical Digital Humanities: The Search for a Methodology.* Champain: University of Illinois Press.

Dostert L (ed.) (1957) *Report of the Eighth Annual Round Table Meeting on Linguistics and Language Studies: Research in Machine Translation.* Washington, D.C.: Georgetown University Press.

Druckrey T (2006) Foreword. In Zielinski S. *Deep Time of the Media: Toward an Archaeology of Hearing and Seeing by Technical Means,* tran. Gloria Custance. Cambridge, MA, London, England: The MIT Press, vii–xii.

Dubé P H (1975) Computer-generated Concordances and their Application to explication de texte. *The Canadian Modern Language Review* 33: 27–31. https://doi.org/10.3138/cmlr.33.1.27.

Dunlop T (2015) *The Bletchley Girls: War, secrecy, love and loss: the women of Bletchley Park tell their story.* London: Hodder Paperbacks.

Dunnage J (2002) *Twentieth Century Italy: A Social History.* London: Routledge.

Duro A (1968) Humanities Computing Activities in Italy. *Computers and the Humanities* 3: 49–52. https://doi.org/10.1007/BF02395450.

Dyer R R (1968) Machine coding for Greek. *Calculi*: 35–37.

Dyer R R (1969) The New Philology: An Old Discipline or a New Science? *Computers and the Humanities* 4: 53–64. https://doi.org/10.1007/BF02393451.

Dyson G (1999) The Undead . *Wired Magazine* 7 (3). http://www.wired.com/wired/archive/7.03/punchcards_pr.html.

EADH (2011) Nominations for Roberto Busa Award. EADH European Association for Digital Humanities. https://eadh.org/news/2011/06/18/nominations-roberto-busa-award.

Earhart A E (2015) *Traces of the Old, Uses of the New: The Emergence of Digital Literary Studies.* Ann Arbor: The University of Michigan Press.

Earhart A, Jones S E, McPherson T, Murray P R and Whitson R (2017) Alternate Histories of the Digital Humanities. ADHO-2017. Hosted at McGill University, Université de Montréal, Canada. 8–11 August. https://dh-abstracts.library.cmu.edu/works/3836.

Eckert W J (1940) *Punched Card Methods in Scientific Computation.* The Thomas J. Watson Astronomical Computing Bureau. New York: Columbia University. https://catalog.hathitrust.org/Record/002523225.

Edgerton D (2019) *The Shock of The Old: Technology and Global History since 1900.* London: Profile Books.

Eichmann-Kalwara N, Jorgensen J and Weingart S B (2018) Representation at Digital Humanities Conferences (2000–2015). In Losh E M and Wernimont J (eds) *Bodies of information: intersectional feminism and digital humanities.* Minneapolis: University of Minnesota Press, 72–92.

Eisenstein E L (1980) *The printing press as an agent of change: communications and cultural transformations in early-modern Europe.* New York: Cambridge University Press.

Ellison J W (1957) *Complete Concordance of the Revised Standard Version Bible.* New York: Thomas Nelson & Sons.

Ensmenger, N (2004). Power to the People: Toward a Social History of Computing. *IEEE Annals of the History of Computing* 26: 96–95 [*sic*]. https://doi.org/10.1109/MAHC.2004.1278876.

Ensmenger N (2012) *The Computer Boys Take Over: Computers, Programmers, and the Politics of Technical Expertise.* Cambridge, London: MIT Press.

Ensmenger N (2015) "Beards, Sandals, and Other Signs of Rugged Individualism": Masculine Culture within the Computing Professions. *Osiris* 30: 38–65. https://doi. org/10.1086/682955.

Ensmenger, N (2021) The Cloud Is a Factory. In Mullaney T S, Peters B, Hicks M and Philip K (eds) *Your Computer Is on Fire*. Cambridge, London: The MIT Press, 29–50. https://doi.org/10.7551/mitpress/10993.003.0005.

Essin C (2015) Unseen Labor and Backstage Choreographies: A Materialist Production History of A Chorus Line. *Theatre Journal* 67: 197–212. https://doi.org/10. 1353/tj.2015.0048.

European Commission (2009) Gender segregation in the labour market. Luxembourg: European Union.

European Commission (2013) Women Active in the ICT Sector. Final Report. Luxembourg: European Union.

Ewers, Stefan Markus (2022) LibGuides: Treaty of Rome: Home. https://consilium -europa.libguides.com/c.php?g=689896&p=4939332.

Fair Cite Initiative (2012) Fair Cite: Towards a Fairer Culture of Citation in Academia. https://faircite.wordpress.com/.

Fisk C (2006) Credit Where It's Due: The Law and Norms of Attribution. *Georgetown Law Journal* 95: 49–117.

Flow chart (1952) *Flow Chart*. Busa Archive. Unaccessioned papers received March 2015. A digitised version is available: http://www.recaal.org/pages/workflow.html.

Fornaciari L (1956) Osservazioni sull'andamento del lavoro femminile in Italia negli ultimi 50 anni. *Rivista Internazionale di Scienze Sociali* 27: 222–240.

Fox M (2014) *Riddle of the Labyrinth: The Quest to Crack an Ancient Code and the Uncovering of a Lost Civilisation*. London: Profile Books.

Fraistat N (2012) The Function of Digital Humanities Centers at the Present Time. In Gold M K (ed.) *Debates in the Digital Humanities*. Minneapolis, London: University of Minnesota.

Fricker M (2007) *Epistemic Injustice: Power and the Ethics of Knowing*. Oxford: Oxford University Press.

Friedan B (1963) *The Feminine Mystique*. New York: Dell Publishing.

Frisch M (2006) *Oral History and the Digital Revolution: Toward a Post-Documentary Sensibility*. In Perks R and Thomson A (eds) The Oral History Reader. Abingdon: Routledge, 102–114.

Gallas A (2018) Introduction: The Proliferation of Precarious Labour in Academia. *Global Labour Journal* 9: 69–74. https://doi.org/10.15173/glj.v9i1.3428.

Game A and Pringle R (1984) *Gender at Work*. London: Pluto Press.

Gao J (2021) Visualising the intellectual and social structures of digital humanities using an invisible college model. Doctoral thesis. University College London.

Gao J, Nyhan J, Duke-Williams O and Mahony S (2022) Gender influences in Digital Humanities co-authorship networks. *Journal of Documentation* 78: 327–350. https:// doi.org/10.1108/JD-11-2021-0221.

General Congregation 34 (1995) Decree 14: Jesuits and the Situation of Women in Church and Civil Society. Jesuitresource.org. https://www.xavier.edu/jesuitresource/ jesuit-a-z/terms-w/decree-14.

Genêt J-P and Zampolli A (1992) *Computers and the humanities*. Aldershot; Brookfield, Vt., USA: Dartmouth; Distributed in the United States by Ashgate Pub.

Gibson S (2002) Fairly Determined. *University of Toronto Magazine*. March 3.

Gieryn T F (1983) Boundary-Work and the Demarcation of Science from Non-Science: Strains and Interests in Professional Ideologies of Scientists. *American Sociological Review* 48: 781–795. https://doi.org/10.2307/2095325.

Gorman M (2005) The Influence of Ignatian Spirituality on Women's Teaching Orders in the United States. In Chapple C (ed.) *The Jesuit Tradition in Education and Missions: A 450 Year Perspective.* Scranton; London: University of Chicago Press, 182–202.

Govoni P (2009) "Donne in un mondo senza donne": le studentesse delle facoltà scientifiche in Italia 1877–2005. *Quaderni Storici* 130 (1): 213–247.

Gray M L and Suri S (2019) *Ghost Work: How to Stop Silicon Valley from Building a New Global Underclass.* Boston; New York: Houghton Mifflin Harcourt.

Green J (1997) *Chasing the Sun: Dictionary-Makers and the Dictionaries They Made.* London: Pimlico.

Greenwald M W (1984) Alice Kessler-Harris. *Out to Work: A History of Wage-Earning Women in the United States* 89: 193. https://doi.org/10.1086/ahr/89.1.193.

Grier D A (1996) The ENIAC, the Verb to Program, and the Emergence of Digital Computers. *IEEE Annals of the History of Computing* 18: 51–55. https://doi.ieee computersociety.org/10.1109/85.476561.

Grier D A (2005) *When Computers Were Human.* Princeton: Princeton University Press.

Griffin G and Hayler M S (2018) Collaboration in Digital Humanities Research – Persisting Silences. *Digital Humanities Quarterly* 12.

Gunnerud Berg N (1997) Gender, place and entrepreneurship. *Entrepreneurship & Regional Development* 9: 259–268. https://doi.org/10.1080/08985629700000015.

Gürer D (2002) Women in computing history. *ACM SIGCSE Bulletin* 34: 116–120. https://doi.org/10.1145/543812.543843.

Gutzwiller M C (1999) Wallace Eckert, Computers, and the Nautical Almanac Office. In Fiala A D and Dick S J (eds) *Proceedings, Nautical Almanac Office Sesquicentennial Symposium*, Washington D.C.: U.S. Naval Observatory, 147–163.

Guzzetti L (1995) *A Brief History of European Union Research Policy.* Luxembourg: European Commission.

Haigh T (2001) The chromium-plated tabulator: institutionalizing an electronic revolution, 1954–1958. *IEEE Annals of the History of Computing* 23 (4): 75–104. https://doi.org/10.1109/85.969965.

Haigh T (2010) *Masculinity and the Machine Man, In ed. Misa T J: Gender Codes: Why Women are Leaving Computing.* Hoboken: John Wiley & Sons, 52–71.

Haigh T (2011) Unexpected connections, powerful precedents, and big questions: the work of Michael Sean Mahoney on the history of computing. In Haigh T (ed.) *Histories of Computing.* Cambridge; London: Harvard University Press, 1–20.

Haigh T (2014) The tears of Donald Knuth. *Communications of the ACM* 58: 40–44. https://doi.org/10.1145/2688497.

Haraway D (1988) Situated Knowledges: The Science Question in Feminism and the Privilege of Partial Perspective. *Feminist Studies* 14 (3): 575–599. https://doi.org/10.2307/3178066.

Hardiman R (2005). Advocating the reform of the reform: Latin Mass or Tridentine Mass? *Pastoral Liturgy* 36: 21–25.

Harding S G (1986) *The Science Question in Feminism.* Ithaca: Cornell University Press.

Hartley J M and Tansey E M (2015) White coats and no trousers: narrating the experiences of women technicians in medical laboratories, 1930–90. *Notes and Records: the Royal Society journal of the history of science* 69: 25–36. https://doi.org/10.1098/rsnr.2014.0058.

Handlist (n.d.). Explanatory handlist compiled by Roberto Busa to facilitate navigation of, and identification of entities, locations and other features of interest pictured in historical photos of CAAL and the Index Thomisticus project. Busa Archive.

Hartman Strom S (1989) "Light Manufacturing": The Feminization of American Office Work, 1900–1930. *Industrial and Labor Relations Review* 43: 53–71. https://doi.org/10.2307/2523208.

Hatton E (2017) Mechanisms of invisibility: rethinking the concept of invisible work. *Work, Employment and Society* 31: 336–351. https://doi.org/10.1177/0950017016674894.

Heide L (2009) *Punched-Card Systems and the Early Information Explosion, 1880–1945*. Baltimore: John Hopkins University Press.

Heller R A (1961) Letter from Roger A. Heller, Head of Centre to Roberto Busa, May 17, 1961. (Gall. Rel. Cult. Est. 1944. Rel. Cult. Germania). Busa Archive.

Heller RA (1997) The Challenge of Keypunching for MT. In *Proceedings of Machine Translation Summit VI: Plenaries*. San Diego: California, 37–38.

Hicks M (2017) *Programmed Inequality: How Britain Discarded Women Technologists and Lost Its Edge in Computing*. Cambridge; London: MIT Press.

Higgins L (2004) *Coeducation but Not Equal Opportunity: Women Enter Boston College*, In Miller-Bernal L and Poulson S L (eds) *Going Coed: Women's Experiences in Formerly Men's Colleges and Universities, 1950–2000*. Nashville: Vanderbilt University Press, 198–218.

Hochschild A (2016) Foreword: Invisible Labor, Inaudible Voice. In Crain M, Poster W and Cherry M (eds) *Invisible Labor. Hidden Work in the Contemporary World*. Berkeley, CA: University of California Press, xi–xiv.

Hockey S (1980) *A Guide to Computer Applications in the Humanities*. Baltimore: John Hopkins University Press.

Hockey S (2000) *Electronic Texts in the Humanities: Principles and Practice*. Oxford; New York: Oxford University Press.

Hockey S M (2004) *The History of Humanities Computing*. In Schreibmann S, Siemens R and Unsworth J (eds) *Companion to Digital Humanities* (Blackwell Companions to Literature and Culture). Oxford: Blackwell Publishing Professional, 1–19.

Hockey S and Nyhan J (2016) *They Took a Chance*. In Nyhan J and Flinn A (eds) *Computation and the Humanities: Towards an Oral History of Digital Humanities*. Cham: Springer International Publishing, 87–97.

Hollings, Christopher, Ursula Martin, and Adrian Rice (2018) *Ada Lovelace: The Making of a Computer Scientist*. Illustrated edition. Oxford: The Bodleian Library.

Humanist Discussion Group (1987/88a) Vol. 1 Num. 47. McCarty, W (ed.) 5/87–85/88. https://humanist.kdl.kcl.ac.uk/Archives/Virginia/v01/.

Humanist Discussion Group (1987/88b) Vol. 1 Num. 49. McCarty, W (ed.) 5/87–85/88 https://humanist.kdl.kcl.ac.uk/Archives/Virginia/v01/.

Hutchins J (2003) *ALPAC: The (In)Famous Report*. In Nirenburg S, Somers H L and Wilks Y (eds) *Readings in Machine Translation*. Cambridge; London: MIT Press, 131–136.

Hutchins, J (2004) *The Georgetown-IBM Experiment Demonstrated in January 1954*. In Frederking R E and Taylor K B (eds) *Machine Translation: From Real Users to Research*: 6th Conference of the Association for Machine Translation in the Americas, AMTA 2004, Washington, DC, USA, September 28–October 2, 2004. Proceedings. Heidelberg: Springer Verlag, Berlin, 102–114.

Hutchins J (2005) The First Public Demonstration of Machine Translation: The Georgetown-IBM System, 7th January 1954. Unpublished Manuscript.

Hutchins W J (1978) Machine translation and machine-aided translation. *Journal of Documentation* 34: 119–159.

Hutchins W J (2000) The First Decades of Machine Translation: Overview, Chronology, Sources. In Hutchins W J (ed.) *Early Years in Machine Translation*, Amsterdam; Philadelphia: John Benjamins Publishing Company, 1–16.

IBM Corporation (1936) Machine Methods of Accounting AM-7. USA.

IBM Corporation (1946) Process Control. IBM data processing management. Form 225-3576-3. 590 Madison Avenue, New York 22, N.Y.

IBM Corporation (1949) Card Punching and Verifying. Form 225-5404-2. 590 Madison Avenue, New York 22 N.Y.

IBM Corporation (1950) IBM Data Processing Customer Executive Program. Information Management. Form 225-3385-6. 590 Madison Avenue, New York 22 N.Y.

IBM Corporation (1952) IBM World Trade News. March.

IBM Corporation (1954) IBM Archives: 701 Translator. TS200. 8 January 1954. //www.ibm.com/ibm/history/exhibits/701/701_translator.html.

IBM Corporation (1955a) Work Loads: IBM Data Processing Management. IBM Corporation.

IBM Corporation (1955b) Manuals of Procedure. Form 225-3707-4. 590 Madison Avenue, New York 22, N.Y.

IBM Corporation (1955c) The New IBM Cardatype Accounting Machine (Brochure).

IBM Corporation (1956) IBM Data Processing Customer Executive Program. Installation Management. R25–1394–0. New York, USA: International Business Machines Corporation (IBM).

IBM Corporation (1957) Philosophy on Punched Cards in Italy. *IBM World Trade News.*

IBM Corporation (1961) Punched Card Data Processing Principles. Section 1: The IBM Card and Its Preparation. IBM Personal Study Program. USA.

IBM Corporation (2003a) Italy Chronology. TS200. 23 January 2003. https://www.ibm.com/ibm/history/exhibits/italy/italy_ch1.html.

IBM Corporation (2003b) Old and new punched cards. TS200. https://www.ibm.com/ibm/history/exhibits/supplies/supplies_5404PH13.html.

Iliffe R (2008) Technicians. *Notes and Records of the Royal Society* 62: 3–16. https://doi.org/10.1098/rsnr.2007.0053.

Irani L (2016) The hidden faces of automation. *XRDS: Crossroads, The ACM Magazine for Students* 23 (2): 34–37. https://doi.org/10.1145/3014390.

Irvine D (2015) From Angel to Agile: The Business of the Digital Humanities. *Scholarly and Research Communication* 6 (4): 1–8. https://doi.org/10.22230/src.2015v6n4a208.

Jackson C M (2016) The Laboratory. In Lightmann B (ed.) *A Companion to the History of Science*. Chichester; Malden: John Wiley & Sons, 296–309.

Jardine L (2015) *Erasmus, Man of Letters: The Construction of Charisma in Print.* Princeton; Oxford: Princeton University Press.

Jockers M (2011) 'Nominations for Busa Prize'. Email. *Humanist Discussion Group 25* (107). https://dhhumanist.org/Archives/Current/Humanist.vol25.txt.

Johnson G (2006) *Miss Leavitt's Stars: The Untold Story of the Woman Who Discovered How to Measure the Universe.* New York: W. W. Norton.

Johnston J (2011) Interrogating the goals of work-integrated learning: Neoliberal agendas and critical pedagogy. *Asia-Pacific Journal of Cooperative Education* 12 (3): 175–182.

Jones S (2016) *Roberto Busa, S. J., and the Emergence of Humanities Computing: The Priest and the Punched Cards.* New York; London: Routledge.

Jones S (2018) Reverse Engineering the First Humanities Computing Center. *Digital Humanities Quarterly* 12 (2).

Jones S E (2019) Foreword. In Nyhan J and Passarotti M (eds) *One Origin of Digital Humanities: Fr Roberto Busa in his own words*. Cham: Springer International Publishing, xiii–xviii.

Jones S et al. (2017) Reconstructing the First Humanities Computing Centre. http://www.recaal.org.

Jordanova L J (2000) *History in practice*. London; New York: Oxford University Press.

Kaltenbrunner W (2014) Infrastructural Inversion as a Generative Resource in Digital Scholarship. *Science as Culture* 24 (1): 1–23. https://doi.org/10.1080/09505431.2014.917621.

Kaltenbrunner W (2015) Scholarly Labour and Digital Collaboration in Literary Studies. *Social Epistemology* 29 (2): 207–233. https://doi.org/10.1080/02691728.2014.907834.

Keller E F and Longino H E (1996) *Feminism and Science*. Oxford: Oxford University Press.

Kessler-Harris A (1982) *Out to work: a history of wage-earning women in the United States*. Oxford; New York: Oxford University Press.

Kirschenbaum M G (2016) *Track changes: a literary history of word processing*. Cambridge: Harvard University Press.

Klein J T (2017) The boundary work of making in Digital Humanities. In Sayers J (ed.) *Making things and drawing boundaries*. Minneapolis: University of Minnesota Press, 21–31.

Kmec J A, McDonald S and Trimble L B (2010) Making Gender Fit and "Correcting" Gender Misfits: Sex Segregated Employment and the Nonsearch Process. *Gender & Society* 24: 213–236. https://doi.org/10.1177/0891243209360531.

Knorr-Cetina K D (1981) *The Manufacture of Knowledge: Essay on the Constructivist and Contextual Nature of Science*. Oxford; New York: Pergamon Press.

Kopstein F F and Shillestad I J (1961) A Survey of auto-instructional devices. ADS Technical Report 61–414. Wright-Patterson Air Force Base, Ohio: United States Air Force.

Krajewski M and Krapp P (2011) *Paper Machines: About Cards & Catalogs, 1548–1929*. Cambridge; London: MIT Press.

L'Italia (1961a) Gallarate – Corso allieve perforatrici. Domenica 18 giugno, 9 [text cited in the body of the book translated by Philip Barras]

L'Italia (1961b) Si formano nuove operatrici contabili. Venerdì 4 agosto, 9 [text cited in the body of the book translated by Philip Barras].

L'Italia (1963) *Un corso speciale del centro automazione*. Tutti preparati gli eredi di industrie a Gallarate. Giovedì 10 gennaio, 9 [text cited in the body of the book translated by Philip Barras].

L'Osservatore Romano (2011) Stop, Reader! Fr Busa Is Dead. 11 August.

La Croix (1957) Cerveaux électroniques et Saint Thomas. 1957. 1 October [text cited in the body of the book translated by Philip Barras].

La Prealpina (1957) Per la prima volta in Italia. Scuola di automazione al Centro di analisi letteraria. 30 November [text cited in the body of the book translated by Philip Barras].

La Prealpina (1958) Alla civica Biblioteca un corso di specializzazione per operatori meccanografici. Venerdì 7 November [text cited in the body of the book translated by Philip Barras].

La Prealpina (1961a) Concorso a 12 posti allieve perforatrici. Venerdì 23 giugno, 2 [text cited in the body of the book translated by Philip Barras].

La Prealpina (1961b) Possibilità ai giovani che desiderano specializzarsi in contabilità aziendale. Mercoledì 26 luglio, 3 [text cited in the body of the book translated by Philip Barras].

La Prealpina (1962) Domenica L'Assegnazione. Le Borse di studio del Centro automazione. Venerdì 21 dicembre, 3 [text cited in the body of the book translated by Philip Barras].

La Prealpina (1963) In costante sviluppo. Il Centro di analisi letteraria assumerà importanza nazionale. Mercoledì 30 gennaio, 4 [text cited in the body of the book translated by Philip Barras].

La Prealpina (1964) Provenienti da Parigi e da Roma. Una Visita di illustri Scienziati al Centro di analisi liguistica. Giovedì 27 febbraio [text cited in the body of the book translated by Philip Barras].

La Prealpina (1965a) Si avvia alla conclusione un imponente Lavoro. L'Opera Omnia di San Tommaso al Centro di analisi linguistica. Martedì 12 ottobre. [text cited in the body of the book translated by Philip Barras].

La Prealpina (1965b) Ieri Mattina. Il Ministro Arnaudi ha visitato il Centro di analisi linguistica. Domenica 26 settembre, 4 [text cited in the body of the book translated by Philip Barras].

La Prealpina (1965c) Ha il maggior numero di schede. Istituti Americani chiedono la collaborazione del Centro linguistico. Domenica 14 novembre, 5 [text cited in the body of the book translated by Philip Barras].

La Prealpina (2020) Chi siamo: La Prealpina. [text cited in the body of the book translated by Giulia D'Agostino].

Lancashire I (1986) Concordance Programs for Literary Analysis. *SIGUE Outlook* 19 (1–2):54–61. https://doi.org/10.1145/951656.951663.

Latour B (1988) *Science in Action: How to Follow Scientists and Engineers Through Society.* Cambridge: Harvard University Press.

Latour B and Woolgar S (1986) *Laboratory Life: The Construction of Scientific Facts.* Princeton: Princeton University Press.

Lawrence P (1994) Women's Silences as a Ritual of Truth: A Study of Literary Expressions in Austen, Bronté, and Woolf. In Hedges E and Fisher Fishkin S (eds) *Listening to Silences: New Essays in Feminist criticism.* New York: Oxford University Press, 156–167.

Lawson M (1948) The Machine Age in Historical Research. *The American Archivist* 11 (2): 141–149. https://doi.org/10.17723/aarc.11.2.k10wv0736708370q.

Legge n. 25 del 19 gennaio (1955) "Gazzetta Ufficiale", n. 36, 14 February. https://www.normattiva.it/uri-res/N2Ls?urn:nir:stato:legge:1955-01-19;25!vig=-01-19;25!vig [text cited in the body of the book translated by Giulia D'Agostino].

Lerner G (1998) *Why History Matters: Life and Thought.* New York; Oxford: Oxford University Press.

Lessard G and Levison M (1997) Introduction: Quo Vadimus? *Computers and the Humanities* 31: 261–269. https://doi.org/10.1023/A:1001022725758.

Lettera Della Sig.Na (1960) Lettera Della Sig.Na a P. Busa in Data 2 1 1960, Unaccessioned papers, received March 2015. Busa Archive [text cited in the body of the book translated by Philip Barras].

Leydesdorff S, Passerini L and Thompson P (2017) *Gender & Memory.* New York: Routledge.

Light J S (1999) When Computers Were Women. *Technology and Culture* 40: 455–483.

Linn P (1987) Gender Stereotypes, Technology Stereotypes. In McNeil M (ed.) *Gender and Expertise*. London: Free Association Books, 127–152.

Liu A (2012) Where is Cultural Criticism in the Digital Humanities. In Gold M K (ed.) *Debates in the Digital Humanities*. Minneapolis: University of Minnesota Press, 490–509.

Livingstone D N (2003) *Putting Science in Its Place: Geographies of Scientific Knowledge*. Chicago: University of Chicago Press.

Losh E M and Wernimont, J (2018) *Bodies of Information: Intersectional Feminism and Digital Humanities*. Minneapolis: University of Minnesota Press.

Lubar S (1992) "Do Not Fold, Spindle or Mutilate": A Cultural History of the Punch Card. *The Journal of American Culture* 15 (4): 43–55. https://doi.org/10.1111/j.1542-734X.1992.1504_43.x.

McDonough J T (1967) Computers and the Classics. *Computers and the Humanities* 2 (1): 37–40. doi:10.1007/BF02402465.

Macdonald R R (1963) *General Report 1952–63*. Georgetown University Occasional Papers on Machine Translation. Washington, D.C.: Georgetown University.

Maddox B (2002) *Rosalind Franklin: The Dark Lady of DNA*. London: HarperCollins.

Mahoney M S (1980) Reading a Machine. https://www.princeton.edu/~hos/h398/readmach/modeltfr.html.

Mahoney M S (2005) The Histories of Computing(s). *Interdisciplinary Science Reviews* 30: 119–135. https://doi.org/10.1179/030801805X25927.

Mahoney, M S (2011) *Histories of Computing*. Edited by Thomas Haigh. Cambridge, Mass: Harvard University Press.

Malagreca, Miguel (2013) Lottiamo Ancora: Reviewing One Hundred and Fifty Years of Italian Feminism. *Journal of International Women's Studies* 7: 69–89.

Mandel L (1967) The Computer Girls. *Cosmopolitan*, April, 52–56.

Martin-Nielsen, J (2010) "This war for men's minds": the birth of a human science in Cold War America. *History of the Human Sciences* 23 (5): 131–155. https://doi.org/10.1177/0952695110378952.

McCarty W (2005) *Humanities computing*. Basingstoke; New York: Palgrave Macmillan.

McCarty W (2013) What Does Turing Have to Do with Busa? In Mambrini F, Passarotti M and Sporleder C (eds) *Proceedings of The Third Workshop on Annotation of Corpora for Research in the Humanities (ACRH-3)*. Sofia: Bulgarian Academy of Sciences, 1–14.

McCarty, W (2014) Getting there from here. Remembering the future of digital humanities Roberto Busa Award lecture 2013. *Literary and Linguistic Computing* 29: 283–306. https://doi.org/10.1093/llc/fqu022.

McDonough J T (1967) Computers and the classics. *Computers and the Humanities* 2: 37–40. https://doi.org/10.1007/BF02402465.

McGillivray B, Alex B, Ames S, Armstrong G, Beavan D, Ciula A et al. (2020) The challenges and prospects of the intersection of humanities and data science: A White Paper from The Alan Turing Institute. The Alan Turing Institute, Online resource. https://doi.org/10.6084/m9.figshare.12732164.v5.

McNamara W J (1967) The Selection of Computer Personnel – Past, Present, Future. *Proceedings of the fifth SIGCPR conference on Computer personnel research June 1967*. Association of Computing Machinery, New York, 52–56. https://doi.org/10.1145/1142662.1142667.

McNamara W J and Hughes J L (1955) The Selection of Card Punch Operators. *Personnel Psychology* 8 (4): 417–427. https://doi.org/10.1111/j.1744-6570.1955.tb01220.x.

McPherson T (2012) Why Are the Digital Humanities so White? Or Thinking the Histories of Race and Computation. In Gold M K (ed.) *Debates in the Digital Humanities*. Minneapolis: University of Minnesota Press, 139–160.

Melloni A (1990) Church History and the Computer. *Computers and the Humanities* 24 (5–6):393–395. https://doi.org/10.1007/BF00186481.

Memorandum (1965) A memorandum-report of meetings held between Dr. Biraghi (Ludovico Biraghi-Losetti, who was general manager at IBM Italia from 1965) and associates of CAAL and Father Busa's college, the Aloisianum, 26 November. http://www.recaal.org/pages/busa.html.

Merkin R (1983) The historical/academic dictionary. In Hartmann R R (ed.) *Lexicography: principles and practice*. London: Academic Press, 123–133.

Miall D S (1992) Estimating Changes in Collocations of Key Words across a Large Text: A Case Study of Coleridge's Notebooks. *Computers and the Humanities* 26: 1–12. https://doi.org/10.1007/BF00114883.

Milkman R (1987) *Gender at Work: The Dynamics of Job Segregation by Sex During World War II*. Urbana: University of Illinois Press.

MLA (2012) Guidelines for Evaluating Work in Digital Humanities and Digital Media. Modern Languages Association. https://www.mla.org/About-Us/Governance/Committees/Committee-Listings/Professional-Issues/Committee-on-Information-Technology/Guidelines-for-Evaluating-Work-in-Digital-Humanities-and-Digital-Media.

Moravec M (2017) Feminist Research Practices and Digital Archives. *Australian Feminist Studies* 32: 186–201. https://doi.org/10.1080/08164649.2017.1357006.

Morus I R (2016) Invisible Technicians, Instrument Makers, and Artisans. In Lightman B (ed.) *A Companion to the History of Science*. Hoboken; Chichester: John Wiley & Sons, 97–110.

Mullaney T S, Peters B, Hicks M and Philip K (eds) (2021) *Your Computer Is on Fire*. Cambridge; London: MIT Press.

n.a. (1961) List of Delegates. International Conference on Machine Translation of Languages and Applied Language Analysis, National Physical Laboratory, Teddington, UK, 5–8 September 1961. Machine Translation Archive. Compiled by John Hutchins for the European Association for Machine Translation on behalf of the International Association for Machine Translation.

n.a. (2002) The Roberto Busa Award. *Computers and the Humanities* 36: 257. https://doi.org/10.1023/A:1016131700839.

Nace J G (1965) Teaching Card Punch Operators Through the Use of Filmed Lessons. *American Annals of the Deaf* 110: 563–570.

Nardozzi G (2003) The Italian "Economic Miracle". *Rivista di storia economica* 2: 139–180. https://doi.org/10.1410/9557.

Nebeker F (2009) *Dawn of the Electronic Age: Electrical Technologies in the Shaping of the Modern World, 1914 to 1945*. Hoboken; Piscataway: John Wiley & Sons; IEEE Press.

Nirenburg S, Somers H L and Wilks Y A (eds) (2003) *Readings in Machine Translation*. Cambridge; London: MIT Press.

Noble D F (1992) *A World without Women: the Christian Clerical Culture of Western Science*. New York Oxford: Oxford University Press.

Noble S U (2018) *Algorithms of Oppression: How Search Engines Reinforce Racism*. New York: NYU Press.

Noble S U (2019) *Toward a Critical Black Digital Humanities.* In Gold M K and Klein L F (eds) *Debates in the Digital Humanities.* Minneapolis: University of Minnesota Press, 27–35.

Norberg A L (1990) High-Technology Calculation in the Early 20th Century: Punched Card Machinery in Business and Government. *Technology and Culture* 31 (4): 753–779. https://doi.org/10.2307/3105906.

Nyhan J (2008) Developing Integrated Editions of Minority Language Dictionaries: The Irish Example. *Literary and Linguistic Computing* 23: 3–12. https://doi.org/10.1093/llc/fqm038.

Nyhan J (ed.) (2012) Hidden Histories: Computing and the Humanities c. 1965–1985. *Digital Humanities Quarterly* 6 (3).

Nyhan J (2014) Gender, Knowledge and Hierarchy: On Busa's Female Punch Card Operators. *Archae logos: notes on the digital humanities and oral history* http://archelogos.hypotheses.org/135.

Nyhan J and Flinn A (2014) Oral History, audio-visual materials and Digital Humanities: a new "grand challenge"?Sound and (Moving) Image in Focus pre-Conference Workshop. Switzerland.

Nyhan J (2016) In Search of Identities in the Digital Humanities: The Early History of Humanist. In Malloy J (ed.) *Social Media Archaeology and Poetics.* Cambridge, London: MIT Press, 227–242.

Nyhan J and Flinn A (2016) *Computation and the Humanities: Towards an Oral History of Digital Humanities.* Cham: Springer International Publishing.

Nyhan J and Passarotti M (eds) (2019) *One Origin of Digital Humanities: Fr Roberto Busa in His Own Words.* Cham: Springer International Publishing.

Nyhart L K (2016) Historiography of the History of Science. In Lightmann B (ed.) *A Companion to the History of Science.* Chichester: John Wiley & Sons Ltd, 7–22.

Oakman R L (1980) *Computer Methods for Literary Research.* Columbia: University of South Carolina Press.

Ó Corráin D (1998) Creating the past: the early Irish genealogical tradition. *Peritia* 12: 177–208. https://doi.org/10.1484/J.Peri.3.329.

Off the Tracks (2011) Collaborators' Bill of Rights. http://mcpress.media-commons.org/offthetracks/part-one-models-for-collaboration-career-paths-acquiring-institutional-support-and-transformation-in-the-field/a-collaboration/collaborators'-bill-of-rights/.

O'Grady D (1966) The Jesuit Who Punches Cards. *U.S. Catholic*, July.

O'Neil Adams M (1995) Punch Card Records: Precursors of Electronic Records. *The American Archivist* 58 (2): 182–201. https://doi.org/10.17723/aarc.58.2.d61078182725616j.

O'Neil C (2016) *Weapons of Math Destruction: How Big Data Increases Inequality and Threatens Democracy.* New York: Crown.

O'Neill J C (1964) Pope Lauds Computer Project: Foreign N.C.W.C. News Service. Issued by the Press Department, National Catholic Welfare Conference. CWC News Service.

Opitz D L (2016) Domestic Space. In Lightmann B (ed.) *A Companion to the History of Science.* Hoboken; Chichester: John Wiley & Sons, 252–267.

Ortolja-Baird A, Pickering V, Nyhan J, Sloan K and Fleming M (2019) Digital Humanities in the Memory Institution: The Challenges of Encoding Sir Hans Sloane's Early Modern Catalogues of His Collections. *Open Library of Humanities* 5: 44. https://doi.org/10.16995/olh.409.

O'Sullivan J (2020) The Digital Humanities in Ireland. *Digital Studies/Le champ numérique* 10 (1). https://doi.org/10.16995/dscn.374.

Otlet P and Rayward W B (1990) *International Organisation and Dissemination of Knowledge: Selected Essays of Paul Otlet.* Amsterdam: Elsevier.

Painter J A (1964) Implications of the Cornell Concordances for Computing. In Bessinger J B and Parrish S M (eds) *Literary Data Processing Conference Proceedings.* White Plains: IBM, 160–171.

Parrish S M (1962) Problems in the Making of Computer Concordances. *Studies in Bibliography,* 15, 1–14. http://www.jstor.org/stable/40371322.

Parrish S M (1967) Computers and the Muse of Literature. In Bowles E A (ed.) *Computers in Humanistic Research: Readings and Perspectives.* Englewood Cliffs: Prentice-Hall, 124–134.

Pasanek B (2019) Extreme Reading: Josephine Miles and the Scale of the Pre-Digital Digital Humanities. *ELH* 86 (2): 355–385. https://doi.org/10.1353/elh.2019.0018.

Passarotti M (2013) One hundred years Ago. In memory of Father Roberto Busa SJ. In Mambrini F, Passarotti M and Sporlederr C (eds) *Proceedings of The Third Workshop on Annotation of Corpora for Research in the Humanities (ACRH-3).* Sofia: Institute of Information and Communication Technologies Bulgarian Academy of Sciences, 15–24.

Passarotti M and Nyhan J (2019) Introduction, or Why Busa Still Matters. In Nyhan J and Passarotti M (eds) *One Origin of Digital Humanities: Fr Roberto Busa in his own words.* Cham: Springer International Publishing, 1–18.

Passerini L (1979) Work Ideology and Consensus under Italian Fascism. *History Workshop Journal* 8: 82–108. https://doi.org/10.1093/hwj/8.1.82.

Paul H (2008) The Epistemic Virtues of Historical Scholarship; or, the Moral Dimensions of a Scholarly Character. *Soundings: An Interdisciplinary Journal* 91 (3/4): 371–387. http://dx.doi.org/10.5325/soundings.91.3-4.0371.

Pawlicka-Deger U (2020) The Laboratory Turn: Exploring Discourses, Landscapes, and Models of Humanities Labs. *Digital Humanities Quarterly* 14.

Pankowicz Z L (1966) Letter from Zbigniew L. Pankowicz to Roberto Busa, 28 April 1966. (Gall. Rel. Cult. Est. 1943. Rel. Cult. USA). Busa Archive.

Perks R and Thomson A (2006) *The Oral History Reader.* London: Routledge.

Perry M E (2010) *Finding Fatima, a Slave Woman of Early Modern Spain.* In Chaudhuri N, Katz S J and Perry M E (eds) *Contesting Archives: Finding Women in the Sources.* Urbana-Champaign: University of Illinois, 3–19.

Perschke S (1968) Machine Translation? The Second Phase of Development. *Endeavour* 27: 97–100.

Pettegree A (2010) *The Book in the Renaissance.* New Haven; London: Yale University Press.

Petrini F (2004) The Common vocational training policy in the EEC from 1961 to 1972. *European Journal* 32: 45–54. https://files.eric.ed.gov/fulltext/EJ734145.pdf.

Pierson R R (1986). *They're Still Women After All: The Second World War and Canadian Womanhood.* Toronto: McClelland and Stewart.

Plumb R K (1954) Russian Is Turned Into English By a Fast Electronic Translator; Calculator Takes on a New Job: Language Translation Language Device Translates Fast. https://www.nytimes.com/1954/01/08/archives/russian-is-turned-into-english-by-a-fast-electronic-translator.html.

Pojmann W (2011) For Mothers, Peace and Family: International (Non)-Cooperation among Italian Catholic and Communist Women's Organisations during the Early

Cold War. *Gender & History* 23 (2): 415–429. https://doi.org/10.1111/j.1468-0424. 2011.01646.x.

Poole A H (2018) "Could My Dark Hands Break through the Dark Shadow?": Gender, Jim Crow, and Librarianship during the Long Freedom Struggle, 1935–1955. *The Library Quarterly* 88 (4): 348–374. https://doi.org/10.1086/699269.

Portelli A (1981) The Peculiarities of Oral History. *History Workshop Journal* 12: 96–107. https://doi.org/10.1093/hwj/12.1.96.

Posner M (2021) Breakpoints and Black Boxes: Information in Global Supply Chains. *Postmodern Culture* 31 (3) https://doi.org/10.1353/pmc.2021.0002.

Poster W R, Crain M and Cherry M A (2016) Introduction: Conceptualizing Invisible Labor. In Crain M G, Poster W R and Cherry M A (eds) *Invisible Labor: Hidden Work in the Contemporary World*. Berkley: University of California Press, 3–27.

Price L and Thurschwell P (eds) (2004) *Literary Secretaries/Secretarial Culture*. Aldershot, Hants, England; Burlington, VT: Routledge.

Pritchard B L (1940) Letter from Belva L. Pritchard to Miss Ida M. Tarbell, 17 January 1940. Allegheny College DSpace Repository.

Pritchard D (2008) Working Papers, Open Access, and Cyber-Infrastructure in Classical Studies. *Literary and Linguistic Computing* 23 (2): 149–162. https://doi.org/10.1093/llc/fqn005.

Prosser W R and Beldecos H J (1967) *Key-punch Practice*. Chicago: H. M. Rowe Co.

Quirke S (2010) *Hidden Hands: Egyptian Workforces in Petrie Excavation Archives, 1880–1924*. London: Bristol Classical Press.

Raben J (1969) The Death of the Handmade Concordance. *Scholarly Publishing* 1: 61–69.

Raben J (1977) *Computer-Assisted Research in the Humanities: A Directory of Scholars Active*. New York: Pergamon Press.

Raben J. (1987) Computers and the Humanities: some Historical Considerations. In Zampolli A, Cappelli A, Cignoni L and Peters C A (eds) *Linguistica Computazionale Studies in Honour of Roberto Busa S. J.* Pisa: Giardini, 225–230.

Raben J (1991) Humanities Computing 25 Years Later. *Computers and the Humanities* 25: 341–350. https://doi.org/10.1007/BF00141184.

Ramsay S (2008) Algorithmic Criticism. In Schreibmann S and Siemens R (eds) *A Companion to Digital Literary Studies*. Oxford: Blackwell Publishing, 477–491.

Ramsay S (2011a) *Reading Machines: Toward and Algorithmic Criticism*. Urbana: University of Illinois Press.

Ramsay S (2011b) A Tribute to Fr Busa, from Stephen Ramsay (Repost). https://thomistica.net/news/2011/8/19/a-tribute-to-fr-busa-from-stephen-ramsay-repost.html

Redacted (1963a) Gallarate 6.6. Unaccessioned papers received March 2015. Busa Archive.

Redacted (1963a) Esame psicoattitudinale del [redacted]. Gallarate 8.6. Unaccessioned papers received March 2015. Busa Archive.

Rhodes I (1962) Letter from Ida Rhodes to Jerome Wiesner, 27 August 1962. (Gall. Rel. Cult. Est. 1943. Rel. USA.) Busa Archive.

Risam R (2016) *Navigating the Global Digital Humanities: Insights from Black Feminism*. In Gold M K and Klein L F (eds) Debates in the Digital Humanities 2016. Minneapolis: University of Minnesota Press, 359–367.

Risam R (2018) *New Digital Worlds: Postcolonial Digital Humaniteis in Theory, Praxis and Pedagogy*. Evanston: Northwestern University Press.

Ritchie D A (2014) *Doing Oral History*. Oxford; New York: Oxford University Press.

Roberts S T (2019) *Behind the Screen: Content Moderation in the Shadows of Social Media*. New Haven; London: Yale University Press.

Rockmael V (1963) The Woman Programmer. *Datamation* 9 (1): 41.

Rockwell G (2011) On the Evaluation of Digital Media as Scholarship. *Profession* 1: 152–168. https://doi.org/10.1632/prof.2011.2011.1.152.

Rockwell G (2013) Tasman: Literary Data Processing. Theoreti.ca. https://theoreti.ca/?p=4571.

Rockwell G (2016) The Index Thomisticus as Project. Theoreti.ca http://theoreti.ca/?p=6096.

Rockwell G and Passarotti M (2019) The Index Thomisticus as a Big Data Project. *Umanistica Digitale* 5: 13–34. https://doi.org/10.6092/issn.2532-8816/8575.

Rockwell G and Sinclair S (2016) *Hermeneutica: Computer-Assisted Interpretation in the Humanities*. Cambridge; London: The MIT Press.

Rockwell G and Sinclair S (2017) Workflow. https://avc.web.usf.edu/images/RECAAL/pages/workflow.html.

Rockwell G and Sinclair S (2020) Tremendous Mechanical Labor: Father Busa's Algorithm. *Digital Humanities Quarterly* 14 (3) http://www.digitalhumanities.org/dhq/vol/14/3/000456/000456.html.

Rockwell G and Sinclair S (2021) Voyant Tools. https://voyant-tools.org/.

Rogers K (2015) Humanities Unbound: Supporting Careers and Scholarship Beyond the Tenure Track. *Digital Humanities Quarterly* 9.

Rossiter M W (1993) The Matthew Matilda Effect in Science. *Social Studies of Science* 23 (2): 325–341. https://doi.org/10.1177/030631293023002004.

Rothschild J (1983) Foreword. In Rothschild J (ed.) *Machina Ex Dea: Feminist Perspectives on Technology*. New York: Pergamon Press, vii–viii.

Rouse M A and Rouse R H (eds) (1991) *Authentic Witnesses: Approaches to Medieval Texts and Manuscripts*. Notre Dame: University of Notre Dame Press.

Ruder S (n.d.) NLP-Progress. Repository to Track the Progress in Natural Language Processing (NLP), Including the Datasets and the Current State-of-the-Art for the Most Common NLP Tasks. http://nlpprogress.com/english/part-of-speech_tagging.html.

Rupert C T (1985) [Review of]: Global Linguistic Statistical Methods (Roma: Ateneo, 1982, Robert Busa (ed.)) *Computers and the Humanities* 19 (3): 185–189. https://doi.org/10.1007/BF02259535.

Russell N C, Tansey E M and Lear P V (2000) Missing Links in the History and Practice of Science: Teams, Technicians and Technical Work. *History of Science* 38 (2): 237–241. https://doi.org/10.1177/007327530003800205.

Rutimann H and Nyhan J (2016) I heard about the arrival of the Computer. In Nyhan J and Flinn A (eds) *Computation and the Humanities: Towards an Oral History of Digital Humanities*. Cham: Springer International Publishing, 167–176.

Rybak J P (1969) St. Mary's IMB Card Punching Program. *American Annals of the Deaf* 114:34–36.

Sadler A G (1958) The Accounting Teacher Turns to Electronic Data Processing. *The Accounting Review* 33: 497–501.

Samson N and Shen A (2018) A history of Canada's full-time faculty in six charts. https://www.universityaffairs.ca/features/feature-article/history-canadas-full-time-faculty-six-charts/.

Sangster J (1994) Telling our stories: feminist debates and the use of oral history. *Women's History Review* 3: 5–28. https://doi.org/10.1080/09612029400200046.

Saresella D (2020) *Catholics and communists in twentieth-century Italy: between conflict and dialogue.* London: Bloomsbury Academic.

Schafer V and Thierry B G (2015) Connecting Gender, Women and ICT in Europe: A Long-Term Perspective. In Schafer V and Thierry B G (eds) *Connecting Women: Women, Gender and ICT in Europe in the Nineteenth and Twentieth Century.* Cham: Springer International Publishing, 1–23.

Schantz H F (1982) *The History of OCR: Optical Character Recognition.* Manchester: Recognition Technologies Users Association.

Scheinfeldt T (2014) The Dividends of Difference: Recognizing Digital Humanities Diverse Family Tree's. *Found History.* http://foundhistory.org/2014/04/the-dividends-of-difference-recognizing-digital-humanities-diverse-family-trees/.

Schiff B, McKim A E and Patron S (eds) (2017) *Life and Narrative: The Risks and Responsibilities of Storying Experience.* New York: Oxford University Press.

Schreibman S, Mandell L and Olsen S (2011) Introduction. *Profession* 1: 123–135.

Schreibman S, Siemens R and Unsworth J (eds) (2008) *A Companion to Digital Humanities.* Oxford: Blackwell Publishing.

Sforzi F (2002) The Industrial District and the 'New' Italian Economic Geography. *European Planning Studies* 10 (4): 439–447. https://doi.org/10.1080/09654310220130167.

Shapin S (1989) The Invisible Technician. *American Scientist* 77 (6): 554–563.

Shapin S and Schaffer S (2011) *Leviathan and the Air-Pump: Hobbes, Boyle, and the Experimental Life.* Princeton: Princeton University Press.

Shavit Y and Westerbeek K (1998) Reforms, Expansion, and Equality of Opportunity. *European Sociological Review* 14: 33–47. https://doi.org/10.1093/oxfordjournals.esr.a018226.

Sherratt T (2019) Hacking Heritage: Understanding the Limits of Online Access. In Lewi H, Smith W, Lehn von D and Cooke S (eds) *The Routledge International Handbook of New Digital Practices in Galleries, Libraries, Archives, Museums and Heritage Sites.* London: Routledge, 116–130.

Shetterly M L (2017) *Hidden Figures: The Untold Story of the African American Women Who Helped Win the Space Race.* London: William Collins.

Short P (2019) Busa Archive Photos. Personal Email communication to Nyhan J. 6 June 2019. Reproduced with kind permission of P. Short.

Siegmund-Schultze, R (2009) *Mathematicians fleeing from Nazi Germany: individual fates and global impact.* Princeton, NJ: Princeton University Press.

Sigmund P E (1987) The Catholic Tradition and Modern Democracy. *The Review of Politics* 49 (4): 530–548. https://doi.org/10.1017/S0034670500035452.

Simons G L (1981) *Women in Computing.* Manchester: National Computing Centre Publications.

Sinclair S (2016) Experiments with Punch Cards. http://stefansinclair.name/punchcard/.

Sinclair S and Rockwell G (2022) Voyant Tools. https://voyant-tools.org/.

Smith D A and Cordell R (2018) A Research Agenda for Historical and Multilingual Optical Character Recognition – Historical and Multilingual Optical Character Recognition. https://ocr.northeastern.edu/report/.

Smith L (2006) *Uses of Heritage.* London; New York: Routledge.

Smith M W A (1985) An Investigation of Morton's Method to Distinguish Elizabethan Playwrights. *Computers and the Humanities* 19: 3–21 https://doi.org/10.1007/BF02259637.

Smithies J and Ciula A (2020) Humans in the Loop: Epistemology & Method in King's Digital Lab. In Schuster K and Dunn S (eds) *Routledge International Handbook of Research Methods in Digital Humanities.* London: Routledge, 155–172.

Smyth H, Nyhan J and Flinn A (2020) Opening the "black box" of digital cultural heritage processes: feminist digital humanities and critical heritage studies. In Schuster K and Dunn S (eds) *Routledge International Handbook of Research Methods in Digital Humanities*. London: Routledge, 295–308.

Spain Daphne (1993) Gendered Spaces and Women's Status. *Sociological Theory* 11 (2): 137–151. https://doi.org/10.2307/202139.

Srigley K, Zembrzycki S and Iacovetta F (2018) *Beyond Women's Words: Feminisms and the Practices of Oral History in the Twenty-First Century*. Abingdon; New York: Routledge.

Srnicek Nick (2017) *Platform Capitalism*. Cambridge; Malden: Polity.

Stanford online (2014) 2014 Kailath Lecture: Stanford Professor Donald Knuth. YouTube. https://www.youtube.com/watch?v=gAXdDEQveKw&feature=youtu.be.

Star S L and Strauss A (1999) Layers of Silence, Arenas of Voice: The Ecology of Visible and Invisible Work. *Computer Supported Cooperative Work* 8: 9–30. https://doi.org/10.1023/A:1008651105359.

Steele C K (2021) *Digital Black Feminism*. New York: New York University Press.

Stevens M E (1959) Letter from Mary Elizabeth Stevens to Roberto Busa, 29 April 1959. (Gal. Rel. Cult. 1940. Rel. Cult. USA) Busa Archive.

Stewart L (2008) Assistants to enlightenment: William Lewis, Alexander Chisholm and invisible technicians in the Industrial Revolution. *Notes and Records of the Royal Society* 62: 17–29. https://doi.org/10.1098/rsnr.2007.0034.

Stibitz G (1985) Lecture. In Campbell-Kelly M and Williams M (eds) *The Moore School Lectures: Theory and Techniques for Design of Electronic Digital Computers*. Cambridge; London: MIT Press, 5–16.

Stillinger J (1991) *Multiple Authorship and the Myth of Solitary Genius*. New York: Oxford University Press.

Strom S H (1989) "Light Manufacturing": The Feminization of American Office Work, 1900–1930. *Industrial and Labor Relations Review* 43: 53–71. https://doi.org/10.1177/001979398904300106.

Strom S H (1992) *Beyond the Typewriter: Gender, Class, and the Origins of Modern American Office Work, 1900–1930*. Urbana: University of Illinois Press.

Suk J C (2018) Feminist Constitutionalism and the Entrenchment of Motherhood. *Studies in Law, Politics and Society* 75: 107–133. https://doi.org/10.1108/S1059-433720180000075004.

Sydell L (2014) The Forgotten Female Programmers Who Created Modern Tech. http://www.npr.org/blogs/alltechconsidered/2014/10/06/345799830/the-forgotten-female-programmers-who-created-modern-tech.

Tasman P (1957) Literary Data Processing. *IBM Journal of Research and Development* 1 (3): 249–256.

Taylor A (2018) The Automation Charade. *Logic Magazine* 5. https://logicmag.io/failure/the-automation-charade/.

Terras M (2013) For Ada Lovelace Day – Father Busa's Female Punch Card Operatives. Melissa Terras' Blog. http://melissaterras.blogspot.com/2013/10/for-ada-lovelace-day-father-busas.html.

Terras M, Nyhan J and Vanhoutte E (eds) (2013) *Defining Digital Humanities: a Reader*. Farnham: Ashgate Publishing Limited.

The Centre for Computing History (2016) Bubbles Whiting. Using Punch Cards – Hollerith and IBM. YouTube. https://www.youtube.com/watch?v=L7jAOcc9kBU.

Thaller M (2017) Between the Chairs: An Interdisciplinary Career. *Historical Social Research, Supplement* 29: 7–109. https://doi.org/10.12759/hsr.suppl.29.2017.7-109.

Thaller M and Nyhan J (2016) It's Probably the only Modestly Widely Used System with a Command Language in Latin. In Nyhan J and Flinn A (eds) *Computation and the Humanities: Towards an Oral History of Digital Humanities*. Cham: Springer International Publishing, 195–208.

Thornton D (1998) *The Scholar in His Study: Ownership and Experience in Renaissance Italy*. New Haven: Yale University Press.

Thornton B D and Zambrana R E (2016) 'Critical Thinking about Inequality: An Emerging Lens'. In McCann C and Seung-kyung K (eds) *Feminist Theory Reader: Local and Global Perspectives*. Fourth Edition. New York and London. Routledge, 182–193.

Treccani (2020) *L'Italia*. https://www.treccani.it/enciclopedia/l-italia.

Turchetti, S (2022). Use, refuse or lock them up? A history of Italian academic refugees in Britain, 1930–1955. Ph.D., England: The University of Manchester (United Kingdom). https://www.proquest.com/docview/1990591178/abstract/9B1CBF0C3DE047EAPQ/1.

Turner A (2014) Women in Tech from ENIAC to MOM. http://nursingclio.org/2014/10/14/women-in-tech-from-eniac-to-mom/.

Ubell E (1954) It's All Done by Machine. Words Go in in Russian, English Sentence Comes Out. *New York Herald Tribune*, 8 January.

Ubell E (1964). Computers and St. Thomas. *New York Herald Tribune*, 10 September.

Unknown (1960) [Premesso che presso il Centro per l'automazione …] 12 March. Busa Archive. Unaccessioned papers received March 2015.

Unknown (n.d.) Relazione Degli Incontri Con La I.B.M. per Le Questioni Riguardanti Il CAAL.

Unsworth J (2004) Forms of Attention: Digital Humanities Beyond Representation. Paper delivered at The Face of Text: Computer-Assisted Text Analysis in the Humanities, the third conference of the Canadian Symposium on Text Analysis (CaSTA), McMaster University, 19–21 November 2004. http://people.lis.illinois.edu/~unsworth/FOA/.

van den Ende J (1994) The Number Factory: Punched-Card Machines at the Dutch Central Bureau of Statistics. *IEEE Annals of the History of Computing* 16 (3): 15–24. https://doi.org/10.1109/MAHC.1994.298417.

van Dongen J and Paul H (eds) (2017) *Epistemic Virtues in the Sciences and the Humanities*. Cham: Springer International Publishing.

Vanhoutte E (2013) The Gates of Hell: History and Definition of Digital | Humanities | Computing. In Terras M M, Nyhan J and Vanhoutte E (eds) *Defining Digital Humanities: A Reader*. Farnham: Ashgate Publishing Limited, 119–156.

Vanhoutte E (2010) Unpublished PhD manuscript. Reproduced with permission of the author.

van Ittersum M J (2011) Knowledge Production in the Dutch Republic: The Household Academy of Hugo Grotius. *Journal of the History of Ideas* 72: 523–548. http://dx.doi.org/10.1353/jhi.2011.0033.

van Ness R G (1963) *Principles of Punched Card Data Processing*. Elmhurst: Business Press.

van Rooij, Arjan (2011) Knowledge, money and data: an integrated account of the evolution of eight types of laboratory. *The British Journal for the History of Science* 44 (3): 427–448.

van Zundert, J J (2015) Screwmeneutics and Hermenumericals. In *A New Companion to Digital Humanities*. Oxford, West Sussex: John Wiley & Sons Ltd, MA, 331–347. https://doi.org/10.1002/9781118680605.ch23.

van Zundert J J (2016) The Case of the Bold Button: Social Shaping of Technology and the Digital Scholarly Edition. *Digital Scholarship in the Humanities* 31 (4): 898–910. https://doi.org/10.1093/llc/fqw012.

van Zundert J J and Haentjens Dekker R (2017) Code, scholarship, and criticism: When is code scholarship and when is it not? *Digital Scholarship in the Humanities* 32: i121–i133. https://doi.org/10.1093/llc/fqx006.

Vasconcellos M (2000) The Georgetown Project and Léon Dostert: Recollections of a Young Assistant. In Hutchins J (ed.) *Early Years in Machine Translation: Manoirs and Biographies of Pioneers*. Amsterdam; Philadelphia: John Benjamins Publishing Company, 87–96.

von Arx J P (2012) Foreword. In Boryczka J M and Petrino E A (eds) *Jesuit and Feminist Education: Intersections in Teaching and Learning for the Twenty-first Century*. Fordham University Press, New York, ix–xiv.

Wajcman J (1996) *Feminism Confronts Technology*. PA: The Pennsylvania State University.

Wajcman J (2010) Feminist theories of technology. *Cambridge Journal of Economics* 34: 143–152. https://doi.org/10.1093/cje/ben057.

Walsh A (1958) Alice Walsh on Behalf of Roberto Busa to Professor Allen Kent. 18 Rel Cult. Busa Archive.

Watson A K (1960) A.K. Watson to Rev. Roberto Busa S. J. 7 April 1960. Busa Archive [consulted in digital form at http://www.recaal.org/pages/busa.html; filename AKW-RB-4-7-60].

Wen S (2014) The Ladies Vanish. *The New Inquiry*. https://thenewinquiry.com/the-ladies-vanish/.

Weingart S B and Eichmann-Kalwara N (2017) What's Under the Big Tent?: A Study of ADHO Conference Abstracts. *Digital Studies / Le champ numérique* 7: 1–17. https://doi.org/10.16995/dscn.284.

Weingart S and Jorgensen J (2013) Computational Analysis of the Body in European Fairy Tales. *Literary and Linguistic Computing* 28 (3): 404–416. https://doi.org/10.1093/llc/fqs015.

Whitley R (2000) *The Intellectual and Social Organization of the Sciences*. Oxford; New York: Oxford University Press.

Whitson R (2016) *Steampunk and Nineteenth-Century Digital Humanities: Literary Retrofuturisms, Media Archaeologies, Alternate Histories*. New York: Routledge.

Wieringa M (2020) What to account for when accounting for algorithms: a systematic literature review on algorithmic accountability. In *FAT* '20: Proceedings of the 2020 Conference on Fairness, Accountability, and Transparency*. New York: Association for Computing Machinery, 1–18.

Williams R V (2002) The Use of Punched Cards in US Libraries and Documentation Centers, 1936–1965. *IEEE Annals of the History of Computing* 24 (2): 16–33. https://doi.org/10.1109/MAHC.2002.1010067.

Wimmer M (2019) Josephine Miles (1911–1985): Doing Digital Humanism with and without Machines. *History of Humanities* 4 (2): 329–334. https://doi.org/10.1086/704850.

Winder W (2002) Industrial Text and French Neo-Structuralism. *Computers and the Humanities* 36 (3): 295–306. https://doi.org/10.1023/A:1016122115490.

Winter T N (1999) Roberto Busa, S.J., and the Invention of the Machine-Generated Concordance. *The Classical Bulletin* 75: 3–20.

Winchester S (2003) *The Meaning of Everything: The Story of the Oxford English Dictionary.* Oxford: Oxford University Press.

Wisbey R (1962) Concordance Making by Electronic Computer: Some Experiences with the "Wiener Genesis". *The Modern Language Review* 57 (2): 161–172. https://doi.org/3720960.

WISE (2012) Women in Science, Technology, Engineering and Mathematics: from Classroom to Boardroom, UK Statistics 2012. http://www.wisecampaign.org.uk/about-us/wise-resources/uk-statistics-2012.

WISE (2014) Growth in women's employment in STEM. http://www.wisecampaign.org.uk/about-us/wise-resources/uk-statistics-2014/september-2014.

Wootton C W and Kemmerer B E (2007) The Emergence of Mechanical Accounting in the U.S., 1880–1930. *The Accounting Historians Journal* 34: 91–124.

Wright R (1972) Hebrew-EDP transliterations: Preliminary proposal. *Ariflamoi* 2: 23.

Wright A (2014) *Cataloging the World: Paul Otlet and the Birth of the Information Age.* Oxford: Oxford University Press.

Wuchty, S, Benjamin F J, and Uzzi B (2007) The Increasing Dominance of Teams in Production of Knowledge. *Science* 316 (5827): 1036–1039.

Wyer M, Barbercheck M, Cookmeyer D, Ozturk H and Wayne M (eds) (2013) *Women, Science, and Technology: A Reader in Feminist Science Studies.* London: Routledge.

Zampolli A (1973) Humanities Computing in Italy. *Computers and the Humanities* 7 (6): 343–360. https://doi.org/10.1007/BF02395110.

Zimmeck M (1986) Jobs for the Girls: The Expansion of Clerical Work for Women, 1850–1914. In John A V (ed.) *Unequal Opportunities: Women's Employment in England 1800–1918.* Oxford: Blackwell, 153–178.

Zuboff S (2019) *The Age of Surveillance Capitalism: The Fight for a Human Future at the New Frontier of Power.* London: Profile Books.

Index

Note: Locators in *italic* refer to figures; Locators followed by "n" indicate endnotes.

Printed in the United States
by Baker & Taylor Publisher Services